T0235406

# Lecture Notes in Artificial Intelligence    11770

Subseries of Lecture Notes in Computer Science

Series Editors

Randy Goebel
   *University of Alberta, Edmonton, Canada*
Yuzuru Tanaka
   *Hokkaido University, Sapporo, Japan*
Wolfgang Wahlster
   *DFKI and Saarland University, Saarbrücken, Germany*

Founding Editor

Jörg Siekmann
   *DFKI and Saarland University, Saarbrücken, Germany*

More information about this series at http://www.springer.com/series/1244

Dimitar Kazakov · Can Erten (Eds.)

# Inductive
# Logic Programming

29th International Conference, ILP 2019
Plovdiv, Bulgaria, September 3–5, 2019
Proceedings

 Springer

*Editors*
Dimitar Kazakov ⓘ
Department of Computer Science
University of York
Heslington, UK

Can Erten
Department of Computer Science
University of York
Heslington, UK

ISSN 0302-9743          ISSN 1611-3349   (electronic)
Lecture Notes in Artificial Intelligence
ISBN 978-3-030-49209-0          ISBN 978-3-030-49210-6   (eBook)
https://doi.org/10.1007/978-3-030-49210-6

LNCS Sublibrary: SL7 – Artificial Intelligence

© Springer Nature Switzerland AG 2020
This work is subject to copyright. All rights are reserved by the Publisher, whether the whole or part of the material is concerned, specifically the rights of translation, reprinting, reuse of illustrations, recitation, broadcasting, reproduction on microfilms or in any other physical way, and transmission or information storage and retrieval, electronic adaptation, computer software, or by similar or dissimilar methodology now known or hereafter developed.
The use of general descriptive names, registered names, trademarks, service marks, etc. in this publication does not imply, even in the absence of a specific statement, that such names are exempt from the relevant protective laws and regulations and therefore free for general use.
The publisher, the authors and the editors are safe to assume that the advice and information in this book are believed to be true and accurate at the date of publication. Neither the publisher nor the authors or the editors give a warranty, express or implied, with respect to the material contained herein or for any errors or omissions that may have been made. The publisher remains neutral with regard to jurisdictional claims in published maps and institutional affiliations.

This Springer imprint is published by the registered company Springer Nature Switzerland AG
The registered company address is: Gewerbestrasse 11, 6330 Cham, Switzerland

# Preface

These proceedings contain all accepted submissions to the conference paper track of the 29th International Conference on Inductive Logic Programming (ILP 2019).[1] ILP is a type of symbolic machine learning in which logic of first or higher order is used to represent both the data and the models (theories) learnt. The main conference was held in Plovdiv, Bulgaria, over three days, 3–5 September 2019, and was followed by two tutorials on 6 September 2019.

The ILP 2019 call for papers solicited several types of submissions. This volume consists of 6 long conference papers of up to 15 pages, as well as 5 shorter, more focused contributions of up to 9 pages. Successful submissions to the journal track of the conference have formed the ILP 2019 special issue of the *Machine Learning Journal*,[2] which was edited by Dimitar Kazakov and Filip Železný. Eight late-breaking, 4-page long abstracts were presented at the conference, and made available on the White Rose Research Online repository.[3] The conference also included invited talks by Atanas Kiryakov and Svetla Boytcheva (Ontotext) on reasoning over knowledge graphs, and Preslav Nakov (QCRI/HBKU) on detecting fake news "before it was written." Presentations of three previously published articles (*New Generation Computing*, IJCAI 2019, JELIA 2019) completed the picture of current ILP research.

The overall evidence is that the field has been advancing in a number of directions. These include work on formalisms other than the most commonly used Horn-clause subset of first order logic, e.g. the use of second order logic in meta-interpretive learning, learning in description logics, or the efficient use of propositionalization. The statistical relational learning and probabilistic logic programming paradigms have continued to attract attention, and some of the underlying formalisms are being extended to handle a broader range of data types. The common issue of high computational complexity has also been addressed through the use of concurrency or more efficient algorithms underlying the refinement operators. A general recent trend has also been reflected in the application of ILP to Ethics in AI.

Two best student paper awards were awarded to contributions to these proceedings thanks to the generous sponsorship of the Machine Learning Journal. The 2019 ILP best student paper in the short papers (conference track) category was awarded to Yin Jun Phua and Katsumi Inoue's contribution *Learning Logic Programs from Noisy State Transition Data*. The 2019 ILP best student paper award in the long papers (conference or journal track) category was won by Stefanie Speichert and Vaishak Belle's contribution *Learning Probabilistic Logic Programs over Continuous Data*. Submissions of the latter type were also eligible for the best paper award, which was sponsored by our publisher, Springer. This award was received by Andrew Cropper and Sophie

---

[1] https://ilp2019.wordpress.com.

[2] https://link.springer.com/journal/10994/.

[3] https://eprints.whiterose.ac.uk/.

Tourret for their article *Logical Reduction of Metarules*, which appeared in the ILP 2019 special issue of the Machine Learning Journal.

We would like to thank the members of the Organizing Committee, Bisera Stoyanova (Medical University of Plovdiv, Bulgaria), Ivanka Vlaeva (South-West University Neofit Rilski, Bulgaria), and Raina Hadjikinova (University of Food Technologies, Bulgaria) for their tireless support; the Plovdiv University of Food Technologies as represented by its Vice-Rector, Prof. DSc Nikolay Menkov, for hosting the hands-on tutorials; and Ms. Svetla Malinova of the Ramada Plovdiv Tri-montium Hotel for her professionalism and all-round assistance. The advice of old hands at organizing ILP was very much appreciated, even if occasionally ignored to our own peril. Lastly, but certainly not least, we are grateful to Springer for the sponsorship and editorial support, which, along with the all-important contribution of all authors and reviewers have made these proceedings and the whole conference possible.

September 2019                                                    Dimitar Kazakov
                                                                      Can Erten

# Organization

## Program Chairs

Dimitar Kazakov      University of York, UK
Can Erten      University of York, UK

## Program Committee

| | |
|---|---|
| Dalal Alrajeh | Imperial College London, UK |
| Annalisa Appice | University of Bari Aldo Moro, Italy |
| Alexander Artikis | NCSR Demokritos, Greece |
| Elena Bellodi | University of Ferrara, Italy |
| Hendrik Blockeel | KU Leuven, Belgium |
| Agnès Braud | University of Strasbourg, France |
| Krysia Broda | Imperial College London, UK |
| James Cussens | University of York, UK |
| Tirtharaj Dash | Birla Institute of Technology and Science, India |
| Saso Dzeroski | Jozef Stefan Institute, Slovenia |
| Nicola Fanizzi | University of Bari Aldo Moro, Italy |
| Nuno Fonseca | European Bioinformatics Institute, UK |
| Tamas Horvath | University of Bonn, Germany |
| Katsumi Inoue | Nagoya Institute of Technology, Japan |
| Nobuhiro Inuzuka | Nagoya Institute of Technology, Japan |
| Nikos Katzouris | NCSR Demokritos, Greece |
| Kristian Kersting | TU Darmstadt, Germany |
| Ross King | The University of Manchester, UK |
| Nicolas Lachiche | University of Strasbourg, France |
| Francesca Alessandra Lisi | University of Bari Aldo Moro, Italy |
| Stephen Muggleton | Imperial College London, UK |
| Aline Paes | Fluminense Federal University, Brazil |
| Jan Ramon | Inria-Lille, France |
| Fabrizio Riguzzi | University of Ferrara, Italy |
| Alessandra Russo | Imperial College London, UK |
| Tomoyuki Uchida | Hiroshima City University, Japan |
| Christel Vrain | University of Orléans, France |
| Stefan Wrobel | Fraunhofer IAIS, Germany and University of Bonn, Germany |
| Gerson Zaverucha | Federal University of Rio de Janeiro, Brazil |
| Riccardo Zese | University of Ferrara, Italy |

# Contents

# CONNER: A Concurrent ILP Learner
# in Description Logic

Eyad Algahtani$^{(\boxtimes)}$ and Dimitar Kazakov

University of York, Heslington, York YO10 5GH, UK
ea922@york.ac.uk, kazakov@cs.york.ac.uk
https://www-users.cs.york.ac.uk/kazakov/

**Abstract.** Machine Learning (ML) approaches can achieve impressive results, but many lack transparency or have difficulties handling data of high structural complexity. The class of ML known as Inductive Logic Programming (ILP) draws on the expressivity and rigour of subsets of First Order Logic to represent both data and models. When Description Logics (DL) are used, the approach can be applied directly to knowledge represented as ontologies. ILP output is a prime candidate for explainable artificial intelligence; the expense being computational complexity. We have recently demonstrated how a critical component of ILP learners in DL, namely, cover set testing, can be speeded up through the use of concurrent processing. Here we describe the first prototype of an ILP learner in DL that benefits from this use of concurrency. The result is a fast, scalable tool that can be applied directly to large ontologies.

**Keywords:** Inductive logic programming · Description logics · Ontologies · Parallel computing · GPGPU

## 1 Introduction

Graphic processing units (GPU) can be used with benefits for general purpose computation. GPU-based data parallelism has proven very efficient in a number of application areas [1]. We have recently proposed a GPU-accelerated approach to the computation of the cover set for a given hypothesis expressed in $\mathcal{ALC}$ description logic, which results in a speed up of two orders of magnitude when compared with a single-threaded CPU implementation [2]. The present article combines this approach with an implementation of a well-studied refinement operator and a search strategy for the exploration of the hypothesis space. The result is the first version of a GPU-accelerated inductive learner, further on referred to as CONNER 1.0 (CONcurrent learNER).

In more detail, here we present the first complete description of the way binary predicates (or *roles* in description logic parlance) are handled by our cover set procedure, which is now extended beyond $\mathcal{ALC}$ to make use of cardinality restrictions (e.g. *OffpeakTrain* $\sqsubseteq$ $\leq 6$ *hasCar.Car*) and data properties (e.g. *Bike* $\sqsubseteq$ *numberOfWheels* $= 2$). We test the speed and accuracy of our

© Springer Nature Switzerland AG 2020
D. Kazakov and C. Erten (Eds.): ILP 2019, LNAI 11770, pp. 1–15, 2020.
https://doi.org/10.1007/978-3-030-49210-6_1

learner on a combination of synthetic and real world data sets. To emphasise the low cost of adoption of this algorithm, we have run the tests on a commodity GPU, Nvidia GeForce GTX 1070.

The rest of this paper is structured as follows: Sect. 2 covers relevant work, Sect. 3 completes the previously published description of how the hypothesis cover set is computed [2] with the algorithms handling value restriction and existential restriction, and tests the speed of their execution. Section 4 extends the list of operators with the algorithms for handling the cardinality restriction and data property operators. Section 5 describes a complete GPU-accelerated ILP learner in DL, CONNER, and evaluates its performance, while Sect. 6 draws conclusions and outlines future work.

## 2 Background

CONNER lays at the intersection of ILP, parallel computation, and description logics (Fig. 1). In this section, we review the notable overlaps between these three areas. Algathani and Kazakov [2] can be further consulted for a suitable overview of the basics of GPU architecture.

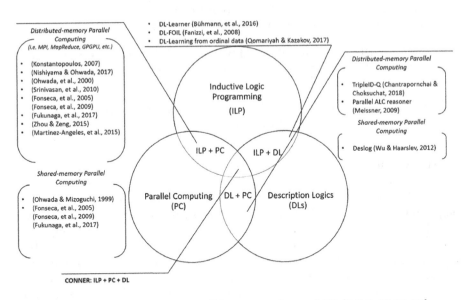

**Fig. 1.** Intersection of ILP, parallel computation and DL [3,5,8–10,16–24].

Arguably, the implementation of an ILP algorithm can be defined by the ways it approaches hypothesis cover set testing, the application of its refinement operator, and the search algorithm used to explore the hypothesis space. While all three are amenable to parallelisation, here we focus our efforts in this direction on the first component, and with a description logic as a hypothesis language.

Description Logics (DL) is a family of subsets of first order logic that are used to represent knowledge in the form of *ontologies*. $\mathcal{ALC}$ (Attributive Language with Complement) is a commonly used subset of DL, which makes use of propositional operators, as well as two binary operators, existential restriction and value restriction. As ontologies continue to gain popularity, e.g. in the form of linked open data, this strengthens the case for learners that can work directly with this type of data. A few notable examples of ILP learners in DL follow.

DL-FOIL [3] is an adaptation of the classical ILP algorithm FOIL [4] to DL as data and hypothesis language. It still uses a top-down refinement operator with search guided by information gain, but the latter is modified to accommodate the use of the Open World Assumption (OWA).

The DL-Learner [5] is a framework for learning in DL. The framework allows the user to select from different reasoners to handle inference. It is also possible to choose from four learning algorithms: OWL Class Expression Learner (OCEL), Class Expression Learning for Ontology Engineering (CELOE), EL Tree Learner (ELTL), and Inductive Statistical Learning of Expressions (ISLE). One can also choose from different refinement operators. The framework provides facilities to handle large datasets by the use of sampling.

APARELL [6] is an ILP algorithm for the learning of ordinal relations (e.g. *better_than* [7]) in DL. The algorithm borrows ideas from the Progol/Aleph pair of algorithms about the way hypothesis search operates. APARELL processes DL data directly from OWL ontologies, and can read any format which is supported by the OWL API.

There have been several attempts to implement reasoners in DL using parallel computation [8,9]. The most relevant effort here is Chantrapornchai and Choksuchat's [10] recently proposed GPU-accelerated framework for RDF query processing, TripleID-Q. The framework maintains a separate hash table for each of the three arguments (*subject, predicate, object*) of the RDF triples. Each triple is represented through the three hash keys (all integers) and stored in the shared memory of the GPU. RDF queries are mapped onto that representation and the data is split among multiple GPU threads to retrieve the matching triples in parallel. In this context, the work of Martínez-Angeles *et al.* on the use of GPU to speed up cover set computation for first-order logic ILP systems, such as Aleph, should also be noted [11].

## 3   Concurrent, GPU-Accelerated Cover Set Computation

A GPU can manipulate matrices very efficiently. Here we complete the description of the GPU-powered approach first presented by Algahtani and Kazakov [2], which aims at speeding up the calculation of the cover set of hypotheses expressed in $\mathcal{ALC}$ description logic. We also present experimental results on the performance of this algorithm.

DL allows one to describe *concepts* $C_i$ defined over a universe of *individuals* $I_i$, and to define *roles* relating individuals to each other. Concept membership can be represented as a Boolean matrix $M$ of size $|C| \times |I|$ (see Fig. 2). Using this representation, it is possible to employ data parallelism for the application of logic operations to concepts. We have already shown how the three propositional operators $\{\sqcap, \sqcup, \neg\}$ can be implemented, and tested the speed with which they are computed [2]. Here we describe the concurrent implementation of the value restriction operator ($\forall r.C$) and the existential restriction operator ($\exists r.C$).

Either restriction operator takes a role and a concept as input, and makes use of the concept matrix $M$ and another matrix, $R$, storing all role assertions (see Fig. 2). The matrix is sorted by the role. As a consequence, all assertions of a given role are stored in a contiguous range of rows. This facilitates a more efficient GPU memory access pattern (namely, coalesced memory access). For each role, the start and end row indices corresponding to its range of rows are stored in a hash table, $H$, and can be retrieved efficiently using the role name as key.

Algorithm 1 shows the implementation of the existential operator. Its first step is to allocate memory for the output array `result` and set all values to 0 (representing `False`). This is done in a concurrent, multi-threaded fashion. The range of rows in $R$ storing all assertions of $Role$ is then looked up in $H$ (in $\mathcal{O}(1)$ time). After that, the role assertions in $R$ within the role range are divided among a number of threads, and for each such assertion, a check in matrix $M$ is made whether `IndvB` belongs to $Concept$ (i.e. the concept in the existential restriction). The result of this step is combined through OR with the current value in row `IndvA` of the output array `result` and stored back there.

This implementation avoids the use of conditional statement, which could slow down the process. At the same time, it is important that an atomic OR is used to avoid a race-condition situation between the individual threads.[1]

|  | C1 | C2 | C3 |  |  | IndvA | Role | IndvB |  |  | DP1 | DP2 | DP3 |
|---|---|---|---|---|---|---|---|---|---|---|---|---|---|
| Indv1 | 0 | 1 | 0 |  |  | 6 | 1 | 46 |  | Indv1 | 3 | 2.5 | 1 |
| Indv2 | 1 | 1 | 0 |  |  | 6 | 1 | 5 |  | Indv2 | 7 | 3.7 | 1 |
| Indv3 | 0 | 0 | 1 |  |  | 9 | 2 | 14 |  | Indv3 | 0 | -0.5 | 0 |

|     (a) Table M     |     (b) Table R     |     (c)  Table D     |

**Fig. 2.** Main data structures in the GPU memory

The implementation of the value restriction operator $\forall Role.Concept$ is analogous to the existential restriction, with the only difference being that all initial values in the $result$ array are set to 1 (i.e. `True`), and an atomic AND operator is applied instead of OR.[2]

---

[1] Here we use the CUDA built-in atomic function `atomicOR(A,B)`, which implements the (atomic) Boolean operation `A := A OR B`.

[2] Note that this implementation returns the correct result for the following special case: if $\nexists IndvB : Role(IndvA, IndvB)$ then $IndvA \in \forall Role.Concept$.

---

**Algorithm 1** Existential Restriction Cover Set ($\exists Role$.Concept)

---

**procedure** PARALLELEXISTENTIALRESTRICTION(CONCEPT,ROLE)

---

```
Given:
M: Boolean 2D matrix of size (individuals x concepts)
R: Integer 2D matrix of size (# of property assertions x 3) // each row
                              // representing a triple: subj,role,obj
HT: hash table // Role -> (Offsets for first and last entries in R)

Concept: Pointer to a column in M
Role: Integer

result: Boolean 1D array of size NumberOfIndividuals

Do:
parallel_foreach thread T_j
| for each individual i in result
| | set result[i] = 0
| endfor
endfor
set role_range := HT[Role] // get range of Role assertions in R from HT
parallel_foreach thread T_j
| foreach roleAssertion in role_range
| | set IndvA := R[row(roleAssertion),1] // first column of roleAssertion
| | set IndvB := R[row(roleAssertion),3] // third column of roleAssertion
| | set local_result := M[row(IndvB),Concept]
| | atomicOR(result[row(IndvA)],local_result)
| endfor
endfor

return result(1..numberOfIndividuals)
```

---

**Table 1.** Execution times for computing the cover sets of $\exists has\_car$.Long and $\forall has\_car$.Long (average of 10).

| Data set size | | | Execution time [ms] | |
|---|---|---|---|---|
| Total number of individuals | Total number of has_car assertions | Total number of all role assertions | $\exists has\_car$.Long mean (stdev) | $\forall has\_car$.Long mean (stdev) |
| 50 | 30 | 149 | 0.49 (0.08) | 0.48 (0.08) |
| 410 | 300 | 1,490 | 0.56 (0.10) | 0.50 (0.10) |
| 4,010 | 3,000 | 14,900 | 0.50 (0.06) | 0.51 (0.08) |
| 40,010 | 30,000 | 149,000 | 0.55 (0.02) | 0.55 (0.03) |
| 400,010 | 300,000 | 1,490,000 | 0.97 (0.02) | 1.02 (0.03) |
| 4,000,010 | 3,000,000 | 14,900,000 | 4.82 (0.05) | 5.85 (0.28) |
| 8,000,010 | 6,000,000 | 29,800,000 | 10.55 (0.34) | 11.38 (0.48) |

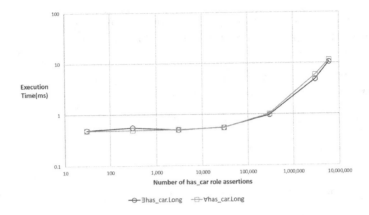

**Fig. 3.** Computing existential (∃) and value (∀) role restrictions

To evaluate the execution times of the two restriction operators, we use a dataset consisting of multiple copies of Michalski's eastbound/westbound trains dataset [12], here in its DL representation [5]. The dataset consists of 12 concepts (unary predicates), and 5 roles (binary predicates); these predicates describe 10 trains (5 eastbound and 5 westbound) and their respective cars. The results are shown in Table 1 and plotted in Fig. 3. It should be noted that only the number of assertions for the given role has an impact on the execution times when matrix R is traversed: while matrix $M$ grows with the number of individuals, access time to each row remains the same as, internally, an individual is represented directly with its row index in $M$. Also, the actual content of the assertions for the role in question makes no difference, which is why this dataset is appropriate here. The results show that the execution times remain virtually constant up to a point, possibly until the full potential for parallel computation in the GPU is harnessed, and then grow more slowly than $\mathcal{O}(n)$ for the range of dataset sizes studied.

## 4   Extending the Hypothesis Language

This section describes how the hypothesis language has now been extended to include cardinality and data property (also known as *concrete role*) restrictions. The result is a type of description logic referred to as $\mathcal{ALCQ}^{(\mathcal{D})}$.

### 4.1   Cardinality Restriction Support

The cardinality operator restricts for a given role the allowed number of assertions per individual. A cardinality restriction can be qualified ($Q$), or unqualified ($N$), where $N$ is a special case of $Q$. In $Q$, any concept can be used in the restriction. While in $N$, only the Top Concept is used. There are three kinds of cardinality restrictions: the minimum ($\geq$), maximum ($\leq$), and the exactly ($==$) restriction. Algorithm 2 implements the first of these three.

---

**Algorithm 2** Qualified Cardinality Restriction Cover Set

---

**procedure** PARALLELCARDINALITYRESTRICTION(CONCEPT,ROLE,N)

```
Given:
M: Boolean 2D matrix of size (individuals x concepts)
R: Integer 2D matrix of size (individuals x 3) // Storing (subj,role,obj)
H: hash table // Role -> (Offsets for first and last entries in R)
Concept: Pointer to a column in M
Role: Integer
n: restriction number
result: Boolean 1D array of size NumberOfIndividuals
Do:
parallel_foreach thread T_j
| for each individual i in result
| | set result[i] = 0
| endfor
endfor
set role_range := H[Role] // retrieve range of Role assertions in R from H
parallel_foreach thread T_j
| foreach roleAssertion in role_range
| | set IndvA := R[row(roleAssertion),1] // first column of roleAssertion
| | set IndvB := R[row(roleAssertion),3] // third column of roleAssertion
| | set local_result := M[row(IndvB),Concept]
| | atomicAdd(result[row(IndvA)],local_result)
| endfor
endfor

parallel_foreach thread T_i
| foreach individual I_j in thread T_i
| | result(row(I_j)):= result(row(I_j)) >= n // OR =< n  OR == n
| endfor
endfor
```

---

**return** result(1..numberOfIndividuals)

---

It first clears the result array (just as in the existential restriction). It then uses the CUDA atomic addition `atomicAdd(A,B)` to increment the counter of the corresponding IndvA for every assertion matching the role and concept. The values in the **result-array** are then compared with the cardinality condition, and the counter for each individual is replaced with 1 or 0 (representing True/False) according to whether the condition in question has been met. The condition in this last loop determines the type of cardinality restriction: min ($\geq$), max ($\leq$), or exactly ($==$).

## 4.2 Data Property Restriction Support

Data properties (or concrete roles) map individuals on to simple values. In this implementation, we (currently) limit the range of values to numerical ones: integer, float and Boolean; supporting other types like Strings, is considered for future work. In order to handle such properties in the GPU, the individuals and their data properties are mapped on to a matrix, $D$ (see Fig. 2), in a way similar to matrix $M$. Each cell in the new 2D matrix, is of float datatype, as it is inclusive to integers and Booleans. As with the cardinality restrictions, there are three kinds of data property restrictions: min, max, and exactly. Algorithm 3 shows how the minimum data property restriction is implemented, with the other two requiring only a trivial variation.

---

**Algorithm 3** Data Property Restriction Cover Set

---

**procedure** PARALLELDATAPROPERTYRESTRICTION(PROPERTY,VALUE)

```
D := 2D matrix (individuals x data properties)
parallel_foreach thread T_i
| foreach individual I_j in thread T_i
| | result(row(I_j)) := D(row(I_j),column(Property)) >= Value //OR =< OR ==
| endfor
endfor
```

---

**return** result(1..numberOfIndividuals)

---

In Algorithm 3, a parallel for loop will iterate through all individuals, and the result—array will be set to 1 for all individuals matching the condition or to 0 otherwise. For the maximum and exactly restriction types, the condition will be changed to $\leq$ (for maximum), and $==$ (for exactly).

## 5  CONNER: All Together Now

The work described in this section was motivated by the desire to incorporate our approach to computing the DL hypothesis cover set in a learner in order to gauge the benefits this approach can offer.

### 5.1  TBox Processing

Every ontology consists of two parts, the so called ABox and TBox. Both of these need to be processed to establish correctly the membership of individuals to concepts. It is possible to employ off-the-shelf reasoners for this purpose. Indeed, this is the approach employed by DL-Learner. While it is expected that CONNER will make the same provision in the next iteration of its development, we have decided to use our own implementation here in order to have full control over how the planned tests are run. The implementation described below is somewhat limited, but sufficient for the test data sets used.

The ABox explicitly lists individuals belonging to a given concept or relation. These are easily processed and matrices $M$ and $R$ updated accordingly. The TBox provides intensional definitions of concepts ($C \equiv \ldots$) and their hierarchy (e.g. $C_1 \sqsubset C_2$). Here we only handle subsumption between single concepts. This information is processed by a dedicated multi-pass algorithm which updates matrix $M$, and is repeated until no further changes in concept definitions occur. Cyclic references are also detected and flagged up as an error. For instance, if the membership of the concept Man is defined extensively, through the ABox, and the TBox contains the statement Man $\sqsubset$ Person, the individuals in Man will also be marked in matrix $M$ as belonging to the concept Person after the TBox is processed (Fig. 4). The TBox needs only be processed once, when the ontology is imported, and represents no overhead on any subsequent computations. The hierarchy of concepts derived from the TBox statements is then used by the refinement operator to generate candidate hypotheses.

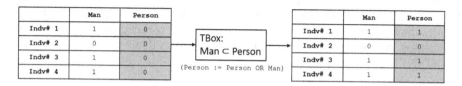

**Fig. 4.** Example of processing the TBox

## 5.2   Refinement Operator and Search Algorithm

CONNER borrows the top-down refinement operators used in DL-Learner. The operator used with $\mathcal{ALC}$ is complete, albeit improper ([13], pp. 69–70). Figure 5 shows a sample $\mathcal{ALC}$ refinement path produced by this operator for a data set discussed in this section. When the hypothesis language is extended to $\mathcal{ALCQ}^{(\mathcal{D})}$, i.e., to include cardinality restrictions and data properties, the corresponding operator is no longer complete ([13], pp. 72–73).

The original operator is capable of producing a hypothesis consisting of a single clause (making use of the disjunction operator, when needed). A refinement step of the type $\top \rightarrow C \sqcup C \sqcup \cdots \sqcup C$ is used to produce a disjunction of concepts that are all subsumed by $C$, e.g. moving from $Car \sqcup Car$ to $Petrol \sqcup Electric$ (potentially excluding $Diesel$). Here the number of copies of $C$ appears to be part of the user input reminiscent of, say, the limit on the maximum length of the target clause used in Progol. We have experimented with alternatives, such as cautious learning where the above step is omitted from the refinement operator, and the disjunction of all consistent clauses found is used in the final hypothesis.

The refinement operator can be used under the closed world assumption (CWA), where test examples not covered by the hypothesis are labelled as negative examples. An example of such use was employed when the DL-Learner was tested by its author on Michalski's trains ([13], pp. 143–146). We have done the same to replicate the results, but we also implement the open world assumption (OWA), which is more commonly used with DL. In this case, two hypotheses $H^+$ and $H^-$ are learned for the target class and its complement (by swapping the positive and negative examples). Test data is labelled as a positive, resp. negative example when either hypothesis is true, and an "I don't know" label is produced when neither or both hypotheses are true.

The learner uses informed search with a scoring function derived from the one used in the OCEL algorithm of the DL-Learner [13]:

$$ocel\_score(N) = accuracy(N) + 0.5.acc\_gain(N) - 0.02.n \qquad (1)$$

Here $acc\_gain(N)$ is the increase in accuracy w.r.t. the parent of $N$, where $N$ is the candidate hypothesis (e.g. conjunction of concepts and/or restrictions), and $n$ is an upper bound on the length of child concepts, which we set to be equal to the number of concepts in the ontology. We extend this function to take into account the length of a hypothesis (i.e. #concepts + #operators) and its depth which represents (here) the refinement steps taken to reach the current hypothesis, not necessarily its depth in the search tree. Thus the scoring function in CONNER is:

$$conner\_score(N) = 10 * ocel\_score(N) - length(N) - depth(N) \qquad (2)$$

The parser currently used to parse the hypotheses tested is Dijkstra's shunting-yard algorithm. The effect of its use here is equivalent to using a binary parse tree, so all conjunctions and disjunctions of three and more concepts are handled as series of applications of the given operator to a pair of concepts. This simplifies the parsing task, but results in a significant drop in performance when compared to simultaneously computing conjunctions or disjunctions of $K$ concepts in the given hypothesis (cf. [2]). A more sophisticated parser or the use of lazy evaluation [2] can be employed with potential benefits, but are not discussed here for reasons of space. We do use *memoization* [14] in the evaluation of each hypothesis, where partial computations are stored and reused.

## 5.3 Evaluation

The overall run time of the learner is first tested under the CWA on data consisting of multiple copies of the Michalski train set (in its DL version distributed with DL-Learner's examples). While the task results in a relatively limited hypothesis space, this artificial data strains the cover set algorithm exactly as much as any real world data set with the same number of instances and assertions. The results are shown in Table 2 and Fig. 6. All experiments are deterministic and the results of multiple runs on the same data are remarkably consistent, so presenting results of single runs was deemed sufficient. Figure 5 shows the search path to the solution found. The solution itself is listed again in Table 3.

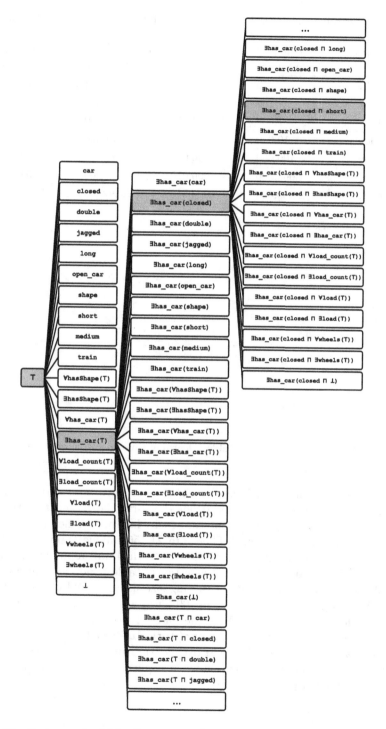

**Fig. 5.** A sample $\mathcal{ALC}$ refinement path to a solution: Michalski's trains

**Table 2.** Learning time vs size of data set (multiple copies of Michalski's trains)

| #Size (by factor) | Training examples | All individuals | #Role assertions | Time [ms] |
|---|---|---|---|---|
| 1x | 10 | 50 | 149 | 227 |
| 10x | 100 | 410 | 1,490 | 233 |
| 100x | 1,000 | 4,010 | 14,900 | 292 |
| 1,000x | 10,000 | 40,010 | 149,000 | 291 |
| 10,000x | 100,000 | 400,010 | 1,490,000 | 712 |
| 100,000x | 1,000,000 | 4,000,010 | 14,900,000 | 2,764 |
| 200,000x | 2,000,000 | 8,000,010 | 29,800,000 | 4,836 |

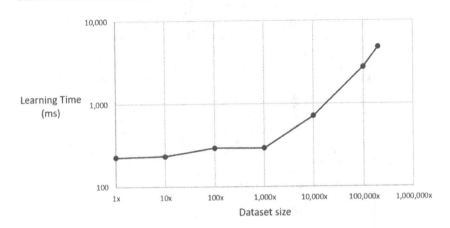

**Fig. 6.** Plot of results in Table 2: learning time vs size of data set

To confirm that all components of the learner have been correctly implemented, and to further test its speed, another artificial data set in the style
of Michalski's trains (here with four cars each) has been generated and used
in a second set of experiments.[3] There are 21,156 unique trains (5,184 eastbound and 15,972 westbound) in the data set, which are represented through
105,780 individuals and 148,092 role assertions. Table 4 shows the average run
times of the learner for data sets of varying size using 10-fold cross-validation.
Under CWA, out-of-sample accuracy of 100% was achieved for all reported samples except for one of the samples of the lowest reported size. The hypothesis
found in most cases is `Train ⊓ ∃has_car(Big ⊓ ∃inFrontOf.Rectangle)`. The
rule `∃has_car.Rectangle ⊓ ∃has_car(Big ⊓ ∃inFrontOf.Rectangle)` is found
by the DL-Learner as its first solution when applied to all data. The two hypotheses are functionally equivalent.

---

[3] The dataset is available from https://osf.io/kf4h6/.

**Table 3.** Solution to Michalski's trains task in DL and FOL

| Description Logic | First Order Logic |
|---|---|
| $\exists$has_car(Closed $\sqcap$ Short) | eastbound(X) $\leftarrow$ $has\_car(X, Y) \wedge$ closed(Y) $\wedge$ short(Y) |

**Table 4.** Learning time vs sample size (21,156 unique trains, 10-fold cross-validation)

| Proportion of data used for training [%] | 0.09 | 0.9 | 90 |
|---|---|---|---|
| Time [ms]: mean (stdev) | 34,106 (90,035) | 1,492 (700) | 1,862 (66) |
| Out-of-sample accuracy [%]: mean (stdev) | 97.64 (0.80) | 100 (0.00) | 100 (0.00) |

We have also tested CONNER on the well-known mutagenesis ILP dataset [15] in its DL representation, using 10-fold cross-validation, with the following results:

Under CWA: $accuracy = 82.61$ $(8.70)\%$

Under OWA: $precision = 96.00$ $(4.63)\%$,
$recall = 80.43$ $(9.22)\%$,
$F\text{-}score = 87.24$ $(6.27)\%$.

## 6   Conclusion and Future Work

This article completes the implementation of the first working prototype of the CONNER algorithm. The results suggest that this GPU-powered ILP learner in DL has a lot of potential to scale up learning from ontologies. We have demonstrated how GPGPU can be used to accelerate the computation of the cover set of a hypothesis expressed in $\mathcal{ALC}$ and $\mathcal{ALCQ}^{(\mathcal{D})}$ description logics. The results add to our previous findings (cf. [2]) that even the use of a commodity GPU can provide the ability to process data sets of size well beyond what can be expected from a CPU-based sequential algorithm of the same type, and within a time that makes the evaluation of hypotheses on a data set with $10^7$–$10^8$ training examples a viable proposition.

Future work should consider provisions for the use of external, off-the-shelf reasoners. However, extending the in-house facilities in this aspect is expected to play an important role when the use of concurrency in the search, and its possible integration with cover set computation are considered. Finally, it should be said that the use of DL as hypothesis language simplifies the task of parallelising the cover set computation when compared to a Horn clause-based hypothesis language. It is clear that some of the problems traditionally tackled through learning in first-order logic can be effectively modelled in DL, and a broader evaluation of the trade-off between expressive power and potential speed up that this choice offers would certainly also provide useful insights.

# References

1. Owens, J.D., et al.: A survey of general-purpose computation on graphics hardware. Comput. Graph. Forum **26**(1), 80–113 (2007)
2. Algahtani, E., Kazakov, D.: GPU-accelerated hypothesis cover set testing for learning in logic. In: CEUR Proceedings of the 28th International Conference on Inductive Logic Programming. CEUR Workshop Proceedings (2018)
3. Fanizzi, N., d'Amato, C., Esposito, F.: DL-FOIL concept learning in description logics. In: Železný, F., Lavrač, N. (eds.) ILP 2008. LNCS (LNAI), vol. 5194, pp. 107–121. Springer, Heidelberg (2008). https://doi.org/10.1007/978-3-540-85928-4_12
4. Quinlan, R.: Learning logical definitions from relations. Mach. Learn. **5**, 239–266 (1990). https://doi.org/10.1007/BF00117105
5. Bühmann, L., Lehmann, J., Westphal, P.: DL-learner - a framework for inductive learning on the semantic web. Web Semant. Sci. Serv. Agents World Wide Web **39**, 15–24 (2016)
6. Qomariyah, N., Kazakov, D.: Learning from ordinal data with inductive logic programming in description logic. In: Programming of the Late Breaking Papers of the 27th International Conference on Inductive Logic, pp. 38–50 (2017)
7. Qomariyah, N., Kazakov, D.: Learning binary preference relations: a comparison of logic-based and statistical approaches. In: Joint Workshop on Interfaces and Human Decision Making for Recommender Systems, Como, Italy (2017)
8. Wu, K., Haarslev, V.: A parallel reasoner for the description logic ALC. In: Proceedings of the 2012 International Workshop on Description Logics (DL 2012) (2012)
9. Meissner, A.: A simple parallel reasoning system for the $\mathcal{ALC}$ description logic. In: Nguyen, N.T., Kowalczyk, R., Chen, S.-M. (eds.) ICCCI 2009. LNCS (LNAI), vol. 5796, pp. 413–424. Springer, Heidelberg (2009). https://doi.org/10.1007/978-3-642-04441-0_36
10. Chantrapornchai, C., Choksuchat, C.: TripleID-Q: RDF query processing framework using GPU. IEEE Trans. Parallel Distrib. Syst. **29**(9), 2121–2135 (2018)
11. Martínez-Angeles, C.A., Wu, H., Dutra, I., Costa, V.S., Buenabad-Chávez, J.: Relational learning with GPUs: accelerating rule coverage. Int. J. Parallel Prog. **44**(3), 663–685 (2015). https://doi.org/10.1007/s10766-015-0364-7
12. Michalski, R.S.: Pattern recognition as rule-guided inductive inference. IEEE Trans. Pattern Anal. Mach. Intell. **PAMI-2**(4), 349–361 (1980)
13. Lehmann, J.: Learning OWL Class Expressions. IOS Press, Amsterdam (2010)
14. Michie, D.: Memo functions and machine learning. Nature **218**, 19–22 (1968)
15. Lavrac, N., Zupanic, D., Weber, I., Kazakov, D., Stepankova, O., Dzeroski, S.: ILPNET repositories on WWW: inductive logic programming systems, datasets and bibliography. AI Commun. **9**(4), 157–206 (1996)
16. Fonseca, N.A., Silva, F., Camacho, R.: Strategies to parallelize ILP systems. In: Kramer, S., Pfahringer, B. (eds.) ILP 2005. LNCS (LNAI), vol. 3625, pp. 136–153. Springer, Heidelberg (2005). https://doi.org/10.1007/11536314_9
17. Fonseca, N.A., Srinivasan, A., Silva, F., Camacho, R.: Parallel ILP for distributed-memory architectures. Mach. Learn. **74**(3), 257–279 (2009). https://doi.org/10.1007/s10994-008-5094-2
18. Fukunaga, A., Botea, A., Jinnai, Y., and Kishimoto, A.: A Survey of Parallel A*. arXiv:1708.05296 (2017)

19. Konstantopoulos, S.K.: A data-parallel version of Aleph. In: Proceedings of the Workshop on Parallel and Distributed Computing for Machine Learning (2007)
20. Nishiyama, H., Ohwada, H.: Yet another parallel hypothesis search for inverse entailment. In: 25th International Conference on ILP (2017)
21. Ohwada, H., Mizoguchi, F.: Parallel execution for speeding up inductive logic programming systems. In: Arikawa, S., Furukawa, K. (eds.) DS 1999. LNCS (LNAI), vol. 1721, pp. 277–286. Springer, Heidelberg (1999). https://doi.org/10.1007/3-540-46846-3_25
22. Ohwada, H., Nishiyama, H., and Mizoguchi, F.: Concurrent Execution of Optimal Hypothesis Search for Inverse Entailment. In: Cussens J., Frisch A. (eds) Inductive Logic Programming. ILP 2000. LNCS, vol. 1866, pp. 165-173. Heidelberg (2000). https://doi.org/10.1007/3-540-44960-4_10
23. Srinivasan, A., Faruquie, T.A., Joshi, S.: Exact data parallel computation for very large ILP datasets. In: The 20th International Conference on ILP (2010)
24. Zhou, Y. and Zeng, J.: Massively parallel A* search on a GPU. 29$^{th}$ AAAI Conference on Artificial Intelligence (2015)

# Towards Meta-interpretive Learning of Programming Language Semantics

Sándor Bartha[1(✉)] and James Cheney[1,2]

[1] Laboratory for Foundations of Computer Science, University of Edinburgh,
Edinburgh, Scotland
sandor.bartha@ed.ac.uk, jcheney@inf.ed.ac.uk
[2] The Alan Turing Institute, London, UK

**Abstract.** We introduce a new application for inductive logic programming: learning the semantics of programming languages from example evaluations. In this short paper, we explore a simplified task in this domain using the Metagol meta-interpretive learning system. We highlight the challenging aspects of this scenario, including abstracting over function symbols, nonterminating examples, and learning non-observed predicates, and propose extensions to Metagol helpful for overcoming these challenges, which may prove useful in other domains.

## 1 Introduction

Large systems often employ idiosyncratic domain specific languages, such as scripting, configuration, or query languages. Often, these languages are specified in natural language, or no specification exists at all. Lack of a clear specification leads to inconsistencies across implementations, maintenance problems, and security risks. Moreover, a formal semantics is prerequisite to applying formal methods or static analysis to the language.

In this short paper, we consider the problem: Given an opaque implementation of a programming language, can we reverse-engineer an interpretable semantics from input/output examples? The outlined objective is not merely of theoretical interest: it is a task currently done manually by experts. Krishnamurthi et al. [7] cite a number of recent examples for languages such as JavaScript, Python, and R that are the result of months of work by research groups. Reverse-engineering a formal specification involves writing a lot of small example programs, then testing their behaviour with an opaque implementation.

Krishnamurthi et al. [7] highlights the importance of this research challenge. They describe the motivation behind learning the semantics of programming languages, and discuss three different techniques that they have attempted, showing that all of them have shortcomings. However, inductive logic programming (ILP) was not one of the considered approaches. A number of tools for computer-aided semantics exploration are already based on logic or relational programming, like λProlog [10] or αProlog [1], or PLT Redex [6].

© Springer Nature Switzerland AG 2020
D. Kazakov and C. Erten (Eds.): ILP 2019, LNAI 11770, pp. 16–25, 2020.
https://doi.org/10.1007/978-3-030-49210-6_2

Inductive logic programming seems like a natural fit for this domain: it provides human-understandable programs, allows decomposing learning problems by providing partial solutions as background knowledge (BK), and naturally supports complex structures such as abstract syntax trees and inference rules, which are the main ingredients of *structural operational semantics* (SOS) [14]. These requirements make other popular learning paradigms, including most statistical methods, hard to apply in this setting.

In this short paper we consider a simplified form of this task: given a base language, learn the rules for different extensions to the language from examples of input-output behavior. We assume that representative examples of the language behaviour are available – we are focusing on the learning part for now. We assume that we already have a parser for the language, and deal with its abstract syntax only. We also assume that the base language semantics (an untyped lambda-calculus) is part of the background knowledge.

We investigated the applicability of meta-interpretive learning (MIL) [12], a state-of-the-art framework for ILP, on this problem. In particular we used Metagol [3], an efficient implementation of MIL in Prolog. Our work is based on previous work on MIL [4]. We especially relied on the inspiring insight of how to learn higher-order logic functions with MIL [2]. Semantics learning is a challenging case study for Metagol, as interpreters are considerably more complex than the classic targets of ILP.

We found that Metagol is not flexible enough to express the task of learning semantic rules from examples. The main contribution of the paper is showing how to solve a textbook example of programming language learning by extending Metagol. The extension, called Metagol$_{PLS}$, can handle learning scenarios with partially-defined predicates, can learn the definition of a single-step evaluation subroutine given only examples of a full evaluation, and can learn rules for predicates without examples and learn multiple rules or predicates from single examples.

We believe that these modifications could prove to be useful outside of the domain of learning semantics. These modifications have already been incorporated to the main Metagol repository [3]. We also discuss additional modifications, to handle learning rules with unknown function symbols and to handle non-terminating examples, which are included in Metagol$_{PLS}$ but not Metagol.

All source code of Metagol$_{PLS}$ and our semantics learning scenarios are available on GitHub: https://github.com/barthasanyi/metagol_PLS.

## 2   A Case Study

Due to space limits, we cannot provide a complete introduction to Metagol and have to rely on other publications describing it [12]. Briefly, in Metagol, an ILP problem is specified using examples, background knowledge (BK), and *meta-rules* that describe possible rule structures, with unknown predicates abstracted as *metavariables*. Given a target predicate and examples, Metagol attempts to solve the positive examples using a meta-interpreter which may instantiate the meta-rules. When this happens, the metarule instances are retained and become part of the candidate solution. Negative examples are used to reject too-general candidate solutions.

First we give a formal definition of the general problem. Let $\mathcal{L}$ be the set of abstract syntax trees represented as Prolog terms. Let $L \subset \mathcal{L}$ be the language whose semantics we wish to learn, and let $V \subset L$ be the set of values (possible outputs). Let the behaviour of the opaque interpreter be represented as a function: $I : L \rightarrow V \cup \{\bot\}$, where $\bot$ represents divergent computations. The function can be assumed to be the identity function on values: $\forall v \in V, I(v) = v$. We do not have the definition of $I$, but we can evaluate it on any $e \in L$ term.

We assume that a partial model of the interpreter is defined in Prolog: let $B$ be the background knowledge, a set of Prolog clauses, which contains a partial definition of the binary **eval** predicate. We wish to extend the **eval** predicate so that it matches the $I$ function. Let $\mathcal{H}$ be the hypothesis space, a set of clauses that contains additional evaluation rules that may extend $B$.

The inputs are $L, I, B$ and $\mathcal{H}$. The expected output is $H \subset \mathcal{H}$, such that

1. $\forall e \in L, v \in V : I(e) = v \Longrightarrow B \cup H \vDash \texttt{eval}(e, v)$
2. $\forall e \in L, v \in V : I(e) \neq v \Longrightarrow B \cup H \nvDash \texttt{eval}(e, v)$
3. $\forall e \in L : I(e) = \bot \Longrightarrow \forall v \in V : B \cup H \nvDash \texttt{eval}(e, v)$

Note that in this learning scenario we cannot guarantee the correctness of the output, as we assumed that $I$ is opaque and we can only test its behaviour on a finite number of examples. We can merely empirically test the synthesized rules on suitable terms against the implementation, possibly adding terms to the examples where we get different results, and restarting the learning process. This actually matches the current practice by humans, as one reason for the tediousness of obtaining the semantics is that the existing implementation of the language is usually not intelligible.

As a case study of the applicability of Metagol to this general task, we chose a classic problem from PL semantics textbooks: extending the small-step structural operational semantics of the $\lambda$-calculus with pairs and its selector functions **fst** and **snd**. By analysing this problem we show how can we represent learning tasks in this domain with MIL, and what modifications of the framework are needed.

In this case the language $L$ contains $\lambda$-terms extended with pairs and selectors, and the background knowledge $B$ is an interpreter (SOS semantics) in Prolog implementing the $\lambda$-calculus:

```
step(app(lam(X,T1),V),T2)   :- substitute(V,X,T1,T2).
step(app(T1,T2),app(T3,T2)) :- step(T1,T3).

eval(E1,E1) :- value(E1).
eval(E1,E3) :- step(E1,E2) , eval(E2,E3).
```

Here, **substitute** is another BK predicate whose definition we omit, which performs capture-avoiding substitution. The **step** predicate defines a single evaluation step, e.g. substituting a value for a function parameter. The **value** predicate recognizes fully-evaluated values, and the `eval` predicate either returns its first argument if it is a value, or evaluates it one step and then returns the result of further evaluation.

We wish to extend our calculus and its interpreter with pairs: a constructor `pair` that creates a pair from two λ-terms, and two built-in operations: `fst` and `snd`, that extract the corresponding components from a pair. We want to learn all of the semantic rules that need to be added to our basic λ-calculus interpreter from example evaluations of terms that contain pairs. For example, we wish to learn that the components of the pair can be evaluated by a recursive call, and that a pair is a value if both of its components are values.

Our main contribution was interpreting this learning problem as a task for ILP. We include the whole interpreter for the λ-calculus in the BK. In MIL the semantic bias is expressed in the form of meta-rules [13]. Meta-rules are templates or schemes for Prolog rules: they can contain predicate variables in place of predicate symbols. We needed to write meta-rules that encompass the possible forms of the small-step semantic rules required to evaluate pairs.

Substitution is tricky on name binding operations, but fairly trivial on any other construct, and can be handled with a general recursive case for all such constructs. We assumed that we only learn language constructs that do not involve name binding, and included a full definition of substitution in the BK.

In general, we consider examples `eval(e,v)` where `e` is an expression and `v` is the value it evaluates to (according to some opaque interpreter). Consider this positive example (Metagol's search is only guided by the positive examples):

```
eval( app( lam(x,fst(var(x))) ,
           pair( app( lam(x,pair( app( lam( z, var(z)),var(x))
                 ,var(y))) , var(z)) , var(x)) ) ,
      pair(var(z),var(y)) )
```

which says that the lambda-term $(\lambda x.\mathtt{fst}(x))\ ((\lambda x.\ (\ (\lambda z.z)x, y))\ z, x)$ evaluates to $(z, y)$. Using just this example, we might expect to learn rules such as:

```
step(fst(pair(A,B)),A).
step(pair(A,B),pair(C,B)) :- step(A,C).
value(pair(A,B)) :- value(A),value(B).
```

The first rule extracts the first component of a pair; the second says that evaluation of a pair can proceed if the first subexpression can take an evaluation step. The third rule says that a pair of values is a value. Note that the example above does not mention `snd`; additional examples are needed to learn its behavior.

Unfortunately, directly applying Metagol to this problem does not work. What are the limitations of the Metagol implementation that prevents it from solving our learning problem? We compared the task to the examples demonstrating the capabilities of Metagol in the official Metagol repository and the literature about MIL, and found three crucial features that are not covered:

1. For semantics learning, we do not know in advance what function symbols should be used in the meta-rules. Metagol allows abstracting over predicate symbols in meta-rules, but not over function symbols.

2. Interpreters for Turing-complete languages may not halt. Moreover, nontermination may give useful information about evaluation order, for example to distinguish lazy and eager evaluation. Metagol does not handle learning nonterminating predicates.

3. In semantics learning, we may only have examples for a relation `eval` that describes the overall input/output behavior of the interpreter, but we wish to learn subroutines such as `value` that recognize when an expression is fully evaluated, and `step` that describes how to perform one evaluation step. Metagol considers a simple learning scenario with a single learned predicate with examples for that predicate.

In the following we investigate each difference, and show amendments to the Metagol framework that let us overcome them.

# 3   Overview of Metagol$_{\text{PLS}}$

## 3.1   Function Variables in the Meta-rules

As a first-order language, Prolog does not allow variables in predicate or function positions of terms. The MIL framework uses predicate variables in meta-rules. In Metagol meta-rules can contain predicate variables because atomic formulas are automatically converted to a list format with the built-in =.. Prolog operator inside meta-rules.

We demonstrated that function variables can be supported in a similar vein in the meta-interpretive learning framework, converting compound terms to lists inside the meta-rules. We added a simple syntactic transformation to Metagol$_{\text{PLS}}$to automate these conversions.

As an example, consider a general rule that expresses the evaluation of the left component under a binary constructor. In this general rule for the fixed `step` predicate there are no unknown predicates. But we do not know the binary constructor of the abstract syntax of the language, which we wish to learn from examples. With logic notation, we can write this general rule as the following:

$$\exists \mathbb{H} \quad \forall L1, L2, R : \texttt{step}(\mathbb{H}(L1, R), \mathbb{H}(L2, R)) \leftarrow \texttt{step}(L1, L2)$$

where $\mathbb{H}$ stands for an arbitrary function symbol. Using lists instead of compound terms, we can write this meta-rule in the following format:

```
metarule(step21,[step,H],([step,[H,L1,R],[H,L2,R]]
   :- [[step,L1,L2]])).
```

## 3.2   Non-terminating Examples

Interpreters for Turing-complete languages are inherently non-total: for some terms the evaluation may not terminate. Any learning method must be able to deal with non-termination, but due to the halting problem it is impossible to do exactly: any solution will be either unsound or incomplete. Nevertheless, a pragmatic approach is to introduce some bound on the evaluation. We added a user definable, global depth limit to Metagol. By using this approach we lose some formal results about learnability, but it seems to work well in practice.

Non-termination can also distinguish lazy and eager evaluation strategies. To able to separate the two evaluation strategies, we used a three-valued semantics for the examples. We distinguished non-termination from failure: in addition to the traditional classification of the examples into positive and negative ones, we introduced a third kind: non-terminating examples.

A non-terminating example means that the evaluation exceeds the depth limit; positive or negative examples are intended to succeed or finitely fail within the depth limit.

### 3.3   Non-observation Predicate and Multi-predicate Learning

Metagol learns one predicate, determined from the examples. The rules synthesized for this predicate can call predicates completely defined in the BK. This is the usual *single-predicate* and *observation predicate learning* scenario.

In our task the examples are provided for the top level predicate `eval`, for which we do not want to learn new rules: it is defined in the BK. The semantic rules themselves that we want to learn are expressed by two predicates: `step` and `value`, called by the `eval` predicate. The `step` and `value` predicates are partially defined in the BK: we have some predefined rules, but we want to learn new ones for the new language constructs.

We found that this more complex learning scenario can be expressed with interpreted predicates [2]. They have been used to learn higher order predicates; we show that they can also be used for *non-observation predicate learning* and *multi-predicate learning*.

We showed that interpreted predicates are useful for first order learning, too: as they are executed by the meta-interpreter, they may refer to predicates that are not completely defined in the BK, but need to be learnt. The meta-interpreter can simply switch back to learning mode from executing mode when it encounters a non-defined or partially defined predicate.

We added support for a special markup for predicate names to Metagol. We required the user to mark which predicates can be used in the head of a meta-rule, and similarly, to mark which predicates can be used in the body of a meta-rule. This change extends the capabilities of Metagol in three ways:

1. Non-observation predicate learning: We can include learned predicates in the BK, and learn predicates lower down in the call hierarchy. The examples can be for a predicate in the BK, and we can learn other predicates, that do not have their own examples.
2. Multi-predicate learning: We can learn more than one predicate, and the examples can be for more than one predicate.

This simple change nevertheless allows more flexible learning scenarios than the standard ILP setup. These changes have been incorporated into the official version of Metagol [3].

## 4   Evaluation

Our modified version of Metagol and the tests are available on GitHub https:// github.com/barthasanyi/metagol_PLS. All tests benefit from the changes that allow a more flexible learning scenario (Sect. 3.3), learning non-terminating predicates (Sect. 3.2), and function metavariables (Sect. 3.1).

We coded three hand-crafted learning scenarios: learning the semantics of pairs, learning the semantics of lists (very similar to pairs), and learning the semantics of a conditional expression (if then else). Additionally we showed in a fourth scenario that we can distinguish eager and lazy evaluation of the $\lambda$-calculus based on a suitable term that terminates with lazy evaluation, but does not terminate with eager evaluation:

```
eval(app(lam(x,var(y)), app(lam(x,app(var(x),var(x))),
                        lam(x,app(var(x),var(x))))),_)
```

All four case studies use the same hypothesis space (the same set of meta-rules), and the same BK. The meta-rules are similar to the one mentioned in Sect. 3.1. The BK contains the interpreter for the $\lambda$-calculus extended with simple integer arithmetic, as well as two predicates that select a component. They are used in the induced rules for pairs, lists and conditionals:

```
left(A,_,A).          right(_,B,B).
```

The evaluation examples are hand-crafted for each case study, and they are similar to the one showed earlier in Sect. 2. The semantic rules are decomposed into multiple predicates in the output, since MIL tends to invent and re-use predicates. We show this through the example of the synthesized semantics of conditionals. Conditionals are represented with two binary predicates in our target language: if(A,thenelse(B,C)). We chose this format to avoid too many extra meta-rules for ternary predicates.

The induced rules for conditionals are (order re-arranged for readability):

```
step(if(A,B),C) :- pred_1(A,B,C).          % Select apprpopriate branch
pred_1(false,A,B) :- pred_3(A,B).
pred_1(true,A,B) :- pred_2(A,B).
pred_2(thenelse(A,B),C) :- left(A,B,C).
pred_3(thenelse(A,B),C) :- right(A,B,C).
step(if(A,B),if(C,B)) :- step(A,C).        % Evaluate condition inside
value(false).                              % Boolean literals are values
value(true).
```

Finally, we demonstrated that the four learning tasks can be learned sequentially: we can learn a set of operational semantic rules from one task and add these to the BK for the next task. We chained all four demonstrations together, synthesizing a quite large set of semantic rules (25 rules total). Metagol does not scale up to learning this many rules in a single learning task: according to our preliminary investigations, the runtime is roughly exponential, which matches the theoretical results [5]. Even synthesizing half as many rules can take hours. Sequential learning has been implemented in Metagol [9], but the flexible learning scenarios required extending this functionality.

The examples run fairly fast: even the combined learning scenario finishes under 0.2 seconds on our machine. However, during our preliminary experiments with hand-crafted examples we found that the running time of Metagol tasks greatly depends on the order of the examples: there can be orders of magnitude running time differences between example sets. Further research is needed to determine how to obtain good example sets.

## 5   Conclusion and Future Work

This research is a first step towards a distant goal. Krishnamurthi et al. [7] make a strong case that the goal is both important and challenging.

We have demonstrated that with modifications MIL can synthesize structural semantic rules for a simple programming language from suitable (hand-crafted) examples. But we only considered relatively simple language semantics learning scenarios, so further work is need to scale up the method to realistic languages.

The most crucial issue is scalability, which is the general problem for MIL. MIL does not scale well to many meta-rules and large programs. In our experiments we found that synthesizing less than 10 rules is fast, but synthesizing more than 20 seems to be impossible. As a comparison, the SOS semantics of real-world languages may contain hundreds of rules. Therefore we need a method to partition the task: to generate suitable examples that characterize the behaviour of the language on a small set of constructs, and to prune the set of meta-rules, which can be large. Our sequential learning case study ensures that once the problem is partitioned, we can learn the rules, but it does not help with the actual partitioning. Alternatively, other ILP systems that support learning recursive predicates, such as XHAIL [15] or ILASP [8], could be tried.

In our artificial example, substitution rules were added to the BK. In the presence of name binding constructs, correct (capture-avoiding) substitution is tricky to implement in Prolog. However, new language features sometimes involve name-binding and real languages sometimes employ non-standard definitions of substitution or binding. Substitution, while ubiquitous, is a not a good target for machine learning to start our investigations in this new domain. One direction could be to include name binding features (following $\lambda$-Prolog [10] or $\alpha$-Prolog [1]) that make it easier to implement substitution.

Another direction is to test the method on more complex semantic rules. Modular structural operational semantics (MSOS) [11] gives us hope that it is possible: it expresses the semantics of complex languages in a modular way, which means that the rules do not need to be changed when other rules change. MSOS can be implemented in Prolog.

For a working system we also need some semi-automatic translation from the concrete syntax of the language to abstract syntax. This is a different research problem, but could also be a suitable candidate for ILP.

Krishnamurthi et al. [7] framed the same general problem differently: they assume that we know the core semantics in the form of an abstract language, and we need to learn syntactic transformations in the form of tree transducers that reduce the full language to this core language. They attempted several learning techniques, each with shortcomings, but did not consider ILP, so applying ILP to their problem could be an interesting direction to take.

**Acknowledgments.** The authors wish to thank Andrew Cropper, Vaishak Belle, and anonymous reviewers for comments. This work was supported by ERC Consolidator Grant Skye (grant number 682315).

# References

1. Cheney, J., Urban, C.: Nominal logic programming. ACM Trans. Program. Lang. Syst. **30**(5), 26:1–26:47 (2008)
2. Cropper, A., Muggleton, S.H.: Learning higher-order logic programs through abstraction and invention. In: IJCAI, pp. 1418–1424. AAAI Press (2016)
3. Cropper, A., Muggleton, S.H.: Metagol System (2016). https://github.com/metagol/metagol
4. Cropper, A., Tamaddoni-Nezhad, A., Muggleton, S.H.: Meta-interpretive learning of data transformation programs. In: Inoue, K., Ohwada, H., Yamamoto, A. (eds.) ILP 2015. LNCS (LNAI), vol. 9575, pp. 46–59. Springer, Cham (2016). https://doi.org/10.1007/978-3-319-40566-7_4
5. Cropper, A., Tourret, S.: Derivation reduction of metarules in meta-interpretive learning. In: Riguzzi, F., Bellodi, E., Zese, R. (eds.) ILP 2018. LNCS (LNAI), vol. 11105, pp. 1–21. Springer, Cham (2018). https://doi.org/10.1007/978-3-319-99960-9_1
6. Felleisen, M., Findler, R.B., Flatt, M.: Semantics Engineering with PLT Redex, 1st edn. The MIT Press, Cambridge (2009)
7. Krishnamurthi, S., Lerner, B.S., Elberty, L.: The next 700 semantics: a research challenge. In: SNAPL (2019)
8. Law, M., Russo, A., Broda, K.: The ILASP system for learning answer set programs (2015). https://www.doc.ic.ac.uk/~ml1909/ILASP
9. Lin, D., Dechter, E., Ellis, K., Tenenbaum, J., Muggleton, S.: Bias reformulation for one-shot function induction. In: ECAI, pp. 525–530 (2014)
10. Miller, D., Nadathur, G.: Programming with Higher-Order Logic, 1st edn. Cambridge University Press, New York (2012)
11. Mosses, P.D.: Modular structural operational semantics. J. Logic Algebraic Program. **60–61**, 195–228 (2004)
12. Muggleton, S.H., Lin, D., Pahlavi, N., Tamaddoni-Nezhad, A.: Meta-interpretive learning: application to grammatical inference. Mach. Learn. **94**(1), 25–49 (2014). https://doi.org/10.1007/s10994-013-5358-3
13. Muggleton, S.H., Lin, D., Tamadoni-Nezhad, A.: Meta-interpretive learning of higher-order dyadic datalog: predicate invention revisited. Mach. Learn. **100**(1), 49–73 (2015)

14. Plotkin, G.D.: A structural approach to operational semantics. J. Logic Algebraic Program. **60–61**, 17–139 (2004)
15. Ray, O.: Nonmonotonic abductive inductive learning. J. Appl. Logic **7**(3), 329–340 (2009). https://doi.org/10.1016/j.jal.2008.10.007

# Towards an ILP Application in Machine Ethics

Abeer Dyoub[1], Stefania Costantini[1], and Francesca A. Lisi[2(✉)]

[1] Dipartimento di Ingegneria e Scienze dell'Informazione e Matematica,
Università degli Studi dell'Aquila, L'Aquila, Italy
Abeer.Dyoub@graduate.univaq.it, Stefania.Costantini@univaq.it
[2] Dipartimento di Informatica & Centro Interdipartimentale di Logica e
Applicazioni (CILA), Università degli Studi di Bari "Aldo Moro", Bari, Italy
FrancescaAlessandra.Lisi@uniba.it

**Abstract.** Machine Ethics is a newly emerging interdisciplinary field which is concerned with adding an ethical dimension to Artificial Intelligent (AI) agents. In this paper we address the problem of representing and acquiring rules of codes of ethics in the online customer service domain. The proposed solution approach relies on the non-monotonic features of Answer Set Programming (ASP) and applies ILP. The approach is illustrated by means of examples taken from the preliminary tests conducted with a couple of state-of-the-art ILP algorithms for learning ASP rules.

**Keywords:** Answer Set Programming · Machine Ethics · ILP Applications

## 1 Introduction

*Motivation and Background.* Robots in elder care, robot nannies, virtual companions, chatbots, robotic weapons systems, autonomous cars, etc. are examples of some of the AI systems currently undergoing research and development. These kinds of systems usually need to engage in complex interactions with humans. To ensure that these systems will not violate the rights of human being and also will carry out only ethical actions (*i.e.*, actions that follow acceptable ethical principles), a combination of AI and ethics has become mandatory. This is the subject for a newly emerging interdisciplinary field known under the name of *Machine Ethics* [9].

Moral decision-making and judgment is a complicated process involving many aspects: it is considered as a mixture of reasoning and emotions. In addition, moral decision making is highly flexible, contextual and culturally diverse. Since the beginning of this century there have been several attempts at implementing ethical decision making into AI agents using different approaches. However, no fully descriptive and widely accepted model of moral judgment and decision-making exists.

© Springer Nature Switzerland AG 2020
D. Kazakov and C. Erten (Eds.): ILP 2019, LNAI 11770, pp. 26–35, 2020.
https://doi.org/10.1007/978-3-030-49210-6_3

Ethics in customer dealings present the company in a good image, and customers will trust the company in the future. Ethics improves the quality of service and promotes positive relationships. Many top leading companies have a booklet called "code of conduct and ethics" and new employees are made to sign it. However, enforcing codes of conduct and ethics is not an easy task. These codes are mostly abstract and general rules, *e.g.* confidentiality, accountability, honesty, inclusiveness, empathy, fidelity, etc. Therefore they are quite difficult to apply. Moreover, they often contain open textured terms that cover a wide range of specific situations [8]. They are subject to interpretations and may have different meanings in different contexts. Thus, there is an implementation problem from the computational point of view. It is difficult to use deductive logic to address such a problem [12]. It is impossible for experts to define intermediate rules to cover all possible situations. Codes of ethics in their abstract form are very difficult to apply in real situations [6]. All the above mentioned reasons make learning from cases and generalization crucial for judgment of future cases and violations.

*Contribution.* In this work and in the view of future ethical chatbots, we propose an approach for addressing the problem of evaluating the ethical behavior of customer service employees for violations w.r.t. the codes of ethics and conduct of their company. Our approach is based on a combination of Answer Set Programming (ASP) and Inductive Logic Programming (ILP). We use ASP for ethical knowledge representation, and ILP for learning the ASP rules needed for reasoning.

Ethical reasoning is a form of *commonsense* reasoning. Ethical rules normally have exceptions like many other rules in real life. Nonmonotonic logic can effectivelly express exceptions which are represented using NAF (Negation-As-Failure). ASP provides an elegant mechanism for handling negation in logic programming (see, *e.g.*, [3] for an overview of ASP and its applications). Logic Programming based on classical Horn logic is not sufficiently expressive for representing incomplete human knowledge, and inadequate for characterizing non-monotonic commonsense reasoning [11]. This in fact nominates non-monotonic logics which simulate common sense reasoning to be used for formalizing different ethical conceptions. In addition, the expressiveness of ASP, the readability of its code and the performance of the available "solvers" gained ASP an important role in the field of AI.

Two very important and desired aspects of Machine Ethics are *explainability* and *accountability*. Among the many machine learning approaches, ILP was chosen because it supports both. Indeed, ILP is known for its explanatory power which is compelling: clauses of the generated rules can be used to formulate an explanation of the choice of a certain decision over others. Moreover, ILP seems better suited than statistical learning methods to domains in which training examples are scarce as in the case of ethical domain. However, traditional ILP is not able to handle exceptions to general rules. Often, the exceptions to the rules themselves follow a pattern, which can be learned as well, resulting in a default theory that describes the underlying model more accurately.

Furthermore, ASP is a highly declarative LP paradigm. ILP systems are not declarative enough. Users need to experiment with ordering of the clauses, this being relevant not only to efficiency but even to termination and correctness [2]. There has been some interest in extending ILP to the ASP framework. In this work we use two systems which have been proposed to learn ASP rules, viz. XHAIL [10], and ILED [7]. XHAIL is a non-monotonic mode-directed ILP approach that integrates abductive, deductive and inductive reasoning in a common learning framework for learning normal logic programs. XHAIL ensures soundness by generalizing all examples in one go. XHAIL is a state-of-the-art system among its Inverse Entailment-based peer algorithms, in terms of completeness. However, a serious obstacle that prevents XHAIL and other similar ILP algorithms from being widely applicable as a machine learning system in real world applications is scalability. XHAIL scales poorly, partly because of the increased computational complexity of abduction, which lies at the core of its functionality, and partly because of the combinatorial complexity of learning whole theories, which may result in an intractable search space. ILED is a novel incremental algorithm based on XHAIL machinery and scales it to large volumes of sequential data, typically suitable for the type of applications that we present in this paper where examples arrive and grow overtime. There are two key features of ILED that contribute towards its scalability: First, reprocessing of past experience is necessary only in the case where new clauses are generated by a revision, and is redundant in the case where a revision consists of refinements of existing clauses only. Second, reprocessing of past experience requires a single pass over the historical memory, meaning that it suffices to revisit each past window exactly once to ensure that the output revised hypothesis $H_{n+1}$ is complete & consistent w.r.t. the entire historical memory.

Several previous works have suggested the use of either ASP (see, *e.g.*, [5]) or ILP (see, *e.g.*, [1]) for programming ethical AI agents. We think that an approach combining the two would have a greater potential than previous proposals.

*Structure.* The paper is organized as follows. In Sect. 2 we present the application we are addressing by means of illustrative examples. Then we conclude with final remarks and future directions in Sect. 3.

## 2   Learning ASP Rules for Ethical Customer Service

Codes of ethics in domains such as customer service are mostly abstract general codes, which refer to notions like confidentiality, accountability, honesty, fidelity, etc. They are subject to interpretations and may have different meanings in different contexts. Therefore it is quite difficult if not impossible to define codes in a manner that they maybe applied deductively. Also it is not possible for experts to define intermediate rules to cover all possible situations to which a particular code applies. In addition, there are many situations in which obligations might conflict. An important question to ask here is how can the company's managers evaluate the ethical behavior of employees in such setting. To achieve this end, and help managers to have detailed rules in place for monitoring the behavior of their employees at customer service for violations of the company's ethical codes, we propose an approach for generating these rules from interactions with customers. So, the new codes of ethics to be used for ethical evaluation are a combination of the existing clear codes (those that give a clear evaluation procedure that can be deductively encoded using ASP) and the newly generated ones. As already mentioned in the introduction, we use ASP for representing the domain knowledge, the ontology of the domain, and scenarios information. In the following we briefly report the results obtained with the implementations of XHAIL[1] and ILED[2] made available by their authors. In the case of ILED we have used the *mongodb* database for the historical memory of our examples.

*Batch learning with XHAIL.* To learn the rules required for ethical reasoning and evaluation of the agent behavior in a certain scenario, we initially use XHAIL system. The inputs to the system are a series of scenarios(cases) in the form of requests and answers, along with the ethical evaluation of the response considering each particular situation. The system remembers the facts about the narratives and the conclusions given to it by the user, and learns to form rules and relations that are consistent with the evaluation given by the user of the responses to the given requests.

To illustrate our approach, let us consider the following scenario:

**case1:** A client contacts the customer service of a company to ask for a particular product of the company, and the employee talks about the product and tries to convince the customer to buy the product. (S)he starts saying that the product is environmentally friendly (which is irrelevant in this case), and this is an advantage of their product over the same products of other companies. It is unethical to make use of irrelevant but sensitive slogans like "environmentally friendly" to attract and provoke the customers to buy a certain product or service. This can be considered a violation of the ethical principle of 'Honesty'.

We can form an ILP task $ILP(B, E = \{E^+, E^-\}, M)$ for our example, where $B$ is the background knowledge, $E$ are the positive and negative examples, and $M$ are The mode declarations. The three steps of XHAIL to derive the hypothesis are shown with the example in Table 1.

Now, let us consider our agent having three cases together, the above mentioned case and the following two cases (scenarios) along with a set of examples for each case.

**case2:** An employee gives information about client1 to client2 without checking or being sure that client2 is authorized to access such information. This behavior is unethical because it violates 'Confidentiality' which is very critical especially when dealing with sensitive products and services like services or products provided to patients with critical medical conditions.

---

[1] https://github.com/cathexis-bris-ac-uk/XHAIL.
[2] https://github.com/nkatzz/ILED.

**Table 1.** Test with XHAIL: input, steps and output theory

| Input | |
|---|---|
| **Facts(part of B)** | **Conclusion(examples E)** |
| ask(customer,infoabout(productx)) | unethical(environmentallyFriendly) |
| answer(environmentallyFriendly) | |
| sensitiveSlogan(environmentallyFriendly) | |
| not_relevant(environmentallyFriendly) | |
| ask(customer,infoabout(productY)) | unethical(xxx) |
| answer(xxx) | |
| sensitiveSlogan(xxx) | |
| not_relevant(xxx) | |
| ask(customer,infoabout(productZ)) | not_unethical(yyy) |
| answer(yyy) | |
| sensitiveSlogan(yyy) | |
| relevant(yyy) | |
| ask(customer,infoabout(productV)) | not_unethical(zzz) |
| answer(zzz) | |
| not_sensitiveSlogan(zzz) | |
| not_relevant(zzz) | |
| **Mode Declarations M:** | **Background Knowledge B:** |
| modeh    unethical(+answer) | not_relevant(X) ← |
| modeb    sensitiveSlogan(+answer) | not relevant(X),answer(X) |
| modeb    not_sensitiveSlogan(+answer) | not_sensitiveSlogan(X) ← |
| modeb    not_relevant(+answer) | not sensitiveSlogan(X),answer(X) |
| modeb    relevant(+answer) | |

**Step1 (Abduction):**

$\Delta 1=$ {unethical(environmentallyFriendly)
        unethical(xxx)
        unethical(yyy)}

**Step2 (Deduction):**

| **Kernel Set K** | **Variabilized Kernel Set $K_v$** |
|---|---|
| unethical(environmentallyFriendly) ← | K1= unethical(X1) ← |
|     answer(environmentallyFriendly), |     answer(X1), |
|     sensitiveSlogan(environmentallyFriendly), |     sensitiveSlogan(X1), |
|     not_relevant(environmentallyFriendly) |     not_relevant(X1) |
| unethical(xxx) ← | K2= unethical(X2) ← |
|     answer(xxx), |     answer(X2), |
|     sensitiveSlogan(xxx), |     sensitiveSlogan(X2), |
|     not_relevant(xxx) |     not_relevant(X2) |

**Step3 (Induction):**

Learned hypothesis:
unethical(V) ← sensitiveSlogan(V), not_relevant(V),
answer(V)

**Learned hypotheses for the three mentioned cases**

unethical(V) ←
        sensitiveSlogan(V),not_relevant(V), answer(V)
unethical(giveinfo(V1,V2)) ←
        context(competitor(V2)), badinfo(V1),
info(V1),company(V2)
unethical(tell(V2,infoabout(V2))) ←
        not_authorized(tell(V1,infoabout(V2))), client(V1),
client(V2)

**case3:** A client contacts the customer service of a certain company to ask to buy a certain product X. In this context the customer asks also about a similar product of a competitor company which is slightly cheaper. Then the employee, in order to convince the customer to buy their product, says that the other company uses substandard materials in their production. This is an unethical answer from the employee, even if it tells the truth. In general, though the employee should be truthful with the customer, the answer given in this scenario is not ethical because bad mouthing competitors is not ethical and not professional.

From these three cases our agent learned the three rules presented in Table 1 for evaluating the employees ethical behavior (for the lack of space we omitted the details). In addition, supposing that our agent already have the rule $b1$ shown in Table 1 as a background knowledge in his/her knowledge base, which says that it is unethical to give incorrect information to the customers. So now our agent has four rules for ethical evaluation (the one that she already have plus the three learned ones). More details about the experiments done with XHAIL can be found in [4]. As mentioned above XHAIL was perfectly able to learn the desired rules. As a matter of fact XHAIL provides an appropriate framework for learning ethical rules needed for ethical evaluation of online customer service employees. However, because of the drawbacks mentioned in the introduction, and also due to the fact that in applications like the one we are considering examples arrive overtime, we need an incremental learning approach.

*Incremental Learning with ILED.* In the second part of the experiments of our approach we use ILED for learning ethical rules incrementally from interactions with customers. ILED starts with an empty hypothesis and empty historical memory and in this case it reduces to XHAIL and operates on Kernel Set of the first arriving window of examples.

In our case study, each window of examples include one single example which is one case scenario resulting from a single interaction of a customer with an online customer service agent. Mode declarations and background knowledge are the same used with XHAIL. Let us take a small example from our experiments for illustration: In our experiment we started ILED with an empty hypothesis and an empty historical memory. The first input example window is $w1$. The currently empty hypothesis does not cover the provided example since in $w1$ an unethical answer to the customer question was given so the example raise unethical flag. Hence ILED starts the process of generating an initial hypothesis. And here as we mentioned earlier ILED reduces to XHAIL and operates on a Kernel Set of $w1$ only. The variabilized Kernel Set in this case is the single-clause program $K1$ shown in Table 1 generated from the corresponding ground clause. Generalizing the Kernel Set results in a minimal hypothesis that covers $w1$. This hypothesis is shown in Table 2. ILED stores $w1$ in $\varepsilon$ and initializes the support set of the newly generated hypothesis by selecting from $K1$ the clauses that $\theta$-subsumed by the running hypothesis [7], in this case $K1$'s single clause. The new window $w2$ arrives next. In $w2$, an unethical answer flag was also raised, so the running hypothesis correctly accounts for it and thus no revision is required. ILED generates a new Kernel Set $K2$ from window $w2$ as shown in Table 1, $H1.supp$ covers $w2$ so remain unchanged also. Now arrives window $w3$, which has no positive examples for raising unethical flag for the employee answer. Hence the running hypothesis need to be revised for window $w3$, since the current hypothesis covers a negative example because it says that

**Table 2.** Test with ILED: input examples and output theory

| **Window w1** | |
|---|---|
| **Facts** | **Conclusion** |
| ask(customer,infoabout(productx)) | unethical(environmentallyFriendly) |
| answer(environmentallyFriendly) | |
| sensitiveSlogan(environmentallyFriendly) | |
| not_relevant(environmentallyFriendly) | |
| **Kernel Set** | **Variabilized Kernel Set** |
| unethical(environmentallyFriendly) ← | K1= (X1) ← |
|     answer(environmentallyFriendly), |     answer(X1), |
|     sensitiveSlogan(environmentallyFriendly), |     sensitiveSlogan(X1), |
|     not_relevant(environmentallyFriendly) |     not_relevant(X1) |
| **Running Hypothesis** | **Support Set** |
| $H1=$ unethical(X1) ← | $H1.supp = \{K1\}$ |
|     answer(X1) | |
| **window w2** | |
| **Facts** | **Conclusion** |
| ask(customer,infoabout(productY)) | unethical(xxx) |
| answer(xxx) | |
| sensitiveSlogan(xxx) | |
| not_relevant(xxx) | |
| **Kernel Set** | **Variabilized Kernel Set** |
| unethical(xxx) ← | K2= unethical(X1) ← |
|     answer(xxx), |     answer(X1), |
|     sensitiveSlogan(xxx), |     sensitiveSlogan(X1), |
|     not_relevant(xxx) |     not_relevant(X1) |
| **Running Hypothesis** | **Support Set** |
| remains unchanged | $H1.supp = \{K1, K2\}$ |
| **window w3** | |
| **Facts** | **Conclusion** |
| ask(customer,infoabout(productZ)) | not_unethical(yyy) |
| answer(yyy) | |
| sensitiveSlogan(yyy) | |
| relevant(yyy) | |
| **Revised Hypothesis** | **Support Set** |
| $H2=$ unethical(X1) ← | $H2.supp = \{K1, K2\}$ |
|     answer(X1), not_relevant(X1) | |
| **window w4** | |
| **Facts** | **Conclusion** |
| ask(customer,infoabout(productV)) | not_unethical(zzz) |
| answer(zzz) | |
| not_sensitiveSlogan(zzz) | |
| not_relevant(zzz) | |
| **Revised Hypothesis** | **Support Set** |
| $H3=$ unethical(X1) ← | $H3.supp = \{K1, K2\}$ |
|     answer(X1), | |
|     not_relevant(X1),sensitiveSlogan(X1) | |

an answer is always un ethical while in $w3$ the employee answer is *not_unethical*. To address this issue, ILED searches $H1.supp$ which serves now as a refinement search space to find a refinement that rejects the negative example. The only choice for a refinement clause that does not cover the negative example in $w3$ and subsumes $H1.supp$ is adding the literal *not_relevant*$(X1)$ as shown in Table 1. A new clause $H2$ replaces the initial one $H1$ in the running hypothesis. Now the hypothesis is complete and consistent throughout $\varepsilon$. It is important here to note that the hypothesis was refined by local reasoning only i.e. reasoning within $w3$ and the support set. The support set of the new hypothesis $H2$ is initialized to a subset of the support set of it's parent clause that is $\theta$-subsumed by $H2$, in this case $H2.supp = H1.supp$. Window $w4$ arrive next, which also has no positive examples for raising unethical flag. The running hypothesis is revisable in $w4$ because $H2$ covers the negative example in $w4$ by saying that an answer that is notrelevant is unethical so is inconsistent. By searching $H2.supp$, ILED finds a refinement by adding the literal *sensitiveSlogan*$(X1)$. After revision a new hypothesis $H3$ that is complete and consisten throwout the historical memory is generated and $H3.supp = H2.supp$ as shown in Table 2.

## 3   Final Remarks and Future Directions

In this article we have reported ongoing work on using a hybrid logic-based app-roach for ethical evaluation of employees behavior in online customer service chat point. This work was done with a future perspective towards ethical chatbots in customer service. Combining ASP with ILP for modeling ethical agents pro-vides many advantages: increases the reasoning capability of our agent; promotes the adoption of hybrid strategy that allow both topdown design and bottom up learning via context sensitive adaptation of models of ethical behavior; allows the generation of rules with valuable expressive and explanatory power which equips our agent with the capacity to give an ethical evaluation and explain the reasons behind this evaluation. In other words, our method supports transparency and accountability of such models, which facilitates instilling confidence and trust in our agent. Furthermore, in our opinion and for the sake of transparency, eval-uating the ethical behavior of others should be guided by explicit ethical rules determined by competent judges or ethicists or through consensus of ethicists. Our approach provides support for developing these ethical rules.

ILP algorithms, unlike neural networks, output rules which are comprehen-sible by humans and can provide an explanation for predictions on a new data sample. Furthermore, if prior knowledge (background knowledge) is extended in these methods, then the entire model needs to be re-learned. Finally, no distinc-tion is made between exceptions and noisy data in these methods. This makes ILP particularly appropriate for scientific theory formation tasks in which the comprehensibility of the generated knowledge is essential. Moreover, in an ill-defined domain like the machine ethics domain, it is infeasible to define abstract codes in precise and complete enough terms to be able to use deductive problem solvers to apply them correctly. A combination of deductive (rule-based) and inductive (case-based learning) is needed.

In [1] the authors used ILP to learn rules to help decide between two or more available actions based on a set of involved ethical prima facie duties. So their approach can be applied to choose the most ethical action when we have specific clear ethical duties involved and to do so we need to assign weights of importance(priority) to these duties for each available action, then the system computes the weighted sum for each action, and the one with highest weighted sum is the best action to do. In this approach it is not really clear the basis of assigning weights to duties(we doubt whether we can really quantify the importance of ethical duties on a grade from 2 to -2 as done in these works), then it is not clear whether the generated rules can be refined incrementally over time. On the other hand, in our approach we use ILP to generate rules for ethical evaluation of actions (in response to requests from customers) based on different facts extracted from cases. In other words ILP is used to learn the relation between the evaluation of an action to be ethical or unethical and the related facts in the case scenario. To this end, different facts are extracted from the case scenario and our system try to find the relation between these facts and the conclusion (ethical or un ethical or probably unknown). We would like to mention that their approach is not applicable to our application, because in our case, the employee response is either ethical or unethical. There is no sense of assigning weights to relevant facts extracted from text representing the level of violation/satisfaction of certain code of ethics. It is not a matter of arriving to equilibrium between conflicting rules, it is a matter '"violate or not violate"'. Our approach can be used to generate ethical rules to follow when there is no ethical rules available in place for evaluation, by considering the involved facts and possibly involving counterfactual reasoning in the evaluation. We think that our approach is more general and can be used to generate ethical rules for any domain (and/or elaborate existing ones) and does cope with the changes of ethics over time because of the use of non-monotonic logic and incremental learning.

Finally, one of the challenges we are facing in this work is the scarcity of training examples. In fact this is a big challenge in the ethical domain in general. We are currently working on creating a big enough dataset for real experiments, where obtaining real world examples is an obstacle due to the rules of privacy. Until now our experiments are limited to a very small datasets of examples created manually. Furthermore, we would like to test our AI agent in a real chat scenario, and to this purpose the whole system will need to be implemented which also involves natural language processing. Finally, as another future direction we would like to investigate the possibility of judging the ethical behavior from a series of related chat sessions.

## References

1. Anderson, M., Anderson, S.L., Armen, C.: MedEthEx: toward a medical ethics advisor. In: Caring Machines: AI in Eldercare, Papers from the 2005 AAAI Fall Symposium, Arlington, Virginia, USA, 4–6 November 2005. AAAI Technical report, vol. FS-05-02, pp. 9–16. AAAI Press (2005). https://www.aaai.org/Library/Symposia/Fall/fs05-02.php

2. Corapi, D., Russo, A., Lupu, E.: Inductive logic programming in answer set programming. In: Muggleton, S.H., Tamaddoni-Nezhad, A., Lisi, F.A. (eds.) ILP 2011. LNCS (LNAI), vol. 7207, pp. 91–97. Springer, Heidelberg (2012). https://doi.org/10.1007/978-3-642-31951-8_12
3. Dyoub, A., Costantini, S., De Gasperis, G.: Answer set programming and agents. Knowl. Eng. Rev. **33**, e19 (2018)
4. Dyoub, A., Costantini, S., Lisi, F.A.: Learning answer set programming rules for ethical machines. In: Proceedings of the 34th Italian Conference on Computational LogicCILC, 19–21 June 2019, Trieste, Italy. CEUR-WS.org (2019). http://ceur-ws.org/Vol-2396/
5. Ganascia, J.G.: Modelling ethical rules of lying with answer set programming. Ethics Inf. Technol. **9**(1), 39–47 (2007)
6. Jonsen, A.R., Toulmin, S.E.: The Abuse of Casuistry: A History of Moral Reasoning. University of California Press, Berkeley (1988)
7. Katzouris, N., Artikis, A., Paliouras, G.: Incremental learning of event definitions with inductive logic programming. Mach. Learn. **100**(2–3), 555–585 (2015). https://doi.org/10.1007/s10994-015-5512-1
8. von der Lieth Gardner, A.: An Artificial Intelligence Approach to Legal Reasoning. MIT Press, Cambridge (1987)
9. Moor, J.H.: The nature, importance, and difficulty of machine ethics. IEEE Intell. Syst. **21**(4), 18–21 (2006)
10. Ray, O.: Nonmonotonic abductive inductive learning. J. Appl. Logic **7**(3), 329–340 (2009). https://doi.org/10.1016/j.jal.2008.10.007
11. Shakerin, F., Salazar, E., Gupta, G.: A new algorithm to automate inductive learning of default theories. TPLP **17**(5–6), 1010–1026 (2017)
12. Toulmin, S.E.: The Uses of Argument. Cambridge University Press, Cambridge (2003)

# On the Relation Between Loss Functions and T-Norms

Francesco Giannini[1]([✉]), Giuseppe Marra[1,2], Michelangelo Diligenti[1], Marco Maggini[1], and Marco Gori[1]

[1] Department of Information Engineering and Mathematical Sciences, University of Siena, Siena, Italy
{fgiannini,diligmic,maggini,marco}@diism.unisi.it
[2] Department of Information Engineering, University of Florence, Florence, Italy
g.marra@unifi.it

**Abstract.** Deep learning has been shown to achieve impressive results in several domains like computer vision and natural language processing. A key element of this success has been the development of new loss functions, like the popular cross-entropy loss, which has been shown to provide faster convergence and to reduce the vanishing gradient problem in very deep structures. While the cross-entropy loss is usually justified from a probabilistic perspective, this paper shows an alternative and more direct interpretation of this loss in terms of t-norms and their associated generator functions, and derives a general relation between loss functions and t-norms. In particular, the presented work shows intriguing results leading to the development of a novel class of loss functions. These losses can be exploited in any supervised learning task and which could lead to faster convergence rates that the commonly employed cross-entropy loss.

**Keywords:** Loss functions · Learning from constraints · T-Norms

## 1 Introduction

A careful choice of the loss function has been pivotal into the success of deep learning. In particular, the **cross-entropy loss**, or log loss, measures the performance of a classifier and increases when the predicted probability of an assignment diverges from the actual label [7]. In supervised learning, the cross-entropy loss has a clear interpretation as it attempts at minimizing the distribution of the predicted and given pattern labels. From a practical standpoint, the main advantage of this loss is to limit the vanishing gradient issue for networks with sigmoidal or softmax output activations.

Recent advancements in Statistical Relational Learning (SRL) [16] allow to inject prior knowledge, often expressed using a logic formalism, into a learner.

This project has received funding from the European Union's Horizon 2020 research and innovation program under grant agreement No 825619.

© Springer Nature Switzerland AG 2020
D. Kazakov and C. Erten (Eds.): ILP 2019, LNAI 11770, pp. 36–45, 2020.
https://doi.org/10.1007/978-3-030-49210-6_4

One of the most popular lines of research in this community attempts at defining frameworks for performing logic inference in the presence of uncertainty. For example, Markov Logic Networks [18] and Probabilistic Soft Logic [1] integrate First Order Logic (FOL) and graphical models. More recently, many attempts have been focusing on integrating reasoning with uncertainty with deep learning [20]. A common solution, followed by approaches like Semantic Based Regularization [4] and Logic Tensor Networks [5], relies on using deep networks to approximate the FOL predicates, and the overall architecture is optimized end-to-end by relaxing the FOL into a differentiable form, which translates into a set of constraints. For the sake of overall consistency, one question that can naturally arise in this context is how the fitting of the supervised examples can be expressed using logic formalism. Following this starting point, this paper follows an orthogonal approach for the definition of a loss function, by studying the relation between the translation of the prior knowledge using t-norms and the resulting loss function. In particular, the notion of t-norm *generator* plays a fundamental role in the behavior of the corresponding loss. Remarkably, the cross-entropy loss can be naturally derived within this framework. However, the presented theoretical results suggest that there is a larger class of loss functions that correspond to the different possible translations of logic using t-norms, and some loss functions are potentially more effective than the cross-entropy to limit the vanishing gradient issue, therefore proving a faster convergence rate.

The paper is organized as follows: Sect. 2 presents the basic concepts about t-norms, generators and aggregator functions. Section 3 introduces the learning frameworks used to represent supervised learning in terms of logic rules, while Sect. 4 presents the experimental results and, finally, Sect. 5 draws some conclusions.

## 2    Fuzzy Aggregation Functions

The aggregation takes place on a set of values typically representing preferences or satisfaction degrees restricted to the unit interval $[0, 1]$ to be aggregated. There are several ways to aggregate them into a single value expressing an overall combined score, according to what is expected from such mappings. The purpose of aggregation functions is to combine inputs that are typically interpreted as degrees of membership in fuzzy sets, degrees of preference or strength of evidence. Aggregation functions have been studied by several authors in the literature [2,3], and they are successfully used in many practical applications, for instance see [8,19]. Please note that the fuzzy aggregation functions that will be covered in this section can be directly applied to the output of a multi-task classifier, when implemented via a neural network with sigmoidal or softmax output units.

**Basic Definitions.** Aggregation functions are defined for inputs of any cardinality, however for simplicity the main definitions are provided only for the binary case. A (binary) aggregation function is a non-decreasing function $A : [0, 1]^2 \rightarrow [0, 1]$, such that: $A(0, 0) = 0$, $A(1, 1) = 1$. An aggregation function $A$

**Table 1.** Fundamental t-norms.

| Gödel | Lukasiewicz | Product |
|---|---|---|
| $T_M(x,y) = \min\{x,y\}$ | $T_L(x,y) = \max\{0, x + y - 1\}$ | $T_\Pi(x,y) = x \cdot y$ |

can be categorized according to the pointwise order in Eq. 1 as: *conjunctive* when $A \leq \min$, *disjunctive* when $\max \leq A$, *averaging* (a *mean*) when $\min < A < \max$ and *hybrid* otherwise; where min and max are the aggregation functions for the *minimum* and *maximum* respectively.

$$A_1 \leq A_2 \quad \text{iff} \quad A_1(x,y) \leq A_2(x,y), \text{ for all } x, y \in [0,1] . \tag{1}$$

Conjunctive and disjunctive type functions combine values as if they were related by a logical AND and OR operations, respectively. On the other hand, averaging type functions have the property that low values can be compensated by high values. Mean computation is the most common way to combine the inputs, since it assumed the total score cannot be above or below any of the inputs, but it depends on all the inputs.

## 2.1 Archimedean T-Norms

Despite averaging functions have nice properties to aggregate fuzzy values, they are not suitable to represent neither a conjunction nor a disjunction, because they do not generalize their boolean counterpart. This is a reason why, we focus on t-norms and t-conorms [11,14], that are *associative*, *commutative* aggregation functions with 1 and 0 as *neutral element*, respectively. Table 1 reports Gödel, Lukasiewicz and Product t-norms, which are referred as the fundamental t-norms because all the continuous t-norms can be obtained as ordinal sums of the two fundamental t-norms [10]. A simple example of a t-norm that is not continuous is given by the Drastic t-norm $T_D$, that is always returning a zero value, except for $T_D(1,1) = 1$. *Archimedean* t-norms [13] are a class of t-norms that can be constructed by means of unary monotone functions, called *generators*.

**Definition 1.** *A t-norm $T$ is said to be* Archimedean *if for every $x \in (0,1)$, $T(x,x) < x$. In addition, $T$ is said* strict *if for all $x \in (0,1)$, $0 < T(x,x) < x$ otherwise is said* nilpotent.

For instance, the Lukasiewicz t-norm $T_L$ is nilpotent, the Product t-norm $T_\Pi$ is strict, while the Gödel one $T_M$ is not archimedean, indeed $T_M(x,x) = x$, for all $x \in [0,1]$. The Lukasiewicz and Product t-norms are enough to represent the whole classes of nilpotent and strict Archimedean t-norms [14].

A fundamental result for the construction of t-norms by *additive* generators is based on the following theorem [12]:

**Theorem 1.** *Let* $g : [0,1] \rightarrow [0,+\infty]$ *be a strictly decreasing function with* $g(1) = 0$ *and* $g(x) + g(y) \in Range(g) \cup [g(0^+),+\infty]$ *for all* $x,y$ *in* $[0,1]$, *and* $g^{(-1)}$ *its pseudo-inverse. Then the function* $T : [0,1] \rightarrow [0,1]$ *defined as*

$$T(x,y) = g^{-1}\left(\min\{g(0^+), g(x) + g(y)\}\right) . \tag{2}$$

*is a t-norm and* $g$ *is said an* additive generator *for* $T$.

Any t-norm $T$ with an additive generator $g$ is Archimedean, if $g$ is continuous then $T$ is continuous, $T$ is strict if and only if $g(0) = +\infty$, otherwise it is nilpotent.

*Example 1.* If we take $g(x) = 1 - x$, then also $g^{-1}(y) = 1 - y$ and we get $T_L$:

$$T(x,y) = 1 - \min\{1, 1 - x + 1 - y\} = \max\{0, x + y - 1\} .$$

*Example 2.* Taking $g(x) = -\log(x)$, we have $g^{-1}(y) = e^{-y}$ and we get $T_\Pi$:

$$T(x,y) = e^{-(\min\{+\infty, -\log(x) - \log(y)\})} = x \cdot y .$$

Equation (2) allows to derive the other fuzzy connectives as function of the generator:

$$\begin{aligned} \text{residuum}: \quad & x \Rightarrow y = g^{-1}\left(\max\{0, g(y) - g(x)\}\right) \\ \text{bi-residuum}: \quad & x \Leftrightarrow y = g^{-1}\left(|g(x) - g(y)|\right) \end{aligned} \tag{3}$$

If $g$ is expressed as a parametric function, it is possible to define families of t-norms, which can be constructed by the generator obtained when setting the parameters to specific values. Several parametric families of t-norms have been introduced [2]. The experimental section of this paper employs the family of Schweizer–Sklar and Frank t-norms, depending on a parameter $\lambda \in (-\infty, +\infty)$ and $\lambda \in [0,+\infty]$ respectively, and whose generators are defined as:

$$g_\lambda^{SS}(x) = \begin{cases} -\log(x) & \text{if } \lambda = 0 \\ \frac{1-x^\lambda}{\lambda} & \text{otherwise} \end{cases} \quad \text{and} \quad g_\lambda^F(x) = \begin{cases} -\log(x) & \text{if } \lambda = 1 \\ 1 - x & \text{if } \lambda = +\infty \\ \log\left(\frac{\lambda-1}{\lambda^x-1}\right) & \text{otherwise} \end{cases} \tag{4}$$

## 3 From Formulas to Loss Functions

A learning process can be thought of as a constraint satisfaction problem, where the constraints represent the knowledge about the functions to be learned. In particular, multi-task learning can be expressed via a set of constraints expressing the fitting of the supervised examples, plus any additional abstract knowledge.

Let us consider a set of unknown task functions $\mathbf{P} = \{p_1, \ldots, p_J\}$ defined on $\mathbb{R}^n$, all collected in the vector $\boldsymbol{p} = (p_1, \ldots, p_J)$ and a set of known functions or predicates $\boldsymbol{S}$. Given the set $\mathcal{X} \subseteq \mathbb{R}^n$ of available data, a learning problem can be generally formulated as $\min_{\boldsymbol{p}} \mathcal{L}(\mathcal{X}, \boldsymbol{S}, \boldsymbol{p})$ where $\mathcal{L}$ is a positive-valued functional denoting a certain loss function. Each predicate is approximated by a neural network providing an output value in $[0, 1]$. The available knowledge about the task functions consists in a set of FOL formulas $KB = \{\varphi_1, \ldots, \varphi_H\}$ and the learning process aims at finding a good approximation of each unknown element, so that the estimated values will satisfy the formulas for the input samples. Since any formula is true if it evaluates to 1, in order to satisfy the constraints we may minimize the following loss function:

$$\mathcal{L}(\mathcal{X}, \boldsymbol{S}, \boldsymbol{p}) = \sum_{h=1}^{H} \lambda_h L\big(f_h(\mathcal{X}, \boldsymbol{S}, \boldsymbol{p})\big) \tag{5}$$

where any $\lambda_h$ is the weight for the $h$-th logical constraint, which can be selected via cross-validation or jointly learned [15,21], $f_h$ is the truth-function corresponding to the formula $\varphi_h$ according to a certain t-norm fuzzy logic and $L$ is a decreasing function denoting the penalty associated to the distance from satisfaction of formulas, so that $L(1) = 0$. In the following, we will study different forms for the $L$ cost function and how it depends on the choice of the t-norm generator. In particular, a *t-norm fuzzy logic* generalizes Boolean logic to variables assuming values in $[0, 1]$ and is defined by its t-norm modeling the logical AND [9]. The connectives can be treated using the fuzzy generalization of first-order logic that was first proposed by Novak [17]. The *universal* and *existential quantifiers* occurring in the formulas in $KB$ allows the aggregation of different evaluations (groundings) of the formulas on the available data. For instance, given a formula $\varphi(x_i)$ depending on a certain variable $x_i \in \mathcal{X}_i$, where $\mathcal{X}_i$ denotes the available samples for the $i$-th argument of one of the involved predicates in $\varphi$, we may convert the quantifiers as the minimum and maximum operations that are common to any t-norm fuzzy logic:

$$\forall x_i \, \varphi(x_i) \implies f_\varphi(X_i, \boldsymbol{S}, \boldsymbol{p}) = \min_{x_i \in \mathcal{X}_i} f_\varphi(x_i, \boldsymbol{S}, \boldsymbol{p})$$

$$\exists x_i \, \varphi(x_i) \implies f_\varphi(X_i, \boldsymbol{S}, \boldsymbol{p}) = \max_{x_i \in \mathcal{X}_i} f_\varphi(x_i, \boldsymbol{S}, \boldsymbol{p})$$

### 3.1   Loss Functions by T-Norms Generators

A quantifier can be seen as a way to aggregate all the possible groundings of a predicate variable that, in turn, are $[0, 1]$-values. Different aggregation functions have also been considered, for example in [5], the authors consider a mean operator to convert the universal quantifier. However this has the drawback that also the existential quantifier has the same semantics conversion and then it is determined by the authors via Skolemization. Even if this choice may yield some learning benefits, it has no direct justification inside a logic theory. Moreover it does not suggest how to map the functional translation of the formula into a constraint. In the following, we investigate the mapping of formulas into constraints by means of generated t-norm fuzzy logics, and we exploited the same additive generator of the t-norm to map the formula into the functional constraints to be minimized, i.e. $L = g$.

Given a certain formula $\varphi(x)$ depending on a variable $x$ that ranges in the set $\mathcal{X}$ and its corresponding functional representation $f_\varphi(x, \boldsymbol{p})$ evaluated on each $x \in \mathcal{X}$, the conversion of universal and existential quantifiers should have semantics equivalent to the AND and OR of the evaluation of the formula over the groundings, respectively. This can be realized by directly applying the t-norm or t-conorms over the groundings. For instance, for the universal quantifier:

$$\forall x \, \varphi(x) \equiv \bigwedge_x \varphi(x) \implies g^{-1}\left(\min\left\{g(0^+), \sum_{x \in \mathcal{X}} g(f_\varphi(x, \boldsymbol{S}, \boldsymbol{p}))\right\}\right), \quad (6)$$

where $g$ is an additive generator of the t-norm $T$ corresponding to the universal quantifier. Since any generator function is decreasing, in order to maximize the satisfaction of $\forall x \, \varphi(x)$ we can minimize $g$ applied to Eq. 6, namely:

$$\min\{g(0^+), \sum_{x \in \mathcal{X}} g(f_\varphi(x, \boldsymbol{S}, \boldsymbol{p}))\} \qquad \text{if } T \text{ is nilpotent} \qquad (7)$$

$$\sum_{x \in \mathcal{X}} g(f_\varphi(x, \boldsymbol{S}, \boldsymbol{p})) \qquad \text{if } T \text{ is strict} \qquad (8)$$

As a consequence, with respect to the convexity of the expressions in Eqs. 7–8, we get the following result, that is an immediate consequence of how the convexity is preserved by function composition.

**Proposition 1.** *If $g$ is a linear function and $f_\varphi$ is concave, Eq. 7 is convex. If $g$ is a convex function and $f_\varphi$ is linear, Eq. 8 is convex.*

*Example 3.* If $g(x) = 1 - x$ (Lukasiewicz t-norm) from Eq. 7 we get:

$$\min(1, \sum_{x \in \mathcal{X}} (1 - (f_\varphi(x, \boldsymbol{S}, \boldsymbol{p}))) .$$

Hence, in case $f_\varphi$ is concave (see [6] for a characterization of the concave fragment of Lukasiewicz logic), this function is convex.
If $g = -\log$ (Product t-norm) from Eq. 8 we get the cross-entropy:

$$-\sum_{x \in \mathcal{X}} \log(f_\varphi(x, \boldsymbol{S}, \boldsymbol{p})) .$$

As we already pointed out in Sect. 2, if $g$ is an additive generator for a t-norm $T$, then the residual implication and the biresidum with respect to $T$ are given by Eq. 3. In particular, if $p_1, p_2$ are two unary predicates functions sharing the same input domain $\mathcal{X}$, and $\boldsymbol{S} = \emptyset$ the following formulas yield the following penalty terms:

$$\forall x \, p_1(x) \implies \min\left\{g(0^+), \sum_{x \in \mathcal{X}} g(p_1(x))\right\}$$

$$\forall x \, p_1(x) \Rightarrow p_2(x) \implies \min\left\{g(0^+), \sum_{x \in \mathcal{X}} \max(0, g(p_2(x)) - g(p_1(x)))\right\}$$

$$\forall x \, p_1(x) \Leftrightarrow p_2(x) \implies \min\left\{g(0^+), \sum_{x\in\mathcal{X}} |g(p_1(x)) - g(p_2(x))|\right\}.$$

## 3.2 Redefinition of Supervised Learning with Logic

In this section, we study the case of supervised learning w.r.t. the choice of a certain additive generator. Let us consider a multi-task classification problem with predicates $p_j, j = 1, \ldots, J$ defined over the same input domain with a supervised training set $\mathcal{T} = \{(x_i, y_i)\}$ where each $y_i \in \{1, 2, \ldots, J\}$ is the output class for the pattern $x_i$ and $\mathcal{X}$ is the overall set of supervised patterns. Finally, the known predicate $S_j$ is defined for each predicate such that $S_j(x_i) = 1$ iff $y_i = j$, and we indicate as $\mathcal{X}_j = \{x_i \in \mathcal{X} : S_j(x_i) = 1\}$ the set of positive examples for the $j$-th predicate. Then, we can enforce the supervision constraints for $p_j$ as:

$$\forall x \, S_j(x) \Leftrightarrow p_j(x) \implies \mathcal{L}(\mathcal{X}, \boldsymbol{S}, p_j) = \sum_{x\in\mathcal{X}} |g(S_j(x)) - g(p_j(x))|$$

In the special case of the predicates implemented by neural networks and exclusive multi-task classification, where each pattern should be assigned to one and only one class, the exclusivity can be enforced using a softmax output activation. Typically, in this scenario, only the positive supervisions are explicitly listed, and since it holds that $g(S_j(x)) = 0, \forall x \in \mathcal{X}_j$, yields:

$$\mathcal{L}^+(\mathcal{X}, \boldsymbol{S}, p_j) = \sum_{x\in\mathcal{X}_j} g(p_j(x)), \tag{9}$$

For instance, in the case of Lukasiewicz and Product logic, we have, respectively:

$$\mathcal{L}_L^+(\mathcal{X}_j, p_j) = \sum_{x\in\mathcal{X}_j} (1 - p_j(x)), \quad \mathcal{L}_\Pi^+(\mathcal{X}_j, p_j) = -\sum_{x\in\mathcal{X}_j} \log(p_j(x))$$

corresponding to the $L_1$ and cross entropy losses, respectively.

## 4  Experimental Results

The proposed framework allows to recover well-known loss functions by expressing the fitting of the supervision using logic and then carefully selecting the t-norm used to translate the resulting formulas. However, a main strength of the proposed theory is that it becomes possible to derive new principled losses starting from any family of parametric t-norms. Driven by the huge impact that cross-entropy gained w.r.t. to classical loss functions in improving convergence speed and generalization capabilities, we designed a set of experiments to investigate how the choice of a t-norm can lead to a loss function with better performances than the cross-entropy loss. The Schweizer–Sklar and the Frank parametric t-norms defined in Sect. 2.1 have been selected for this experimental evaluation, given the large spectrum of t-norms that can be generated by varying

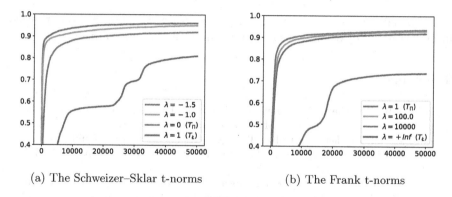

(a) The Schweizer–Sklar t-norms          (b) The Frank t-norms

**Fig. 1.** Convergence speed of multiple generated loss functions on the MNIST classification task for different values of the parameter $\lambda$ of Eq. 4. The well-known cross-entropy loss is equivalent to the loss obtained by the $T_{\Pi}$ generator.

their $\lambda$ parameter. The well known MNIST dataset is used as benchmark for all the presented experiments. In order to have a fair comparison, the same neural network architecture is used during all the runs: a 1-hidden layer neural network with 50 hidden ReLU units and 10 softmax output units. The softmax activation function allows to express only positive supervisions, like commonly done in mutually exclusive classification using the cross-entropy loss. Optimization is carried on using Vanilla gradient descent with a fixed learning rate of 0.01.

Results are shown in Fig. 1, that reports the accuracy on the test set of a neural network trained on the MNIST dataset. Specific choices of the parameter $\lambda$ recover classical loss functions, like the cross-entropy loss, which is equivalent to the loss obtained using $T_{\Pi}$. The results confirm that the cross-entropy loss converges faster than the $L_1$ obtained when using $T_L$. However, there is a wide range of possible choices for the parameter $\lambda$ that brings an even faster convergence and better generalization than the widely adopted used cross-entropy.

## 5    Conclusions

This paper presents a framework to embed prior knowledge expressed as logic statements into a learning task, showning how the choice of the t-norm used to convert the logic into a differentiable form defines the resulting loss function used during learning. When restricting the attention to supervised learning, the framework recovers popular loss functions like the cross-entropy loss, and allows to define new loss functions corresponding to the choice of the parameters of t-norm parametric forms. The experimental results show that some newly defined losses provide a faster convergence rate that the commonly used cross-entropy loss. Future work will focus on testing the loss functions in more structured learning tasks, like the one commonly addressed with Logic Tensor Networks and Semantic based Regularization. The parametric form of the loss functions allows to define joint learning tasks, where the loss parameters are co-optimized during learning, for example using maximum likelihood estimators.

# References

1. Bach, S.H., Broecheler, M., Huang, B., Getoor, L.: Hinge-loss markov random fields and probabilistic soft logic. J. Mach. Learn. Res. **18**, 1–67 (2017)
2. Beliakov, G., Pradera, A., Calvo, T.: Aggregation Functions: A Guide for Practitioners, vol. 221. Springer, Heidelberg (2007). https://doi.org/10.1007/978-3-540-73721-6
3. Calvo, T., Kolesárová, A., Komorníková, M., Mesiar, R.: Aggregation operators: properties classes and construction methods. In: Calvo, T., Mayor, G., Mesiar, R. (eds.) Aggregation Operators, pp. 3–104. Springer, Heidelberg (2002). https://doi.org/10.1007/978-3-7908-1787-4_1
4. Diligenti, M., Gori, M., Sacca, C.: Semantic-based regularization for learning and inference. Artif. Intell. **244**, 143–165 (2017)
5. Donadello, I., Serafini, L., d'Avila Garcez, A.: Logic tensor networks for semantic image interpretation. In: IJCAI International Joint Conference on Artificial Intelligence, pp. 1596–1602 (2017)
6. Giannini, F., Diligenti, M., Gori, M., Maggini, M.: On a convex logic fragment for learning and reasoning. IEEE Trans. Fuzzy Syst. **27**, 1407–1416 (2018)
7. Goodfellow, I., Bengio, Y., Courville, A., Bengio, Y.: Deep Learn., vol. 1. MIT Press, Cambridge (2016)
8. Grabisch, M., Marichal, J.L., Mesiar, R., Pap, E.: Aggregation functions: means. Inf. Sci. **181**(1), 1–22 (2011)
9. Hájek, P.: Metamathematics of Fuzzy Logic, vol. 4. Springer, Dordrecht (2013). https://doi.org/10.1007/978-94-011-5300-3
10. Jenei, S.: A note on the ordinal sum theorem and its consequence for the construction of triangular norms. Fuzzy Sets Syst. **126**(2), 199–205 (2002)
11. Klement, E.P., Mesiar, R., Pap, E.: Triangular norms. position paper i: basic analytical and algebraic properties. Fuzzy Sets Syst. **143**(1), 5–26 (2004)
12. Klement, E.P., Mesiar, R., Pap, E.: Triangular norms. position paper ii: general constructions and parameterized families. Fuzzy Sets Syst. **145**(3), 411–438 (2004)
13. Klement, E.P., Mesiar, R., Pap, E.: Triangular norms position paper iii: continuous t-norms. Fuzzy Sets Syst. **145**(3), 439–454 (2004)
14. Klement, E.P., Mesiar, R., Pap, E.: Triangular Norms, vol. 8. Springer, Dordrecht (2013). https://doi.org/10.1007/978-94-015-9540-7
15. Kolb, S., Teso, S., Passerini, A., De Raedt, L.: Learning SMT (IRA) constraints using smt solvers. In: IJCAI. pp. 2333–2340 (2018)
16. Koller, D., et al.: Introduction to Statistical Relational Learning. MIT Press, Cambridge (2007)
17. Novák, V., Perfilieva, I., Mockor, J.: Mathematical Principles of Fuzzy Logic, vol. 517. Springer, New York (2012). https://doi.org/10.1007/978-1-4615-5217-8
18. Richardson, M., Domingos, P.: Markov logic networks. Mach. Learn. **62**(1), 107–136 (2006)
19. Torra, V., Narukawa, Y.: Modeling Decisions: Information Fusion and Aggregation Operators. Springer, Heidelberg (2007). https://doi.org/10.1007/978-3-540-68791-7

20. Xu, J., Zhang, Z., Friedman, T., Liang, Y., Broeck, G.V.d.: A semantic loss function for deep learning with symbolic knowledge. arXiv preprint arXiv:1711.11157 (2017)
21. Yang, F., Yang, Z., Cohen, W.W.: Differentiable learning of logical rules for knowledge base reasoning. In: Advances in Neural Information Processing Systems, pp. 2319–2328 (2017)

# Rapid Restart Hill Climbing for Learning Description Logic Concepts

Yingbing Hua[1]([⊠]) [iD] and Björn Hein[1,2] [iD]

[1] Karlsruhe Institute of Technology, 76131 Karlsruhe, Germany
{yingbing.hua,bjoern.hein}@kit.edu
[2] Karlsruhe University of Applied Science, 76131 Karlsruhe, Germany

**Abstract.** Recent advances in learning description logic (DL) concepts usually employ a downward refinement operator for space traversing and hypotheses construction. However, theoretical research proved that ideal refinement operator does not exist for expressive DLs, including the language $\mathcal{ALC}$. The state-of-the-art learning framework DL-Learner suggests to use a complete and proper refinement operator and to handle infiniteness algorithmically. For example, the CELOE algorithm follows an iterative widening approach to build a search tree of concept hypotheses. To select a tree node for expansion, CELOE adopts a simple greedy strategy that neglects the structure of the search tree. In this paper, we present the *Rapid Restart Hill Climbing* (RRHC) algorithm that selects a node for expansion by traversing the search tree in a hill climbing manner and rapidly restarts with one-step backtracking after each expansion. We provide an implementation of RRHC in the DL-Learner framework and compare its performance with CELOE using standard benchmarks.

**Keywords:** Concept learning · Description logics · Hill Climbing

## 1 Introduction

The research area of concept learning devotes to develop supervised machine learning algorithms for inducing concept definitions from labeled data. In description logics (DL), such concept definitions are logical expressions that are built using DL constructors. For each concept $C$ of interest, positive data examples represent members of $C$ while negative ones are not. The goal of a learning algorithm is to find a logical expression that correctly classifies the data examples while being as simple as possible.

The theoretical foundation of learning in description logics is based on the study of suitable space traversing operators, so-called refinement operators [12]. One can distinguish between downward and upward refinement operators that

This work has been supported from the European Union's Horizon 2020 research and innovation programme under grant agreement No 688117 "Safe human-robot interaction in logistic applications for highly flexible warehouses (SafeLog)".

© Springer Nature Switzerland AG 2020
D. Kazakov and C. Erten (Eds.): ILP 2019, LNAI 11770, pp. 46–61, 2020.
https://doi.org/10.1007/978-3-030-49210-6_5

either specialize the most general concept $\top$ or generalize the most specific concept $\bot$. Following a learning-by-searching paradigm, concept learning algorithms use the refinement operator to generate concept hypotheses for the learning problem and utilize heuristic functions to assess the quality of the hypotheses.

DL-Learner is a popular concept learning framework that implements several algorithms based on refinement operators [2]. In particular, CELOE is a top-down learning algorithm that employs a complete but infinite refinement operator $\rho^{cl}$ in the language $\mathcal{ALC}$ with the support of concrete roles and cardinality restrictions [11]. To handle the infiniteness of $\rho^{cl}$, CELOE follows the iterative widening [5] approach to span a search tree of concept hypotheses and adopts a simple greedy strategy to select the most promising tree node for expansion. The expansion is controlled by a length upper bound of new refinements that is increased successively during a revisit of the same tree node. However, this simple greedy selection strategy does not utilize the structure of the search tree well and may rapidly lead to a local optimum. Another problem of DL-Learner is the number of parameters used to implement the heuristic. During the empirical evaluation of CELOE, we noticed that different settings of these parameters significantly affect the learning performance, and there is often no clear indication of how they can be mediated for individual learning problems.

In this paper, we present the Rapid Restart Hill Climbing (RRHC) algorithm to tackle these problems. In contrast to the simple greedy strategy adopted by CELOE, RRHC selects a node for expansion by traversing the search tree in a hill climbing fashion. RRHC uses the heuristic proposed in [13] which has only two parameters. For the expansion, RRHC commits to the iterative widening approach for producing a finite set of refinements. Unlike conventional hill climbing techniques used in Inductive Logic Programming (ILP), RRHC rapidly restarts with one-step backtracking after the expansion. We provide an implementation of RRHC in the DL-Learner framework[1] and use CELOE as the baseline for our experiments. In the most learning problems provided by DL-Learner, we show that RRHC generally performs better than CELOE.

The rest of the paper is organized as follows. Section 2 discusses related work in concept learning. Section 3 gives a formal definition of the learning problem and elaborates some details of CELOE that are necessary for presenting RRHC in Sect. 4. We compare the performance of RRHC with CELOE in Sect. 5. Finally, Sect. 6 concludes the paper with future works.

## 2 Related Work

The most related work on top-down concept learning in description logics is the DL-Learner framework [2]. DL-Learner provides an expressive refinement operator $\rho^{cl}$ for the language $\mathcal{ALC}$ which is later extended to cover concrete roles and cardinality restrictions for the Web Ontology Language[2] (OWL). Besides other practical features e.g. knowledge fragment segmentation and approximate

---

[1] https://github.com/kit-hua/DL-Learner/tree/hua/ilp2019.

[2] https://www.w3.org/TR/owl2-overview/.

coverage test, DL-Learner implements two algorithms OCEL [13] and CELOE [11] for learning concepts in OWL. In this paper, we are interested in CELOE, which is a top-down learning algorithm using the operator $\rho^{cl}$. CELOE employs a heuristic to evaluate the quality of concept hypotheses and iteratively searches for a better solution using a simple greedy strategy. It is also worth noting that while DL adopts the Open-World Assumption (OWA), CELOE implements a partially closed world reasoner for learning universal restrictions, negations and cardinality restrictions. Section 3.3 elaborates more details of CELOE, especially on the procedure of search tree construction.

We also discuss other approaches that make explicit use of refinement operators. Badea and Nienhuys-Cheng proposed a refinement operator for top-down concept learning in the language $\mathcal{ALER}$ and showed a basic learning procedure based on this operator [1]. YINGYANG is a learning system for $\mathcal{ALC}$ [6,7,10]. In contrast to a standard refinement-based approach as DL-Learner, YINGYANG uses an upward refinement operator to generalize approximated MSCs (most specific concepts). Afterwards, the so-called counterfactuals and a non-deterministic downward refinement operator are used to remove overly generalized hypotheses. Because MSCs need to be approximated for $\mathcal{ALC}$ and more expressive DL languages, YINGYANG tends to produce unnecessarily long concepts [13].

PArCEL and SPArCEL are recent works on learning in OWL and are built on top of DL-Learner [15,16]. More specifically, both algorithms are parallelized by adopting a separate-and-conquer strategy. While both PArCEL and SPArCEL show the great advantage of parallelism, they use DL-Learner as a subroutine for the top-down refinement and can potentially also be improved by our approach.

DL-FOIL is another DL learning system that adopts the separate-and-conquer strategy [8,9]. As opposed to PArCEL and SPArCEL, DL-FOIL is a DL variant of the FOIL algorithm [14]. The inner loop of DL-FOIL uses a refinement operator for specializing partial solutions of the learning problem, while the outer loop combines the partial solutions with disjunctions. The specialization procedure acts as a hill climbing search with a predefined upper bound of refinement steps, therefore does not construct a search tree as with CELOE.

The hill climbing search adopted by DL-FOIL originated in the well-known ILP system FOIL. In fact, hill climbing is one of the most commonly used search algorithm in ILP, although it suffers from the so-called *myopia* problem [4]. Yet we have a fundamentally different setting in the learning procedure, as our refinement operator is infinite and the heuristic of a concept hypothesis decreases after each refinement (see Sect. 3.3). Thus, we do not run hill climbing search until a solution or a dead end is found, but rapidly restart the search after each refinement step. Our approach shares some similar ideas with the *rapid random restarts* (RRR) algorithm [18], but it does not use computational resource as the condition for the restart and has a deterministic nature for node selection.

# 3    Concept Learning in DL

In this section, we first give the formal definition of the learning problem we are looking at and then describe CELOE more in detail regarding the search tree construction.

## 3.1    The Concept Learning Problem

We use the definition of the learning problem as proposed in [13]:

**Definition 1 (concept learning in description logics).** *Let* Target *be a concept name and* $\mathcal{K}$ *be a knowledge base (not containing* Target*). Let* $E = E^+ \cup E^-$ *be a set of examples, where* $E^+$ *are the positives examples and* $E^-$ *are the negative examples and* $E^+ \cap E^- = \emptyset$*. The learning problem is to find a concept* $C \equiv$ Target *with* $\mathcal{K} \cup C \models E^+$ *and* $\mathcal{K} \cup C \not\models E^-$*.*

In this definition, we call a learned concept $C$ a *hypothesis* of Target. We say that a learned concept $C$ *covers* an example $e \in E$ if $e$ is an instance of $C$ with respect to the knowledge base $\mathcal{K}$, i.e. $K \models C(e)$. A hypothesis $C$ is *complete* if it covers all positive examples $e \in E^+$, is *consistent* if it does not cover any negative example $e \in E^-$, and is *correct* if it is both complete and consistent. Besides the correctness, another criteria of the solution is the length of the concept hypothesis. For concepts in $\mathcal{ALC}$, the length is defined as follows:

**Definition 2 (length of an $\mathcal{ALC}$ concept).** *Let $A$ be an atomic concept, $r$ be a role, and $D, E$ be concepts in $\mathcal{ALC}$, the length operator $|\cdot|$ is defined as:*

$$|A| = |\top| = |\bot| = 1$$
$$|\neg D| = |D| + 1$$
$$|D \sqcup E| = |D \sqcap E| = 1 + |D| + |E|$$
$$|\exists r.D| = |\forall r.D| = 2 + |D|$$

## 3.2    Refinement Operators

Refinement operators formulate the theoretical foundation of concept learning in description logics. They are used to traverse the concept space and to construct appropriate concept hypotheses. In the literature of learning in DL, the subsumption relation $\sqsubseteq$ is usually taken as a quasi-ordering of the search space. A downward (upward) refinement operator specializes (generalizes) a concept $C$ to $C'$ with $C' \sqsubseteq C$ ($C \sqsubseteq C'$), respectively. As this paper focuses on top-down learning algorithms, we briefly discuss some critical characteristics of downward refinement operators.

**Definition 3 (properties of downward refinement operators).** *A refinement operator $\rho$ for a DL language $\mathcal{L}$ is called:*

- **complete** *if for all concepts* $C, D$ *with* $C \sqsubseteq D$, *there is a concept* $E$ *with* $E \in \rho(D)$ *and* $E \equiv C$.
- **weakly complete** *if for all concepts* $C \sqsubseteq \top$, *there is a concept* $E$ *with* $E \in \rho(\top)$ *and* $E \equiv C$.
- **(locally) finite** *if for all concepts* $C$, $\rho(C)$ *is finite*
- **proper** *if for all concepts* $C, D$ *with* $D \in \rho(C)$, $C \not\equiv D$

In this paper, we use the refinement operator $\rho^{cl}$ from the DL-Learner framework. Lehmann and Hitzler showed that $\rho^{cl}$ is weakly complete, complete, and proper [13]. Additionally, $\rho^{cl}$ does not reduce the length of a concept, i.e. $\forall D \in \rho^{cl}(C) : |D| \geq |C|$. These properties provide the basis for developing learning algorithms that are guaranteed to find a correct solution. However, $\rho^{cl}$ is infinite and requires algorithmic handling during the learning procedure.

### 3.3   CELOE

In this section, we show some essential properties of CELOE that are necessary for introducing the RRHC algorithm. CELOE is a top-down learning algorithm based on the refinement operator $\rho^{cl}$. The main part of CELOE iteratively builds a search tree of the concept space in the following steps:

1. **Selection**: Find a tree node $n$ with the maximum heuristic score in the search tree. CELOE implements this by using a global priority queue of all tree nodes, sorted by their score.
2. **Refinement**: Invoke $\rho^{cl}$ to generate new refinements of the node $n$. Since $\rho^{cl}$ is infinite, CELOE adopts an iterative widening approach [5] that restricts the number of refinements using a length upper bound. This upper bound is called the *horizontal expansion* of the node $n$. Upon a revisit of the node $n$, its horizontal expansion is increased by one. Note that because the horizontal expansion limits the length of refinements, there might be no refinement for a certain iteration.
3. **Expansion**: New refinements generated in the last step are tested against redundancy and completeness. A refinement $C$ is ignored if the search tree already contains a concept $C'$ which is weakly equal to $C$ (redundant), or $C$ does not cover all positive examples $E^+$ (too weak). Refinements that are neither redundant nor too weak are added as child nodes to the current node $n$, and CELOE starts over with the selection step.

The basic form of the heuristic employed for assessing the quality of a node $n$ was first proposed in [13] as follows:

$$score(n) = accuracy(C) + \alpha \cdot acc\_gain(n) - \beta \cdot he \quad (\alpha \geq 0, \beta \geq 0) \quad (1)$$

In Eq. 1, $C$ is the concept hypothesis of node $n$, $acc\_gain$ is the accuracy gain compared with $n$'s parent, and $he$ is the horizontal expansion. The two parameters $\alpha, \beta$ control the expansion behavior of the search tree: larger $\alpha$ tends to exploit better hypotheses while larger $\beta$ favors less explored areas.

One major drawback of CELOE is that the selection phase handles the search tree as a single priority queue, and the *global* best tree node is selected for further refinement. We emphasize on the term *global* since CELOE does not traverse the search tree in any form, but tracks the best node in the queue. While this simple greedy approach is fast, it neglects the structure of the search tree and may rapidly lead to a local optimum in the lower part of the tree. Because there are often much more nodes in the lower part of the tree, significant effort is required to regret previous radical decisions.

The concrete implementation of CELOE tries to handle this problem by using two additional parameters in the heuristic. One is the *start node bonus* that gives extra value to the start node $\top$ for a hopefully sufficient exploration in the upper part of the tree, and another one is the *refinement penalty* that penalizes tree nodes proportionally to the number of their child nodes.

Nevertheless, consider the combination with the gain bonus and expansion penalty, we argue that finding a proper setting of these parameters is laborious. More importantly, different learning problems do not share these parameters. We explain this more in detail with the Uncle example from the `family` benchmark provided by DL-Learner. With the default configuration, CELOE was able to find the following solution in 4 s 301 ms.

$$
\begin{aligned}
\mathsf{Uncle} \equiv ((\exists \mathsf{hasSibling}.(\exists \mathsf{hasChild}.\top))\sqcup \\
(\exists \mathsf{married}.(\exists \mathsf{hasSibling}.(\exists \mathsf{hasChild}.\top)))) \sqcap (\neg \mathsf{Female})
\end{aligned}
\tag{2}
$$

This solution is correct and reads, "An uncle is <u>not a female</u> and <u>has a sibling who has a child</u> or <u>is married to someone that has a sibling who has a child</u>." To better illustrate the learning process, we assign an ID for each node in the search tree as follows.

**Definition 4 (ID of a tree node).** *An ID of a tree node n describes its position in the search tree. It is a sequence of position numbers connected by the hyphen as $P_0\text{-}P_1\text{-}P_2\text{-}\cdots$. Each position number $P_i$ represents the index of the branch located at the depth level i that contains n as a descendant node.*

For example, the solution in Eq. 2 has the ID 0-2-52-9-17-9, which means that it is the 9th child of its parent 0-2-52-9-17.

Figure 1 shows the tree depth of expanded nodes for learning the concept of Uncle with CELOE. First, we can see that most expansions occurred at a level lower than 3 (depth larger than 3). In particular, from the iteration 1000 to 9150, CELOE visited level 2 very rarely and put much effort to search from level 3 to 6. After this extensive searching of lower levels, the algorithm realized that a better solution originated in the less explored areas from the upper part of the tree and therefore started to explore level 2 from the iteration 9150. Indeed, a good seed for the solution was the tree node 0-2-52 with the hypothesis $(\exists \mathsf{hasSibling}.\top \sqcup \exists \mathsf{married}.\top) \sqcap (\neg \mathsf{Female})$. As the ID indicates, 0-2-52 was the 52nd child of the level 1 hypothesis $\neg \mathsf{Female}$, while $\neg \mathsf{Female}$ itself was the second child of $\top$. CELOE came back to 0-2-52 in the iteration 9303 and was able to find the solution within 40 further iterations.

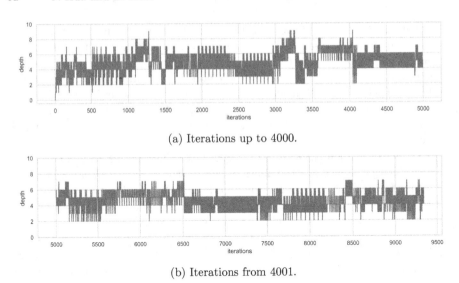

(a) Iterations up to 4000.

(b) Iterations from 4001.

**Fig. 1.** The tree depth of expanded nodes for learning the concept of Uncle with the default setting of CELOE.

**Table 1.** The configurations of learning algorithms used for comparison.

| Configuration | Exp. penalty | Gain bonus | Ref. penalty | Start bonus |
|---|---|---|---|---|
| ori | 0.02/0.1 | 0.3 | 0.0001 | 0.1 |
| spa | 0.05 | 0.2 | 0.0001 | 0.1 |
| ori_v1 | 0.02/0.1 | 0.3 | 0 | 0 |
| ori_v2 | 0.03 | 0.3 | 0.00005 | 0.1 |
| ori_v3 | 0.02 | 0.2 | 0 | 0 |
| rrhc-default | 0.02 | 0.2 | 0 | 0 |

To demonstrate the effects of different parameter settings, we compare the performance of various CELOE configurations for the Uncle example, as shown in Table 1. The configuration ori is the default setting provided by DL-Learner. ori has different expansion penalty for individual learning problems and is set to 0.02 for the Uncle problem. The configuration spa is suggested by Tran et al. in [15]. We also consider three futher variants of ori: ori_v1 and ori_v3 are intended to test the influence of the refinement penalty and the start bonus, while ori_v2 slightly modifies the expansion and refinement penalty.

For each of these configurations, Table 2 summarizes measurements collected until the first correct solution was found. On the one hand, while ori, ori_v1 and ori_v3 had comparatively good performance, they still differ in the number of tested expressions and in the tree depth. In particular, the results of ori_v1 and ori_v3 indicated that the refinement penalty and the start bonus

**Table 2.** The learning performance of four different CELOE configurations for the Uncle example. All statistics are collected until the first correct solution is found.

|        | Time (s) | #iterations | #expressions | #tree nodes | Tree depth | Length |
|--------|----------|-------------|--------------|-------------|------------|--------|
| ori    | 4.301    | 9342        | 16584        | 6655        | 9          | 16     |
| spa    | 177.863  | 429207      | 526022       | 322902      | 12         | 15     |
| ori_v1 | 4.550    | 9346        | 10912        | 7088        | 10         | 15     |
| ori_v2 | 42.808   | 55206       | 115141       | 46546       | 11         | 16     |
| ori_v3 | 4.325    | 9342        | 10457        | 6655        | 10         | 15     |

were unnecessary for learning the definition of Uncle. However, as we will show later in Sect. 5, it is not always the case for other learning problems. More importantly, ori_v1 and ori_v3 found a slightly better solution than ori that replaced ¬Female in Eq. 2 with Male. On the other hand, the terrible performance of both ori_v2 and spa suggested that the (slightly) higher expansion penalty is fatal in the Uncle example.

## 4 Rapid Restart Hill Climbing (RRHC)

RRHC inherits the main idea of CELOE but adopts a different selection strategy. Algorithm 1 illustrates the skeleton of RRHC that has two nested loops. For a current node $n$, the inner loop selects a tree node for expansion in a hill-climbing manner (line 4–11) while the outer loop expands the selected node $n$ using the refinement operator $\rho^{cl}$. The horizontal expansion of the node $n$ is increased by one after the refinement (line 18), so that a revisit of $n$ could generate new refinements. Because the heuristic in Eq. 1 depends on the horizontal expansion, the score of $n$ drops after each refinement such that $n$ might not be the best one among its siblings. Therefore, the algorithm backtracks to $n$'s parent (line 20) and rapidly restarts without checking the new refinements.

In Fig. 2, we compare the tree construction process of RRHC and CELOE. For the sake of simplicity, we use the Mother example from the family benchmark. The numbers on the upper left corner of each tree node illustrate the sequence of refinement generation. The tree node marked as green depicts the solution found by the algorithms.

We observe two major differences between Fig. 2a and 2b. The first one is that CELOE committed to the refinement chain ⊤ ⤳ Person ⤳ Mother ⤳ ··· while RRHC preferred ¬Male rather than Person. In fact, RRHC also generated Female in the early phase but decided to go back to the upper layer instead of exploiting the high score of Female, because the score of Person decreased after one refinement and did not show any advantage against the root node. After discovering the node ¬Male, RRHC insisted on refining it since its score is higher than Person, even after three times of expansion (step 5 to 7). One reason is that ¬Male has the same individuals (instances) as Female, although their semantic equivalence is not explicitly stated in the knowledge base.

---

**Algorithm 1.** Rapid Restart Hill Climbing (RRHC)

---

**Input:** background knowledge $\mathcal{K}$, positive examples $E^+$, negative examples $E^-$
**Output:** best concept found
 1: initialize a search tree $ST$ with the root node $(\top, |\top|)$
 2: let the current node $n = (C, he)$ be the root node with $C = \top, he = |\top|$
 3: **while** Solution not found <u>or</u> timeout not triggered **do**
 4:     **while** $size(n.children) \neq 0$ **do**
 5:         select a node $child$ with the best score among $n.children$
 6:         **if** $score(child) > score(n)$ **then**
 7:             $n \leftarrow child$
 8:         **else**
 9:             break
10:         **end if**
11:     **end while**
12:     let $refinements = \{D \mid D \in \rho^{cl}(C), |D| \leq he\}$
13:     **for** $D \in refinements$ **do**
14:         **if** $D$ is complete <u>and</u> $D$ is not redundant **then**
15:             add $(D, |D|)$ as a child of $n$
16:         **end if**
17:     **end for**
18:     increase the horizontal expansion of $n$ by 1
19:     **if** $n \neq root$ **then**
20:         $n \leftarrow n.parent$
21:     **end if**
22: **end while**
23: **return** concept with best accuracy

---

The second difference is that CELOE found a better solution than RRHC regarding the concept length. However, as we have shown in Table 2, the solution found by CELOE depends on its parameter setting. In fact, with the configurations spa and ori_v2, CELOE generated the same solution as RRHC.

After explaining the learning procedure of RRHC, we want to analyze its theoretical properties. Proposition 1 shows that RRHC is correct in $\mathcal{ALC}$.

**Proposition 1 (Correctness in $\mathcal{ALC}$).** *If a learning problem has a solution in $\mathcal{ALC}$, then Algorithm 1 terminates and finds a correct solution.*

*Proof.* We first briefly repeat the correctness proof for OCEL/CELOE in [12], and then extend it for Algorithm 1.

Suppose that the learning problem has a solution $D$ in $\mathcal{ALC}$, then the weak completeness of the refinement operator $\rho^{cl}$ guarantees a refinement path in the form of $\top \rightsquigarrow D_1 \rightsquigarrow D_2 \rightsquigarrow \cdots \rightsquigarrow D_n = D$. The basic heuristic in Eq. 1 has the property that $score(D) \geq -|D|$ for $\beta \in [0, 1]$, since the first two terms in Eq. 1 are positive, and the horizontal expansion of $D$ is initialized to $|D|$. Moreover, $score(D_i) \geq -|D|$, since $\rho^{cl}$ does not reduce the length of a refined hypothesis. On the other hand, because $\beta > 0$, a hypothesis $D'$ with a sufficiently high horizontal expansion would have a score lower than $-|D|$ and would not exist in

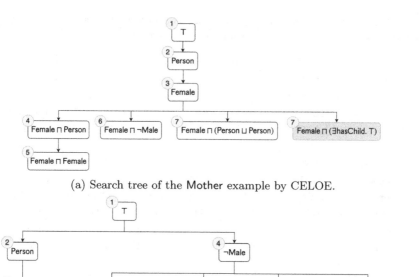

(a) Search tree of the Mother example by CELOE.

(b) Search tree of the Mother example by RRHC.

**Fig. 2.** The search tree constructed for learning the concept of Mother with the default setting of CELOE and RRHC.

the chain above. As OCEL/CELOE greedily selects the global best node from the tree, $D'$ would never be selected until all concepts in the chain above are sufficiently refined. Thus, either $D$ or another solution will be found.

Now we extend this proof for Algorithm 1, since RRHC employs a different selection strategy. Essentially, we need to show that RRHC would not select a node $D'$ that has no chance to refine to $D$, i.e. $score(D') < -|D|$. We proof this by deriving a contradiction. Suppose that $D'$ would be selected, then $-|D| > score(D') \geq score(D^*)$ for each $D^*$ that is a sibling of $D'$. In other words, no sibling node of $D'$ can be refined to the concept $D$. Furthermore, let $D'_p$ be the parent of $D'$, then $-|D| > score(D') > score(D'_p)$, since otherwise Algorithm 1 would choose $D'_p$ and restart. Consider the layers above $D'$, it is evident that the score of all predecessors of $D'$ and the siblings of those are lower than $score(D')$ and therefore lower than $-|D|$, including the root node $\top$. As a consequence, even with sufficiently high horizontal expansion, $\rho^{cl}$ can not generate $D$ from $\top$, which leads to a contradiction of the weak completeness of $\rho^{cl}$.  □

## 5  Experiments

In this section, we conduct extensive comparisons of RRHC and CELOE using the standard benchmarks provided by DL-Learner. Table 3 enumerates the

**Table 3.** Statistics of used benchmarks. `Moral reasoner` and `poker` have two different versions which are shown with two values in each column.

| Benchmarks | Language | #classes | #ind | #op | #dp | #axioms | Category |
|---|---|---|---|---|---|---|---|
| arch | $\mathcal{ALC}$ | 8 | 19 | 5 | 0 | 80 | simple |
| carcinogenesis | $\mathcal{ALC}(\mathbf{D})$ | 142 | 22372 | 4 | 15 | 74566 | hard |
| family | $\mathcal{AL}$ | 4 | 202 | 4 | 0 | 1343 | simp./med. |
| forte | $\mathcal{ALIF}$ | 3 | 86 | 3 | 0 | 347 | medium |
| lymphography | $\mathcal{AL}$ | 53 | 148 | 0 | 0 | 2197 | simp./hard |
| moral reasoner | $\mathcal{ALC}/\mathcal{ALC}$ | 41/44 | 43/202 | 0/0 | 0/0 | 1047/4710 | simple |
| mutagenesis | $\mathcal{AL}(\mathbf{D})$ | 86 | 14145 | 5 | 6 | 62066 | hard |
| poker | $\mathcal{AL}/\mathcal{AL}$ | 2/2 | 311/347 | 6/6 | 0/0 | 1334/1418 | simple |
| semantic bible | $\mathcal{SHOIN}(\mathbf{D})$ | 49 | 724 | 29 | 9 | 4434 | simple |
| trains | $\mathcal{ALC}$ | 10 | 50 | 5 | 0 | 288 | simple |
| yinyang | $\mathcal{ALI}$ | 3 | 31 | 3 | 0 | 157 | simple |

ontologies of these benchmarks with the statistics of their classes, individuals, roles (object properties and data properties in OWL), and axioms[3].

For each benchmark, there can be several learning problems, such as Mother and Uncle in the `family` benchmark. We categorize the learning problems by the learning time required to find the first correct solution: *simple* problems can be solved by both algorithms within 3 s, *medium* problems require more than 3 s by at least one algorithm, and *hard* problems can not be solved within 300 s (timeout) by at least one algorithm. The last column of Table 3 shows the difficulty of each benchmark. Note that some benchmarks have mixed difficulties such as `family`. To assess the performance of algorithms more fairly, we choose a different evaluation criteria for each category as follows:

- *simple*: since both algorithms found the solution very fast, we use the size of the search tree to compare the learning efficiency in order to avoid the impact of oscillations of the computing power.
- *medium*: in this case, the time required for the first solution is used.
- *hard*: in all hard cases, we compare the accuracy of the best concept found by both algorithms.

### 5.1   Results and Discussions

The benefit of using the basic heuristic in Eq. 1 is that we were able to choose a default configuration `rrhc-default` for RRHC empirically (last row in Table 1). It does not mean that the default configuration was always the best one, but it performed statistically well throughout all learning problems. For CELOE, we chose the configurations that are summarized in Table 1. Note that `ori_v3` has exactly the same setting as `rrhc-default`.

---

[3] The statistics are obtained using the Protégé editor.

We run the experiments on a machine with a 2.6 GHz CPU and 16 GB memory. The timeout for all learning problems is 300 s. We explicitly disallow *noise percentage* in all experiments, therefore only complete concept hypotheses are considered as potential solutions. For both algorithms, *predictive accuracy* is used to compute the accuracy of hypotheses [13]. Figures 3 and 4 show the comparisons of RRHC and CELOE regarding the performance criteria mentioned above. In all plots, the blue line or bar depicts the value of RRHC while the others represent different CELOE configurations.

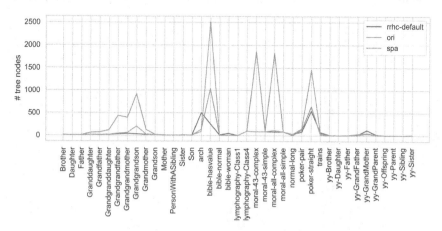

(a) Tree size of `rrhc-default`, `ori`, `spa` for simple learning problems.

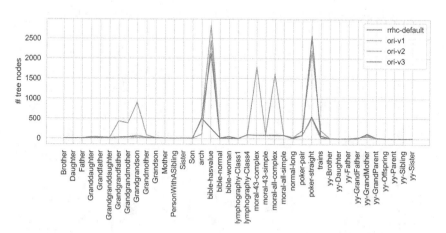

(b) Tree size of `rrhc-default`, `ori v1`, `ori v2`, `ori v3` for simple learning problems.

**Fig. 3.** Comparison of RRHC and CELOE in simple learning problems. (Color figure online)

For the simple learning problems, Fig. 3 shows the number of tree nodes when the first solution is found. Besides some trivial ones in which both algorithms had very similar results, RRHC generally performed better than CELOE. One exception is the `arch` benchmark, which strongly prefers large expansion penalty, such as 0.05/0.1 from `ori, spa`, and `ori_v1`. Note that in Fig. 3b, `ori_v3` performed well for all problems in `family`, but worked unsatisfyingly in some other problems, e.g. `hasValue` in `semantic bible` and `straight` in `poker`.

For the medium learning problems, Fig. 4a shows the time required (in seconds) for constructing the first solution, and RRHC was always the best one. For the hard cases, Fig. 4b shows the accuracy of the best solution found within

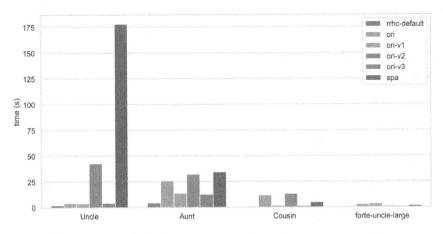

(a) Time required of all configurations for medium learning problems.

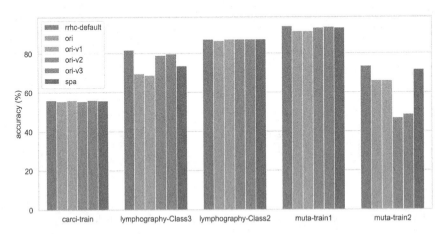

(b) Best accuracy obtained from all configurations for hard learning problems.

**Fig. 4.** Comparison of RRHC and CELOE in medium and hard learning problems. (Color figure online)

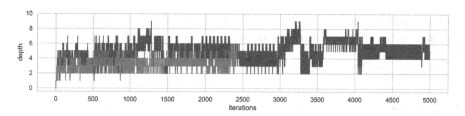

**Fig. 5.** Comparison of RRHC (orange) and CELOE (blue) regarding the expanded nodes in the Uncle example. Iterations from 5001 are omitted since RRHC found a solution in iteration 2418. (Color figure online)

300 s. Apparently, the performance of RRHC was either comparable to or better than the best CELOE configuration.

One extremely hard benchmark is `carcinogenesis`, which is very noisy so that both algorithms had poor results. Among the CELOE configurations, it is evident that no single setting was significantly better than the others. Interestingly, `ori_v3` performed well in most cases except the `muta-train2` problem.

Recall the Uncle example from the `family` benchmark. Figure 5 shows the comparison of RRHC (orange) and CELOE (blue) regarding the tree depth of expanded nodes. Besides that RRHC tended to explore the upper part of the tree, its behavior was also more stable than CELOE regarding depth changes. However, it is worth noting that RRHC is fundamentally different to a breadth-first search, as an exhaustive expansion of any tree node is not viable due to the infiniteness of the refinement operator. Principally, heuristic still guides the search. However, the restart mechanism requires a sequence of good candidates from the root node ⊤ to the selected one. Consequently, RRHC also spent quite much time in level 3 and 4, since the score of the node `0-2-52` was lower than its siblings. However, because the upper part of the tree has much fewer nodes than the lower part, RRHC was able to expand `0-2-52` in iteration 2382, compared with iteration 9303 in the case of CELOE.

## 6 Conclusion and Future Work

In this paper, we presented the Rapid Restart Hill Climbing (RRHC) algorithm for learning DL concepts. We identified the drawbacks of the simple greedy strategy employed in the CELOE algorithm and showed that RRHC generally performs better than CELOE in standard benchmarks of DL-Learner. Moreover, RRHC enjoys a small number of parameters, and a default setting was provided empirically for future research.

While the results look promising, we did not look into the *myopia* problem of hill climbing. One reason is that our heuristic is rather dynamic, i.e. the score of a tree node changes after its concept is refined. In future work, we want to study how the myopia problem affects RRHC for learning DL concepts, and plan to extend RRHC using advanced techniques that can be borrowed from the ILP community. For example, *macros* were introduced for tackling the problem of *non-discriminating* relations in ILP [3]. A similar adaptation of the refinement operator $\rho^{cl}$ can thus require the consumer (filler) in any quantification to be a specialization of $\top$. For noisy data sets, e.g. `carcinogenesis`, one can consider to introduce random selections during the hill climbing search [17].

# References

1. Badea, L., Nienhuys-Cheng, S.-H.: A refinement operator for description logics. In: Cussens, J., Frisch, A. (eds.) ILP 2000. LNCS (LNAI), vol. 1866, pp. 40–59. Springer, Heidelberg (2000). https://doi.org/10.1007/3-540-44960-4_3

2. Bühmann, L., Lehmann, J., Westphal, P.: DL-learner - a framework for inductive learning on the semantic web. Web Semant. **39**(C), 15–24 (2016)

3. Castillo, L.P., Wrobel, S.: Macro-operators in multirelational learning: a search-space reduction technique. In: Elomaa, T., Mannila, H., Toivonen, H. (eds.) ECML 2002. LNCS (LNAI), vol. 2430, pp. 357–368. Springer, Heidelberg (2002). https://doi.org/10.1007/3-540-36755-1_30

4. Castillo, L.P., Wrobel, S.: A comparative study on methods for reducing myopia of hill-climbing search in multirelational learning. In: Proceedings of the Twenty-first International Conference on Machine Learning, ICML 2004. ACM (2004)

5. Cazenave, T.: Iterative widening. In: Proceedings of the 17th International Joint Conference on Artificial Intelligence, IJCAI 2001, vol. 1, pp. 523–528. Morgan Kaufmann Publishers Inc., San Francisco (2001)

6. Esposito, F., Fanizzi, N., Iannone, L., Palmisano, I., Semeraro, G.: Knowledge-intensive induction of terminologies from metadata. In: McIlraith, S.A., Plexousakis, D., van Harmelen, F. (eds.) ISWC 2004. LNCS, vol. 3298, pp. 441–455. Springer, Heidelberg (2004). https://doi.org/10.1007/978-3-540-30475-3_31

7. Fanizzi, N., Ferilli, S., Iannone, L., Palmisano, I., Semeraro, G.: Downward Refinement in the $\mathcal{ALN}$ description logic. In: Fourth International Conference on Hybrid Intelligent Systems (HIS 2004), pp. 68–73, December 2004

8. Fanizzi, N., d'Amato, C., Esposito, F.: DL-FOIL concept learning in description logics. In: Železný, F., Lavrač, N. (eds.) ILP 2008. LNCS (LNAI), vol. 5194, pp. 107–121. Springer, Heidelberg (2008). https://doi.org/10.1007/978-3-540-85928-4_12

9. Fanizzi, N., Rizzo, G., d'Amato, C., Esposito, F.: DLFoil: class expression learning revisited. In: Faron Zucker, C., Ghidini, C., Napoli, A., Toussaint, Y. (eds.) EKAW 2018. LNCS (LNAI), vol. 11313, pp. 98–113. Springer, Cham (2018). https://doi.org/10.1007/978-3-030-03667-6_7

10. Iannone, L., Palmisano, I., Fanizzi, N.: An algorithm based on counterfactuals for concept learning in the Semantic Web. Appl. Intell. **26**(2), 139–159 (2007)

11. Lehmann, J., Auer, S., Bühmann, L., Tramp, S.: Class expression learning for ontology engineering. J. Web Semant. **9**, 71–81 (2011)

12. Lehmann, J., Hitzler, P.: Foundations of refinement operators for description logics. In: Blockeel, H., Ramon, J., Shavlik, J., Tadepalli, P. (eds.) ILP 2007. LNCS (LNAI), vol. 4894, pp. 161–174. Springer, Heidelberg (2008). https://doi.org/10.1007/978-3-540-78469-2_18

13. Lehmann, J., Hitzler, P.: Concept learning in description logics using refinement operators. Mach. Learn. **78**(1), 203 (2009)

14. Quinlan, J.R., Cameron-Jones, R.M.: Induction of logic programs: FOIL and related systems. New Gener. Comput. **13**(3), 287–312 (1995)

15. Tran, A.C., Dietrich, J., Guesgen, H.W., Marsland, S.: Parallel symmetric class expression learning. J. Mach. Learn. Res. **18**(64), 1–34 (2017)
16. Tran, A.C., Dietrich, J., Guesgen, H.W., Marsland, S.: An approach to parallel class expression learning. In: Bikakis, A., Giurca, A. (eds.) RuleML 2012. LNCS, vol. 7438, pp. 302–316. Springer, Heidelberg (2012). https://doi.org/10.1007/978-3-642-32689-9_25
17. Železný, F., Srinivasan, A., Page, C.D.: Randomised restarted search in ILP. Mach. Learn. **64**(1), 183–208 (2006)
18. Železný, F., Srinivasan, A., Page, D.: Lattice-search runtime distributions may be heavy-tailed. In: Matwin, S., Sammut, C. (eds.) ILP 2002. LNCS (LNAI), vol. 2583, pp. 333–345. Springer, Heidelberg (2003). https://doi.org/10.1007/3-540-36468-4_22

# Neural Networks for Relational Data

Navdeep Kaur[1]([✉]), Gautam Kunapuli[1], Saket Joshi[2], Kristian Kersting[3], and Sriraam Natarajan[1]

[1] The University of Texas at Dallas, Richardson, USA
{Navdeep.Kaur,Gautam.Kunapuli,Sriraam.Natarajan}@utdallas.edu
[2] Amazon Inc., Seattle, USA
saketjoshi@gmail.com
[3] TU Darmstadt, Darmstadt, Germany
kersting@cs.tu-darmstadt.de

**Abstract.** While deep networks have been enormously successful, they rely on flat-feature vector representations. Using them in structured domains requires significant feature engineering. Such domains rely on relational representations to capture complex relationships between entities and their attributes. Thus, we consider the problem of learning neural networks for relational data. We distinguish ourselves from current approaches that rely on expert hand-coded rules by learning higher-order random-walk features to capture local structural interactions and the resulting network architecture. We further exploit parameter tying, where instances of the same rule share parameters. Our experimental results demonstrate the effectiveness of the proposed approach over multiple neural net baselines as well as state-of-the-art relational models.

**Keywords:** Neural networks · Relational models

## 1 Introduction

Probabilistic Logic/Statistical Relational Models [1,3] allows them to model complex data structures such as graphs far more easily and interpretably than basic propositional representations. While expressive, these models do not incorporate or discover latent relationships between features as effectively as deep networks. There has been focus on achieving the dream team of symbolic and statistical learning methods such as *relational neural networks* [2,7,11,15,16]. While specific architectures differ, these methods generally employ *an expert* or Inductive Logic Programming (ILP, [10]) to identify domain structure/rules which are then instantiated to learn a neural network. We improve upon these methods in two ways: (1) we employ a rule learner to automatically extract *interpretable* rules that are then employed as hidden layer of the neural network; (2) we exploit *parameter tying* similar to SRL models [14] that allow multiple instances of the same rule share the same parameter. These two extensions significantly improve the adaptation of neural networks (NNs) for relational data.

We employ *Relational Random Walks* [9] to extract relational rules from a database, which are then used as the first layer of the NN. These random walks

© Springer Nature Switzerland AG 2020
D. Kazakov and C. Erten (Eds.): ILP 2019, LNAI 11770, pp. 62–71, 2020.
https://doi.org/10.1007/978-3-030-49210-6_6

have the advantages of being learned from data (as against time-consumingly hand-coded features) and interpretable (they are rules in a database schema). Given evidence (facts), our network ensure two key features. First, relational random walks are learned and instantiated (grounded); parameter tying ensures that groundings of the same random walk share the same parameters resulting in far fewer learnable network parameters. Next, for combining outputs from different groundings of the *same clause*, we employ combination functions [4, 14]. Finally, once the network weights are appropriately constrained by parameter tying, they can be learned using standard techniques such as backpropagation.

We make the following contributions: (1) we learn a NN that can be fully trained from data and with no significant engineering, unlike previous approaches; (2) we combine the successful paradigms of relational random walks and parameter tying allowing the resulting NN to faithfully model relational data while being fully learnable; (3) we evaluate the approach and demonstrate its efficacy.

## 2  Related Work

Our work is closest to Lifted Relational Neural Networks (LRNN, [15]) due to Šourek et al. LRNN uses expert hand-crafted rules, which are then instantiated and rolled out as a ground network. While Šourek et al., exploit tied parameters across facts, we share parameters *across multiple instances* of the same rule. LRNN supports weighted facts due to the fuzzy notion that they adapt; we take a more standard approach with Boolean facts. Finally, while the previous difference appears to be limiting, in our case it leads to a *reduction in the number of network weights*. Šourek et al., extended their work to learn network structure using predicate invention [16]; our work learns relational random walks as rules for the network structure. As we show in our experiments, NNs can easily handle large numbers of random walks as weakly predictive intermediate layers capturing local features. This allows for learning a more robust model than the induced rules, which take a more global view of the domain.

Another recent approach is due to Kazemi and Poole [7], who proposed a relational neural network by adding hidden layers to their Relational Logistic Regression [6] model. A key limitation of their work is that they are restricted to unary relation predictions. Other recent approaches such as CILP++ [2] and Deep Relational Machines [11] incorporate relational information as network layers. However, such models propositionalize relational data into flat-feature vector while we learn a lifted model.

## 3  Neural Networks with Relational Parameter Tying

A relational neural network $\mathcal{N}$ is a set of $M$ weighted rules $\{R_j, w_j)\}_{j=1}^M$. Relational rules are conjunctions of the form $h \Leftarrow b_1 \wedge \ldots \wedge b_\ell$, where the head $h$ is the target of prediction and the body $b_1 \wedge \ldots \wedge b_\ell$ corresponds to conditions that make up the rule. We are given evidence: atomic facts $\mathcal{F}$ and labeled relational examples $\{(\mathbf{x}_i, y_i)\}_{i=1}^{\ell}$. We seek to learn a relational neural network $\mathcal{N} \equiv \{\mathbf{R}_j, w_j)\}_{j=1}^{M}$ to predict a **Target** relation: $y = \mathtt{Target}(\mathbf{x})$. This consists of two steps: structure learning, to learn the architecture of $\mathcal{N}$ and parameter learning, to identify (tied) network parameters of $\mathcal{N}$.

### 3.1  Generating Lifted Random Walks

The architecture is determined by the *set of induced clauses from the domain*. While previous approaches employed carefully hand-crafted rules, we use relational random walks to define the network architecture and local qualitative structure of the domain. Relational data is often represented using a lifted graph, which defines the domain's schema; in such a representation, a relation $\mathtt{Predicate}(\mathtt{Type}_1, \mathtt{Type}_2)$ can be understood as a predicate edge between two type nodes: $\mathtt{Type}_1 \xrightarrow{\mathtt{Predicate}} \mathtt{Type}_2$. A relational random walk through a graph is a chain of such edges corresponding to a conjunction of predicates.

For a random walk to be semantically sound, the input type (argument domain) of the $(i + 1)$-th predicate must be the same as the output type (argument range) of the $i$-th predicate. For example, in a movie domain, the body of the rule $\mathtt{ActedIn}(\mathtt{P}_1, \mathtt{G}_1) \wedge \mathtt{SameGenre}(\mathtt{G}_1, \mathtt{G}_2) \wedge \mathtt{ActedIn}^{-1}(\mathtt{G}_2, \mathtt{P}_2) \wedge$ $\mathtt{SamePerson}(\mathtt{P}_2, \mathtt{P}_3) \Rightarrow \mathtt{WorkedUnder}(\mathtt{P}_1, \mathtt{P}_3)$ is a lifted random walk $\mathtt{P}_1 \xrightarrow{\mathtt{ActedIn}} \mathtt{G}_1 \xrightarrow{\mathtt{SameGenre}} \mathtt{G}_2 \xrightarrow{\mathtt{ActedIn}^{-1}} \mathtt{P}_2 \xrightarrow{\mathtt{SamePerson}} \mathtt{P}_3$, between two entities $\mathtt{P}_1 \rightarrow \mathtt{P}_3$ in the target predicate, $\mathtt{WorkedUnder}(\mathtt{P}_1, \mathtt{P}_3)$. This walk contains an *inverse predicate* $\mathtt{ActedIn}^{-1}$, which is distinct from $\mathtt{ActedIn}$ (its arguments are reversed).

We use path-constrained random walks [9] approach to generate $M$ lifted random walks $\mathbf{R}_j, j = 1, \ldots, M$. These random walks form the backbone of the lifted neural network, as they are templates for various feature combinations in the domain. They can also be interpreted as *domain rules* as they impart localized structure, or a qualitative description of the domain. When these lifted random walks have weights associated with them, we are then able to endow them with a quantitative influence on the target. A key component of network instantiation with these rules is *rule-based parameter tying*, which reduces the number of learnable parameters significantly, while still effectively maintaining the quantitative influences as described by the relational random walks.

### 3.2  Network Instantiation

The relational random walks ($\mathbf{R}_j$) generated above are the relational features of the lifted relational NN, $\mathcal{N}$. Our goal is to unroll and ground the network with several intermediate layers that capture the relationships expressed by these random walks. A key difference in network construction between our proposed work and recent approaches [15] is that we *do not perform an exhaustive grounding* to generate all possible instances before constructing the network. Instead, we only ground as needed leading to a much more compact network (cf. Figure 1).

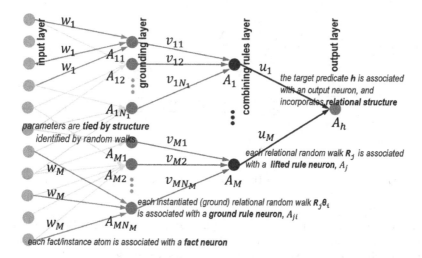

**Fig. 1.** The relational neural network is unrolled in three stages, ensuring that the output is a function of facts through two hidden layers: the combining rules layer (with lifted random walks) and the grounding layer (with instantiated random walks). Weights are tied between the input and grounding layers based on which fact/feature ultimately contributes to which rule in the combining rules layer.

**Output Layer:** For the `Target`, which is also the head **h** in all the rules $\mathbf{R_j}$, introduce an output neuron called the *target neuron*, $A_\mathbf{h}$. With one-hot encoding of the target labels, this architecture can handle multi-class problems. The target neuron uses the *softmax activation function*. Without loss of generality, we describe the rest of the network unrolling assuming a single output neuron.

**Combining Rules Layer:** The target neuron is connected to $M$ *lifted rule neurons*, each corresponding to one of the lifted relational random walks, $(\mathbf{R_j}, w_j)$. Each rule $\mathbf{R_j}$ is a conjunction of predicates defined by random walks:

$$\mathbf{Q_1^j(X, \cdot)} \wedge \ldots \wedge \mathbf{Q_L^j(\cdot, Z)} \ \Rightarrow \ \mathbf{Target(X, Z)}, \ j = 1, \ldots, M,$$

and corresponds to the lifted rule neuron $A_j$. This layer of neurons is fully connected to the output layer to ensure that all the lifted random walks (that capture the domain structure) influence the output. The extent of their influence is determined by learnable weights, $u_j$ between $A_j$ and the output neuron $A_\mathbf{h}$.

In Fig. 1, we see that the rule neuron $A_j$ is connected to the neurons $A_{ji}$; these neurons correspond to $N_j$ *instantiations* of the random-walk $\mathbf{R_j}$. The lifted rule neuron $A_j$ aims to *combine the influence of the groundings of the random-walk feature* $\mathbf{R_j}$ that are true in the evidence. Thus, each lifted rule neuron can also be viewed as a *rule combination neuron*. The activation function of a rule combination neuron can be any *aggregator or combining rule* [14]. This can include *value aggregators* such as **weighted mean, max** or *distribution aggregators* (if inputs to the this layer are probabilities) such as **Noisy-Or**. For instance, combining rule instantiations out$(A_{ji})$ with a weighted mean will

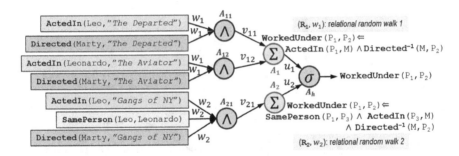

**Fig. 2.** Example: unrolling the network with relational parameter tying.

require learning $v_{ji}$, with the nodes using unit functions for activation. This layer is more general and subsumes LRNN [15], which uses a max combination layer.

**Grounding Layer:** For each ground random walk $\mathbf{R}_j\boldsymbol{\theta}_i$, $i = 1, \ldots, N_j$, we introduce a *ground rule neuron*, $A_{ji}$. This ground rule neuron represents the $i$-th instantiation (grounding) of the body of the $j$-th rule, $\mathbf{R}_j\boldsymbol{\theta}_i: \mathbf{Q}_1^j\boldsymbol{\theta}_i \wedge \ldots \wedge \mathbf{Q}_\ell^j\boldsymbol{\theta}_i$. The activation function of a ground rule neuron is a *logical AND* $(\wedge)$; it is only activated when all its constituent inputs are true. This requires all the constituent facts $\mathbf{Q}_1^j\boldsymbol{\theta}_i, \ldots, \mathbf{Q}_\ell^j\boldsymbol{\theta}_i$ to be in the evidence. Thus, the $(j, i)$-th ground rule neuron is connected to all the *fact neurons* that appear in its corresponding instantiated rule body. A key novelty is relational parameter tying: the weights of connections between the fact and grounding layers are *tied* by the rule these facts appear in together. This is described in detail further below.

**Input Layer:** Each grounded predicate is a *fact*, that is $\mathbf{Q}_k^j\boldsymbol{\theta}_i \in \mathcal{F}$. For each such instantiated fact, we create a *fact neuron* $A_f$, ensuring that each unique fact in evidence has only one single neuron associated with it. Every example is a collection of facts, that is, example $\mathbf{x}_i \equiv \mathcal{F}_i \subset \mathcal{F}$. Thus, an example is input into the system by simply activating its constituent facts in the input layer.

**Relational Parameter Tying:** We employ *rule-based parameter tying* for the weights between the grounding layer and the input/facts layer. Parameter tying ensures that instances corresponding to an example all share the same weight $w_j$ if they occur in the same lifted rule $\mathbf{R}_j$. The shared weights $w_j$ are propagated through the network in a bottom-up fashion, ensuring that weights in the succeeding hidden layers are influenced by them. Our approach to parameter tying is in sharp contrast to LRNN, where weights between the output and combining rules layers are learned. This approach also differs from our previous work [5] where we used relational random walks as features for an RBM. The relational RBM formulation has significantly more edges, and many more parameters to optimize during learning as its architecture is a bipartite graph.

We illustrate network construction with an example: two lifted random walks $(R_1, w_1)$ and $(R_2, w_2)$ for the target predicate $\texttt{WorkedUnder}(P_1, P_2)$ (Fig. 2):

$$\texttt{WorkedUnder}(P_1, P_2) \Leftarrow \texttt{ActedIn}(P_1, M) \wedge \texttt{Directed}^{-1}(M, P_2),$$

$$\texttt{WorkedUnder}(P_1, P_2) \Leftarrow \texttt{SamePerson}(P_1, P_3) \wedge \texttt{ActedIn}(P_3, M) \wedge \texttt{Directed}^{-1}(M, P_2).$$

The **output layer** consists of a single neuron $A_h$ corresponding to $\texttt{WorkedUnder}$. The **lifted rule layer** has two lifted rule nodes $A_1$ corresponding to rule $R_1$ and $A_2$ corresponding to rule $R_2$. These rule nodes combine inputs corresponding to instantiations that are true in the evidence. The network is unrolled based on the specific training example, for instance: $\texttt{WorkedUnder}(\texttt{Leo}, \texttt{Marty})$. For this example, the rule $R_1$ has two instantiations that are true in the evidence. Then, we introduce a ground rule node for each such instantiation:

$$A_{11} : \texttt{Act}(\texttt{Leo}, \texttt{"TheDeparted"}) \wedge \texttt{Dir}^{-1}(\texttt{"TheDeparted"}, \texttt{Marty}),$$

$$A_{12} : \texttt{Act}(\texttt{Leo}, \texttt{"TheAviator"}) \wedge \texttt{Dir}^{-1}(\texttt{"TheAviator"}, \texttt{Marty}).$$

The rule $R_2$ has only one instantiation, and consequently only one node:

$$A_{21} : \texttt{SamPer}(\texttt{Leo}, \texttt{Leonardo}) \wedge \texttt{Act}(\texttt{Leo}, \texttt{"TheDeparted"}) \wedge \texttt{Dir}^{-1}(\texttt{"TheDeparted"}, \texttt{Marty}).$$

The **grounding layer** consists of ground rule nodes corresponding to instantiations of rules that are true in the evidence. The edges $A_{ji} \rightarrow A_j$ have weights $v_{ji}$ that depend on the combining rule implemented in $A_j$. In this example, the combining rule is *average*, so we have $v_{11} = v_{12} = \frac{1}{2}$ and $v_{21} = 1$. The **input layer** consists of atomic fact in evidence: $f \in \mathcal{F}$. The fact nodes $\texttt{ActedIn}(\texttt{Leo}, \texttt{"TheAviator"})$ and $\texttt{Directed}^{-1}(\texttt{"TheAviator"}, \texttt{Marty})$ appear in the grounding $R_1 \theta_2$ and are connected to the corresponding ground rule neuron $A_{12}$. Finally, parameters are tied between the facts layer and the grounding layer. This ensures that all facts that ultimately contribute to a rule are pooled together, which increases the influence of the rule during weight learning. This ensures that a rule that holds strongly in the evidence gets a higher weight.

## 4    Experiments

We aim to answer the following questions about our method, *Neural Networks with Relational Parameter Tying* (NNRPT):[1] **Q1:** How does NNRPT compare to the state-of-the-art SRL models ? **Q2:** How does NNRPT compare to propositionalization models ? **Q3:** How does NNRPT compare to relational neural networks in literature?

---

[1] https://github.com/navdeepkjohal/NNRPT.

**Table 1.** Data sets used in our experiments. The last column is the number of sampled groundings of random walks per example for NNRPT.

| Domain | Target | #Facts | #Pos | #Neg | #RW | #Samp/RW |
|--------|--------|--------|------|------|-----|----------|
| Uw-Cse | advisedBy | 2817 | 90 | 180 | 2500 | 1000 |
| Mutagenesis | MoleAtm | 29986 | 1000 | 2000 | 100 | 100 |
| Cora | SameVenue | 31086 | 2331 | 4662 | 100 | 100 |
| Imdb | WorkedUnder | 914 | 305 | 710 | 80 | - |
| Sports | TeamPlaysSport | 7824 | 200 | 400 | 200 | 100 |

To answer **Q1**, we compare NNRPT with state-of-the-art relational gradient-boosting methods, RDN-Boost[13], MLN-Boost [8], and relational RBMs (RRBM-E, RRBM-C, [5]). As the random walks chain binary predicates in NNRPT, we convert unary and ternary predicates into binary predicates for all data sets. We use these binary predicates across *all our baselines*. We run RDN-Boost and MLN-Boost with their default settings and learn 20 trees for each model. We train RRBM-E and RRBM-C according to the settings recommended in [5]. For NNRPT, we generate random walks by considering each predicate and its inverse to be two distinct predicates. Also, we avoid loops in the random walks by enforcing sanity constraints on the random walk generation (Table 1). When *exhaustive grounding becomes prohibitively expensive*, we *sample groundings* for each random walk for large data sets. For all experiments, we set the positive to negative ratio to be $1:2$ for training, set combination function to "average" and perform 5-fold cross validation. For NNRPT, we set the learning rate to be 0.05, batch size to 1, and number of epochs to 1. We train our model with $L_1$-regularized AdaGrad.

To answer **Q2**, we generated flat feature vectors by Bottom Clause Propositionalization (BCP, [2]), according to which one bottom clause is generated for each example. BCP considers each predicate in the body of the bottom clause as a unique feature when it propositionalizes bottom clauses to flat feature vector. We use PROGOL [12] to generate bottom clauses. After propositionalization, we train two models: a propositionalized RBM (BCP-RBM) and a propositionalized NN (BCP-NN). The NN has two hidden layers, which makes BCP-NN model a modified version of CILP++ [2] that has one hidden layer. Hyper-parameters of both models were optimized by line search on a validation set. To answer **Q3**, we compare NNRPT with LRNN [15]. To ensure fairness, we perform structure learning by using PROGOL and input the *same clauses* to both LRNN and NNRPT. PROGOL learned 4 clauses for Cora, 8 clauses for Imdb, 3 clauses for Sports, 10 clauses for Uw-Cse and 11 clauses for Mutagenesis in our experiment.

Table 2 compares NNRPT to state-of-the-art SRL methods. NNRPT is significantly better than RRBM for Cora and Sports, and performs comparably on other data sets. It also performs better than MLN-Boost, RDN-Boost on Imdb and Cora, and comparably on other data sets. Broadly, **Q1** can be answered affirmatively: NNRPT performs comparably to or better than state-of-the-art SRL.

**Table 2.** Comparison with different SRL algorithms.

| Data Set | Measure | RDN-Boost | MLN-Boost | RRBM-E | RRBM-C | NNRPT |
|---|---|---|---|---|---|---|
| Uw-Cse | AUC-ROC | $0.973 \pm 0.014$ | $0.968 \pm 0.014$ | $0.975 \pm 0.013$ | $0.968 \pm 0.011$ | $0.959 \pm 0.024$ |
| | AUC-PR | $0.931 \pm 0.036$ | $0.916 \pm 0.035$ | $0.923 \pm 0.056$ | $0.924 \pm 0.040$ | $0.896 \pm 0.063$ |
| Imdb | AUC-ROC | $0.955 \pm 0.046$ | $0.944 \pm 0.070$ | $1.000 \pm 0.000$ | $0.997 \pm 0.006$ | $0.984 \pm 0.025$ |
| | AUC-PR | $0.863 \pm 0.112$ | $0.839 \pm 0.169$ | $1.000 \pm 0.000$ | $0.992 \pm 0.017$ | $0.951 \pm 0.082$ |
| Cora | AUC-ROC | $0.895 \pm 0.183$ | $0.835 \pm 0.035$ | $0.984 \pm 0.009$ | $0.867 \pm 0.041$ | $0.952 \pm 0.043$ |
| | AUC-PR | $0.833 \pm 0.259$ | $0.799 \pm 0.034$ | $0.948 \pm 0.042$ | $0.825 \pm 0.050$ | $0.899 \pm 0.070$ |
| Mutag. | AUC-ROC | $0.999 \pm 0.000$ | $0.999 \pm 0.000$ | $0.999 \pm 0.000$ | $0.998 \pm 0.001$ | $0.981 \pm 0.024$ |
| | AUC-PR | $0.999 \pm 0.000$ | $0.999 \pm 0.000$ | $0.999 \pm 0.000$ | $0.997 \pm 0.002$ | $0.970 \pm 0.039$ |
| Sports | AUC-ROC | $0.801 \pm 0.026$ | $0.806 \pm 0.016$ | $0.760 \pm 0.016$ | $0.656 \pm 0.071$ | $0.780 \pm 0.026$ |
| | AUC-PR | $0.670 \pm 0.028$ | $0.652 \pm 0.032$ | $0.634 \pm 0.020$ | $0.648 \pm 0.085$ | $0.668 \pm 0.070$ |

**Table 3.** Comparison of NNRPT with propositionalization-based approaches.

| Data Set | Measure | BCP-RBM | BCP-NN | NNRPT |
|---|---|---|---|---|
| Uw-Cse | AUC-ROC | $0.951 \pm 0.041$ | $0.868 \pm 0.053$ | $0.959 \pm 0.024$ |
| | AUC-PR | $0.860 \pm 0.114$ | $0.869 \pm 0.033$ | $0.896 \pm 0.063$ |
| Imdb | AUC-ROC | $0.780 \pm 0.164$ | $0.540 \pm 0.152$ | $0.984 \pm 0.025$ |
| | AUC-PR | $0.367 \pm 0.139$ | $0.536 \pm 0.231$ | $0.951 \pm 0.082$ |
| Cora | AUC-ROC | $0.801 \pm 0.017$ | $0.670 \pm 0.064$ | $0.952 \pm 0.043$ |
| | AUC-PR | $0.647 \pm 0.050$ | $0.658 \pm 0.064$ | $0.899 \pm 0.070$ |
| Mutag. | AUC-ROC | $0.991 \pm 0.003$ | $0.945 \pm 0.019$ | $0.981 \pm 0.024$ |
| | AUC-PR | $0.995 \pm 0.001$ | $0.973 \pm 0.012$ | $0.970 \pm 0.039$ |
| Sports | AUC-ROC | $0.664 \pm 0.021$ | $0.543 \pm 0.037$ | $0.780 \pm 0.026$ |
| | AUC-PR | $0.532 \pm 0.041$ | $0.499 \pm 0.065$ | $0.668 \pm 0.070$ |

Table 3 compares NNRPT with two propositionalization models: BCP-RBM and BCP-NN. NNRPT performs better than BCP-RBM on all data sets except Mutagen-esis, where the two are comparable. NNRPT performs better than BCP-NN on all data sets. It should be noted that BCP feature generation sometimes introduces a large positive-to-negative example skew (for example, in the Imdb data set), which can sometimes gravely affect the performance of propositional models. This emphasizes the need for models, like ours, that can handle relational data without propositionalization. **Q2** can now be answered affirmatively: that NNRPT performs better than propositionalization models.

Table 4 compares NNRPT and LRNN when both use clauses learned by PRO-GOL. NNRPT performs better on Uw-Cse, Sports evaluated using AUC-PR. This result is especially significant because these data sets are considerably skewed. NNRPT also outperforms LRNN on Cora and Mutagenesis. The reason for this big performance gap between the two models on Cora is likely because LRNN could not build effective models with the fewer number of clauses typically learned by PROGOL (four, here). In contrast, even with very few clauses, NNRPT

**Table 4.** Comparison of NNRPT and LRNN on AUC-ROC and AUC-PR on different data sets. Both the models were provided clauses learnt by PROGOL, [12].

| Model | Measure | Uw-Cse | Imdb | Cora | Mutagen. | Sports |
|-------|---------|--------|------|------|----------|--------|
| LRNN | AUC-ROC | $0.923 \pm 0.027$ | $0.995 \pm 0.004$ | $0.503 \pm 0.003$ | $0.500 \pm 0.000$ | $0.741 \pm 0.016$ |
|  | AUC-PR | $0.826 \pm 0.056$ | $0.985 \pm 0.013$ | $0.356 \pm 0.006$ | $0.335 \pm 0.000$ | $0.527 \pm 0.036$ |
| NNRPT | AUC-ROC | $0.700 \pm 0.186$ | $0.997 \pm 0.007$ | $0.968 \pm 0.022$ | $0.532 \pm 0.019$ | $0.657 \pm 0.014$ |
|  | AUC-PR | $0.910 \pm 0.072$ | $0.992 \pm 0.017$ | $0.943 \pm 0.032$ | $0.412 \pm 0.032$ | $0.658 \pm 0.056$ |

outperforms LRNN. This helps us answer **Q3**, affirmatively: NNRPT offers many advantages over state-of-the-art relational neural networks.

Our experiments show the benefits of parameter tying as well as the expressivity of relational random walks in tightly integrating with a neural network model across a variety of domains and settings. The key strengths of NNRPT are that it can (1) efficiently incorporate a large number of relational features, (2) capture local qualitative structure through relational random walk features, (3) tie feature weights to capture global quantitative influences.

## 5    Conclusion and Future Work

We considered the problem of learning neural networks from relational data. Our proposed architecture exploits parameter tying: instances of the same rule share the same parameters for the same training example. In addition, we explored relational random walks as relational features for training these neural nets. Further experiments on larger data sets could yield insights into the scalability of this approach. Integration with an approximate-counting method could potentially reduce the training time. Finally, understanding the use of such random-walk-based NN as a function approximator can allow for efficient and interpretable learning in relational domains with minimal feature engineering.

**Acknowledgements.** SN, GK & NK gratefully acknowledge AFOSR award FA9550-18-1-0462. The authors acknowledge the support of Amazon faculty award. KK acknowledges the support of the RMU project DeCoDeML. Any opinions, findings, and conclusion or recommendations expressed in this material are those of the authors and do not necessarily reflect the view of the AFOSR, Amazon, DeCoDeML or the US government.

## References

1. De Raedt, L., Kersting, K., Natarajan, S., Poole, D.: Statistical Relational Artificial Intelligence: Logic, Probability, and Computation. Morgan & Claypool (2016)
2. França, M.V.M., Zaverucha, G., d'Avila Garcez, A.S.: Fast relational learning using bottom clause propositionalization with artificial neural networks. MLJ (2014)
3. Getoor, L., Taskar, B.: Introduction to Statistical Relational Learning. MIT Press, Cambridge (2007)

4. Jaeger, M.: Parameter learning for relational bayesian networks. In: ICML (2007)
5. Kaur, N., Kunapuli, G., Khot, T., Kersting, K., Cohen, W., Natarajan, S.: Relational restricted Boltzmann machines: a probabilistic logic learning approach. In: ILP (2017)
6. Kazemi, S.M., Buchman, D., Kersting, K., Natarajan, S., Poole, D.: Relational logistic regression. In: KR (2014)
7. Kazemi, S.M., Poole, D.: RelNN: a deep neural model for relational learning. In: AAAI (2018)
8. Khot, T., Natarajan, S., Kersting, K., Shavlik, J.: Learning Markov logic networks via functional gradient boosting. In: ICDM (2011)
9. Lao, N., Cohen, W.: Relational retrieval using a combination of path-constrained random walks. In: JMLR (2010)
10. Lavrac, N., Džeroski, V.: Inductive Logic Programming: Techniques and Applications. Prentice Hall, New Jersey (1993)
11. Lodhi, H.: Deep relational machines. In: ICONIP (2013)
12. Muggleton, S.: Inverse entailment and Progol. New Generation Computing (1995)
13. Natarajan, S., Khot, T., Kersting, K., Guttmann, B., Shavlik, J.: Gradient-based boosting for statistical relational learning: relational dependency network case. MLJ (2012)
14. Natarajan, S., Tadepalli, P., Dietterich, T.G., Fern, A.: Learning first-order probabilistic models with combining rules. ANN MATH ARTIF INTEL (2008)
15. Šourek, G., Aschenbrenner, V., Železny, F., Kuželka, O.: Lifted relational neural networks. In: NeurIPS Workshop (2015)
16. Šourek, G., Svatoš, M., Železný, F., Schockaert, S., Kuželka, O.: Stacked structure learning for lifted relational neural networks. In: ILP (2017)

# Learning Logic Programs from Noisy State Transition Data

Yin Jun Phua[1,2(✉)] and Katsumi Inoue[1,2]

[1] Department of Informatics, SOKENDAI (The Graduate University
for Advanced Studies), Tokyo, Japan
[2] National Institute of Informatics, Tokyo, Japan
{phuayj,inoue}@nii.ac.jp

**Abstract.** Real world data are often noisy and fuzzy. Most traditional logical machine learning methods require the data to be first discretized or pre-processed before being able to produce useful output. Such shortcoming often limits their application to real world data. On the other hand, neural networks are generally known to be robust against noisy data. However, a fully trained neural network does not provide easily understandable rules that can be used to understand the underlying model. In this paper, we propose a Differentiable Learning from Interpretation Transition ($\delta$-LFIT) algorithm, that can simultaneously output logic programs fully explaining the state transitions, and also learn from data containing noise and error.

**Keywords:** Neural network · Machine learning · Interpretability · LFIT

## 1 Introduction

Learning from Interpretation Transition (LFIT) is an algorithm that learns explainable rules of a dynamic system [7]. Given a series of state transitions from the observed dynamic system, the LFIT algorithm outputs a normal logic program (NLP) which realizes the given state transitions. LFIT has many applications in different areas. In the robotics field, being able to learn the model of the surrounding enables the agent to perform planning [8]. In the field of biology, learning the model of how each gene influence each other can lead to development of medicine and curing of diseases [9].

The LFIT algorithm has largely been implemented in two different methods, symbolic method [10] and the neural network method [5]. The symbolic method utilizes logical operations to learn and induce logic programs. However, there are also significant limits when utilizing logical operations. One such limit is that the logical operations currently employed by the symbolic LFIT method lacks ambiguous notations. This means that any error or noise present in the data is reflected directly in the output, synonymous to the garbage in, garbage out problem.

© Springer Nature Switzerland AG 2020
D. Kazakov and C. Erten (Eds.): ILP 2019, LNAI 11770, pp. 72–80, 2020.
https://doi.org/10.1007/978-3-030-49210-6_7

To employ some ambiguity in LFIT, the neural network method was developed. Deep learning and various other statistical machine learning methods have been shown to be relatively robust against noisy data [11,12]. Prior work using neural network has shown that it is possible to perform the LFIT algorithm with neural networks [5]. Although robustness against noise was not proven in [5], experiments showed that the neural network was able to generalize despite only given a smaller number of state transitions as training data.

In this paper, we propose the Differentiable Learning from Interpretation Transition ($\delta$-LFIT) algorithm. The $\delta$-LFIT algorithm is an end-to-end differentiable implementation of the LFIT algorithm. With $\delta$-LFIT, we attempt to address both the problems of symbolic machine learning methods and the problems of neural network methods. It is robust to noisy and ambiguous data, generalizes well from very few training data, and the output is a human-readable, interpretable model.

This paper is structured as follows: first we cover some necessary background on logic programming, LFIT and neural networks in Sect. 2. Next, we present the $\delta$-LFIT algorithm in Sect. 3. Following that, we present some experiments and observations in Sect. 4. In Sect. 5, we discuss some prior works that are related to our contribution. Finally, we summarize our work and discuss some future research directions that are possible with this work.

## 2   Background

The main goal of LFIT is to learn an NLP describing the dynamics of the observed system. To describe the dynamics of a changing system with respect to time, we can use time as an argument. In particular, we will consider the state of an atom $A$ at time $t$ as $A(t)$. Thus, we consider a dynamic rule as follows:

$$A(t+1) \leftarrow A_1(t) \wedge \cdots \wedge A_m(t) \wedge \neg A_{m+1}(t) \wedge \cdots \wedge \neg A_n(t) \qquad (1)$$

which means that, if $A_1, A_2, \ldots, A_m$, denoted as $b^+$ is true at time $t$ and $A_{m+1}$, $A_{m+2}, \ldots, A_n$, denoted as $b^-$ is false at time $t$, then the head $A$ will be true at time $t+1$. We can simulate the state transition of a dynamical system with the $T_P$ operator.

An Herbrand interpretation $I$ is a subset of the Herbrand base $\mathcal{B}$. For a logic program $P$ and an Herbrand interpretation $I$, the immediate consequence operator (or $T_P$ operator) is the mapping $T_P : 2^{\mathcal{B}} \rightarrow 2^{\mathcal{B}}$:

$$T_P(I) = \{h(R) \mid R \in P, b^+(R) \subseteq I, b^-(R) \cap I = \emptyset\}. \qquad (2)$$

Given a set of Herbrand interpretations $E$ and $\{T_P(I) \mid I \in E\}$, the LFIT algorithm outputs a logic program $P$ which completely represents the dynamics of $E$.

The LFIT algorithm, in its simplest form, can be described as an algorithm that requires an input of a set of state transitions $E$ and an initial NLP $P_0$, then outputs an NLP $P$ such that $P$ is consistent with the input $E$.

# 3    δ-LFIT

In this section, we describe our core contribution: a differentiable implementation of the LFIT algorithm. Broadly speaking, the δ-LFIT model can be seen as a classifier, classifying whether each rule is present in the system.

## 3.1    Rule Classification

To build a classifier, we first have to know all the possible rules that a system can have given the Herbrand base $\mathcal{B}$. There can be an infinite number of rules possible if we consider the combination of each atoms and placing them in the form (1). Therefore, we have to place some restrictions in the rules that we are classifying.

First, we'll define an operation that allows us to simplify a rule.

**Definition 1 (Simplification of Rules).** *A rule can be simplified according to the following operations:*

- *$a \wedge a$ is simplified to $a$*
- *$\neg a \wedge \neg a$ is simplified to $\neg a$*
- *$a \wedge \neg a$ and $\neg a \wedge a$ is simplified to $\perp$*

*where $a$ is an atom.*

$\perp$ is the equivalent of having an empty body $a \leftarrow$.

**Definition 2 (Minimal Rule).** *A rule is considered to be minimal, if its logical formula cannot be simplified further.*

For every Herbrand base $\mathcal{B}$, we can generate a finite ordered set of rules $\tau(\mathcal{B})$ that contains all possible minimal rules for any system that has Herbrand base $\mathcal{B}$. In a classification scenario, we want to know which class corresponds to which rule. To ease this mapping, we define a deterministic approach of mapping each rules to an index, which corresponds to the class.

**Definition 3 (Length of a rule).** *The length of a rule $R \in \tau(\mathcal{B})$ is defined as $\|b(R)\|$.*

**Definition 4 (Index of element in ordered set).** *Let $S$ be an ordered set, the index of element $e \in S$, is defined as $\sigma_S(e) = \|S_{<e}\|$, where $\sigma_S : S \mapsto \mathbb{N}$ and $S_{<e} = \{x \mid x < e, x \in S\}$.*

**Definition 5 (Ordered Herbrand Base).** *The ordered Herbrand base $\mathcal{B}_o$ contains the same elements as $\mathcal{B}$ except each element has an ordered relation $<$.*

The relation $<$ on $\mathcal{B}_o$ can be defined arbitrarily, but in most cases, the lexicographical ordering is the most convenient, and is the one that we will be using throughout this paper. Now, consider a set of rules $\tau_l(\mathcal{B}_o)$, where $\tau_l(\mathcal{B}_o) = \{R \mid \|b(R)\| \leq l, R \in \tau(\mathcal{B}_o)\} \subseteq \tau(\mathcal{B}_o)$ which contains all rules that are less than or equal to length $l$. The number of rules in $\tau_l(\mathcal{B}_o)$ can be given by the following formula:

$$\|\tau_l(\mathcal{B}_o)\| = \begin{cases} 1 & \text{if } l = 0, \\ \|\tau_{l-1}(\mathcal{B}_o)\| + \binom{n}{l} \times 2^l & \text{if } l > 0. \end{cases}$$

where $n = \|\mathcal{B}_o\|$ is the number of elements in the Herbrand base and $\binom{n}{k}$ represents the binomial coefficient.

Also consider the ordered set $\widetilde{\tau}_l(\mathcal{B}_o) = \{R \mid \|b(R)\| = l, R \in \tau(\mathcal{B}_o)\}$ containing all the rules $R$ that are exactly of length $l$. The ordered relation for $\widetilde{\tau}_l$ is defined by first ordering the negation by marking the negative literals as 1s and positive literals as 0s. With that, the position of negations in the literals can be mapped into a binary number. Note that there is no information loss here, as the binary number mapping is only used for ordering. Next, we look at each atom in the rule and order them according to $\mathcal{B}_o$. In this relation, $\{a, b\} < \{a, c\} < \{\neg a, b\} < \{\neg b, c\} < \{\neg a, \neg c\}$.

The index of a rule $R$ $\sigma_{\tau(\mathcal{B}_o)}(R)$ can be obtained by performing the following calculation:

$$\sigma_{\tau(\mathcal{B}_o)}(R) = \|\tau_{l-1}(\mathcal{B}_o)\| + \sigma_{\widetilde{\tau}_l(\mathcal{B}_o)}(R)$$

where $l = \|b(R)\|$ is the length of the rule $R$.

If we consider that in a rule, an atom can be present as a positive literal, as a negative literal, or not be present, then the number of possible rules for an $n$-variable system ($n = \|\mathcal{B}\|$) is $\|\tau_n(\mathcal{B}_o)\| = 3^n$. Thus, for an $n$-variable system, the number of classes the $\delta$-LFIT model is classifying is $3^n \times n$, with each variable in the system taking the head of the rules.

To encode normal logic programs (NLP) into a matrix, we consider only the minimal form, where a minimal form is a formula that cannot be further reduced.

By enumerating all possible rules that take only the minimal form, we can construct a matrix where the rows represent the head of the rules, and the columns represent the body. Note that heads with multiple rules, which are disjunctions in the NLP semantics, can be encoded by marking their respective rows as 1, therefore each rows are not strictly one-hot encoding.

## 3.2 Model

In this section, we describe our core model, which is the differentiable implementation of the LFIT approach. The main concept is being able to accept a series of state transitions, and being able to output the corresponding rules that are found within the transitions. Therefore, we opted to use the LSTM (Long-Short Term Memory) [6] model to handle the input, and a feed-forward neural network that will give us the output. This is depicted in Fig. 1. Unfortunately, LSTM does not handle varying dimensions in the input. Therefore, we would not be able to use a trained 3-variable $\delta$-LFIT model on a 5-variable system, we would instead have to retrain the model from scratch.

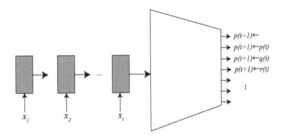

**Fig. 1.** The $\delta$-LFIT Architecture.

For each rule $r$, given the state transitions $T$, our model outputs the conditional probability $p(r|T)$. The aim is to output for each rule $r$ that appears within the logic program $P$ be $p(r|T) = 1$ and those that don't appear in $P$ be $p(r|T) = 0$. Therefore, the goal is to minimize the expected negative log likelihood:

$$\text{LFIT loss} = -\mathbb{E}_{(r,T)\sim\Lambda}(r \times \log p(r|T) + (1-r) \times \log(1 - p(r|T)))$$

In addition to this, we would also like to capture the subsumption relation between rules. Consider a set of rules $S$ such that for every rule $R \in S$, there is another rule $R' \in S$ that subsumes $R$. A set $\mathbb{S}$ of all $S$ possible in the Herbrand base $\mathcal{B}$, a softmax cross entropy loss is added. For $S$, the loss is defined as follows:

$$\text{Subsumption Loss}_S = -\sum_{r\in S} \left( r \times \log p(r|T) + (1-r) \times \log(1 - p(r|T)) \right)$$

Thus, the loss for which we are optimizing is:

$$\text{loss} = \text{LFIT loss} + \lambda_1 \sum_{S\in \mathbb{S}} \text{Subsumption Loss}_S + \lambda_2 \|\theta\|^2$$

where $\lambda_1$ and $\lambda_2$ are the hyperparameters that control the weight for the losses, and $\|\theta\|^2$ is the $L_2$-regularization of all the parameters.

### 3.3 Generating Training Data

Gathering good training data is usually the most important aspect in statistical machine learning [14]. In terms of the $\delta$-LFIT task, we are attempting to solve a classification problem. Thus a training data for that allows identification for each separate rule is required. Unfortunately, this is very difficult to obtain from real world data. Therefore, the training data that we are going to use will be artificially generated.

To generate the training data set, first a logic program $P_o$ is constructed. $P_o$ must contain the rule $R$ for which we are constructing the training data set for. Next, a random initial state is selected and a series of state transition $T$ is generated based on $P_o$. Next, based on the state transition generated a logic program $P_l$ is learned based on the algorithm described in [10]. If $R$ is present in $P_l$, then the data pair $(T, P_l)$ is accepted, otherwise it is rejected and a next initial state is selected.

## 4    Experiments

We first verify that our model is capable of producing the expected logic programs when given a series of state transition. Next, we perform several experiments that focus mainly on the ability to handle noisy data and also erroneous data.

We implemented our model in Tensorflow [1]. We prepared several experiments to verify the performance of our model. As far as we are aware, there are no other works that perform similar tasks, therefore we were not able to do any comparison. Instead, we will show the precise results that we obtained in our experiments.

### 4.1    Experimental Methods

Table 1. The MSE for the state transitions generated by the predicted logic programs.

| Boolean Network | MSE (Discrete) | MSE (Fuzzy) |
|---|---|---|
| 3-node (a) | 0.095 | 0.137 |
| 3-node (b) | 0.054 | 0.057 |
| Raf | 0.253 | 0.217 |
| 5-node | 0.142 | 0.147 |

We generated 500,000 $(T, P)$ pairs for each training data set. For some rules, the amount of training data required was generated relatively quickly. However for some rules, the generation took 10 h. In total, the whole process for generating this training dataset took 27 h on a 28-core Intel i9-7940X. The model is then trained for 10 epochs on this data sets while attempting to minimize the loss. The training process only took 4 h.

Once $\delta$-LFIT has finished training, we get the probability of the rules. To turn it into a human-readable logic program, we just have to take for each $p(R) \geq \theta$, where $\theta$ is a threshold, use the reverse lookup $\sigma^{-1}_{\tau(\mathcal{B}_O)}(R)$ and combine them.

We tested $\delta$-LFIT on 4 boolean networks taken from [13]. Three of them are 3-variable systems and one of them is a 5-variable system. We could only test on small systems currently, mainly due to memory constraints because larger systems require a larger neural network architecture. Another factor is that the training data generation takes too long to be practical beyond 5 variables.

First, we fed $\delta$-LFIT discrete, error-free data. From the predicted logic program that was obtained from $\delta$-LFIT, we attempted to reproduce the same state transition sequence. Then, we calculated the mean squared error (MSE) between the original input sequence and the generated sequence.

Next, we test $\delta$-LFIT with fuzzy data. We map the values of the transition being fed into $\delta$-LFIT from $1 \rightarrow [0.5, 1]$ and $0 \rightarrow [0, 0.5]$ randomly on a normal distribution. Note that both ranges include 0.5, this is done deliberately to test the model's robustness.

The full results for the experiments we have performed is detailed in Table 1. In general, we notice that $\delta$-LFIT was not able to perform as well when the data is fuzzy, except for Raf, which has several attractors. We provide some analysis into why this is the case in Sect. 4.2.

Here, we describe in detail the experiment for the network 3-node (a). This is a toy network that contains 3 nodes. Its corresponding logic program is described as below:

$$v_1(t+1) \leftarrow \neg v_1(t) \wedge \neg v_2(t). \quad v_2(t+1) \leftarrow \neg v_1(t) \wedge v_2(t). \quad v_3(t+1) \leftarrow \neg v_1(t).$$
$$v_1(t+1) \leftarrow \neg v_1(t) \wedge \neg v_3(t). \qquad\qquad\qquad\qquad\qquad\qquad v_3(t+1) \leftarrow v_2(t).$$

This network has two attractors and one steady state. We plugged every possible initial state ($2^3$ states) and produced a series of 15 state transitions for every initial state. These series were then fed into $\delta$-LFIT to obtain the corresponding logic program. After $\delta$-LFIT predicted the logic program, we then used the predicted logic program to generate a series of 15 state transitions. Those transitions were then compared with the original transitions.

The mean squared error (MSE) in this task for all the state transitions were 0.095. More precisely, out of 8 possible series of state transitions, there were 2 series of state transitions for which the predicted logic program couldn't reproduce accurately. $\delta$-LFIT predicted the following logic program that was consistent with the input:

$$v_1(t+1) \leftarrow v_2(t). \quad v_2(t+1) \leftarrow v_2(t). \quad v_3(t+1) \leftarrow v_2(t).$$
$$v_1(t+1) \leftarrow \neg v_1(t). \quad v_2(t+1) \leftarrow \neg v_1(t) \wedge v_3(t). \quad v_3(t+1) \leftarrow \neg v_1(t).$$
$$v_1(t+1) \leftarrow \neg v_3(t). \quad v_2(t+1) \leftarrow v_1(t) \wedge \neg v_3(t). \quad v_3(t+1) \leftarrow \neg v_3(t).$$

Notice that even though the predicted logic program was longer than the original logic program, none of the rules subsume each other. We attribute this to the subsumption loss that was added to the loss function.

## 4.2 Discussion

Our aim was to utilize neural network's ability to handle ambiguous data to produce models that fully explain the system that we were trying to observe. While we were able to show that when passing discrete data, $\delta$-LFIT was able to perform very well. Performance on ambiguous and fuzzy data were slightly worse. We attribute this to the fact that we did not train our neural networks to learn to handle fuzziness in the data. We speculate that adding fuzziness to the training data should be able to help $\delta$-LFIT generalize better to ambiguity.

We were also not able to scale the neural network beyond 5 variables. Mainly because the amount of expressiveness required beyond that point far exceeds the computation capability we currently possess. To train a 7-variable model, we would require $7 \times 3^7 = 15,309$ datasets, which would take several weeks to generate and would require more than 24GB RAM on the GPU. This grows exponentially with the number of variables.

Also, on all 4 of the experiments, $\delta$-LFIT was not able to output a logic program that was consistent with the input when the input was within an attractor. However, the performance improved by slightly when fuzzy data was given for Raf, which had more attractors than the other boolean networks. We attribute this to the low variance nature of an attractor as an input.

## 5    Related Work

Currently, there are not many works that attempt to construct generalized neural network architecture that could learn logic programs without retraining the neural networks itself. In [4], the authors proposed a method to use neural networks to learn symbolic examples, then extract symbolic knowledge based on what the neural networks have learned. In [3], the authors provided a method to extract symbolic knowledge from neural networks, provided certain constraints on the neural network itself. These work place constraints on the neural network architecture itself and require retraining of the neural network when a new logic program has to be learned.

Enguerrand, et. al. [5] presented an algorithm that performs LFIT by extracting logic programs from a feed-forward neural network after learning. This method only trains one neural network to learn one specific system, while our work trains one neural network to learn many systems of the same number of variables.

Evans, et. al. [2] introduced the $\delta$-ILP framework, which incorporates a differentiable machine learning approach and the symbolic ILP approach. The main difference between $\delta$-ILP and $\delta$-LFIT is that, in $\delta$-ILP, the authors proposed a framework that uses differentiable methods to also perform the ILP task at hand, while simultaneously learning to produce the logic program that could solve the ILP task itself. In contrast, we constructed a differentiable method to learn the logic program, while not imposing any trainable parameters to resemble the logic program.

## 6    Conclusion

In this work, we have advocated an approach to performing symbolic logical learning with neural network. We described our method for enumerating all possible rules and mapping them to classes. We then showed our approach to learning logic programs by using only off-the-shelf neural network architectures.

We performed several experiments to evaluate the model that we have proposed. We found that $\delta$-LFIT was able to perform well when discrete error-free data that has high variance was given, however when the data given was fuzzy, ambiguous and only contained steady states, $\delta$-LFIT struggled to produce accurate results.

As future work, we plan to adapt some of the state-of-the-art multiclass-multilabel classification problem to allow our framework to scale to a higher number of variables.

# References

1. Abadi, M., Agarwal, A., Barham, P., et al.: TensorFlow: large-scale machine learning on heterogeneous systems (2015). https://www.tensorflow.org/, software available from tensorflow.org
2. Evans, R., Grefenstette, E.: Learning explanatory rules from noisy data. CoRR abs/1711.04574 (2017). http://arxiv.org/abs/1711.04574
3. d'Avila Garcez, A.S., Broda, K., Gabbay, D.M.: Symbolic knowledge extraction from trained neural networks: a sound approach. Artif. Intell. **125**(1), 155–207 (2001)
4. d'Avila Garcez, A.S., Zaverucha, G.: The connectionist inductive learning and logic programming system. Appl. Intell. **11**(1), 59–77 (1999)
5. Gentet, E., Tourret, S., Inoue, K.: Learning from interpretation transition using feed-forward neural network. In: Proceedings of ILP 2016, CEUR Proceedings 1865, pp. 27–33 (2016)
6. Hochreiter, S., Schmidhuber, J.: Long short-term memory. Neural Comput. **9**(8), 1735–1780 (1997). https://doi.org/10.1162/neco.1997.9.8.1735
7. Inoue, K., Ribeiro, T., Sakama, C.: Learning from interpretation transition. Mach. Learn. **94**(1), 51–79 (2013). https://doi.org/10.1007/s10994-013-5353-8
8. Martínez, D., Alenyà, G., Ribeiro, T., Inoue, K., Torras, C.: Relational reinforcement learning for planning with exogenous effects. J. Mach. Learn. Res. **18**(78), 1–44 (2017). http://jmlr.org/papers/v18/16-326.html
9. Ribeiro, T., Magnin, M., Inoue, K., Sakama, C.: Learning multi-valued biological models with delayed influence from time-series observations. In: 2015 IEEE 14th International Conference on Machine Learning and Applications (ICMLA), pp. 25–31, December 2015. https://doi.org/10.1109/ICMLA.2015.19.
10. Ribeiro, T., Inoue, K.: Learning prime implicant conditions from interpretation transition. In: Davis, J., Ramon, J. (eds.) ILP 2014. LNCS (LNAI), vol. 9046, pp. 108–125. Springer, Cham (2015). https://doi.org/10.1007/978-3-319-23708-4_8
11. Rolnick, D., Veit, A., Belongie, S., Shavit, N.: Deep learning is robust to massive label noise (2018). https://openreview.net/forum?id=B1p461b0W
12. Seltzer, M.L., Yu, D., Wang, Y.: An investigation of deep neural networks for noise robust speech recognition. In: 2013 IEEE International Conference on Acoustics, Speech and Signal Processing (ICASSP), pp. 7398–7402. IEEE (2013)
13. Streck, A., Siebert, H., Klarner, H.: PyBoolNet: a python package for the generation, analysis and visualization of boolean networks. Bioinformatics **33**(5), 770–772 (2016). https://doi.org/10.1093/bioinformatics/btw682
14. Sun, C., Shrivastava, A., Singh, S., Gupta, A.: Revisiting unreasonable effectiveness of data in deep learning era. CoRR abs/1707.02968 (2017). http://arxiv.org/abs/1707.02968

# A New Algorithm for Computing Least Generalization of a Set of Atoms

Hien D. Nguyen[1,3] and Chiaki Sakama[2(✉)]

[1] University of Information Technology, Ho Chi Minh City, Vietnam
hiennd@uit.edu.vn
[2] Wakayama University, Wakayama, Japan
sakama@wakayama-u.ac.jp
[3] Vietnam National University, Ho Chi Minh City, Vietnam

**Abstract.** This paper provides a new algorithm of computing a least generalization of a set of atoms. Our algorithm is based on the notion of *anti-combination* that is the inverse substitution of a combined substitution. In contrast to an anti-unification algorithm that computes a least generalization of two atoms, anti-combination can compute a least generalization of (more than two) atoms in parallel. We evaluate the proposed algorithm using randomly generated data and show that anti-combination outperforms the iterative application of an anti-unification algorithm in general.

**Keywords:** Anti-unification · Anti-combination · Least generalization

## 1 Introduction

For a definite program $P$ and a goal $G$, a computed answer $\theta$ for $P \cup \{G\}$ is the substitution obtained by restricting the *composition* $\theta_1 \cdots \theta_n$ to the variables of $G$, where $\theta_1, \ldots, \theta_n$ is the sequence of mgu's used in an SLD-refutation of $P \cup \{G\}$ [10]. In an SLD-derivation, each $\theta_i$ is an mgu used for deriving a new goal $G_i$ from its preceding goal $G_{i-1}$ and a parent clause in $P$. Thus, $\theta_1, \ldots, \theta_n$ are computed sequentially and an answer substitution is computed by composing mgus one by one. As such, the composition operation is not very efficient, and furthermore, it is often unintuitive or inadequate [13]. Yamasaki *et al.* [17] introduce a new resolution method based on *combination* of mgus. The method has the unique feature that resolution is performed by manipulation of substitutions, and mgus used in combination are computed independently of one another. Palamidessi [13] introduces a compositional operational semantics of definite logic programs based on combination of mgus and addresses its application to concurrent logic programming. Compared with the composition operation, however, the combination operation is not well-known and is of relatively little use in automated reasoning and logic programming, although the original idea is date back to [1,15]. Eder [4] formulates algebraic properties of substitutions and shows that combination is obtained as the greatest lower bound of mgus. In contrast to

© Springer Nature Switzerland AG 2020

D. Kazakov and C. Erten (Eds.): ILP 2019, LNAI 11770, pp. 81–97, 2020.
https://doi.org/10.1007/978-3-030-49210-6_8

composition that is only associative, combination is commutative, associative and idempotent, so that it has potential for parallel computation of symbolic reasoning.

In this paper we use the combination operation for computing a *least generalization* (lg) of a set of atoms. Plotkin [14] and Reynolds [16] introduce algorithms for *anti-unification* of two atoms. Plotkin argues that the algorithm is iteratively applied to computing a least generalization of a set of atoms: for a set of atoms $\{A_1, \ldots, A_n\}$, its least generalization is computed as $lg(A_1, lg(A_2, \ldots, lg(A_{n-1}, A_n) \cdots))$ where $lg(A_i, A_j)$ computes a least generalization of $A_i$ and $A_j$. Such serial computation is inefficient when the number of atoms increases. We show that it is computed in parallel using combination of substitutions.

This paper is an extension of the preliminary report [18], which sketches the idea while implementation and evaluation are left. The current paper develops an algorithm and provides experimental evaluation. The rest of this paper is organized as follows. Section 2 reviews basic notions and formal properties of substitutions. Section 3 introduces a method of computing a least generalization by combination of substitutions, and presents an algorithm based on it. Section 4 provides experimental evaluation. Section 5 discusses related issues and Sect. 6 summarizes the paper.

## 2   Preliminaries

A *first-order language* consists of an alphabet and all formulas defined over it. The definition is the standard one in the literature [1,10]. Variables are represented by letters $x, y, z, \ldots$; constants are represented by letters $a, b, c, \ldots$; function symbols (of arities $>0$) are represented by letters $f, g, h, \ldots$; and predicate symbols are represented by letters $P, Q, R, \ldots$. A *term* is either (i) a constant, (ii) a variable, or (iii) $f(t_1, \ldots, t_m)$ where $f$ is an $m$-ary ($m \geq 1$) function symbol and $t_1, \ldots, t_m$ are terms. An *atom* is a formula $P(t_1, \ldots, t_n)$ ($n \geq 1$) where $P$ is an $n$-ary predicate and $t_i$'s are terms. An *expression* is either a term or an atom. Two atoms are *compatible* if they have the same $n$-ary predicate. The set of all variables (resp. terms, atoms) in the language is denoted by $Var$ (resp. $Term$, $Atom$). The set $Atom$ also contains the special elements $\top$ and $\bot$. The set of all expressions is defined as $Exp = Term \cup Atom$. The set of variables occurring in an expression $e$ (resp. a set $E$ of expressions) is denoted by $\mathcal{V}(e)$ (resp. $\mathcal{V}(E)$). The following definitions and results are due to [1,4,9,13,16].

**Definition 1 (substitution).** A *substitution* is a mapping $\sigma$ from $Var$ into $Term$ such that the set $\Gamma = \{\langle x, \sigma(x) \rangle \mid x \neq \sigma(x) \text{ and } x \in Var\}$ is finite. When $\sigma(x_i) = t_i$ for $i = 1, \ldots, n$, it is also written as $\sigma = \{t_1/x_1, \ldots, t_n/x_n\}$.[1] The set of all substitutions in the language is denoted by $Sub$. The set $\mathcal{D}(\sigma) = \{x \mid \langle x, t \rangle \in \Gamma\}$ is the *domain* of $\sigma$ and the set $\mathcal{R}(\sigma) = \{t \mid \langle x, t \rangle \in \Gamma\}$ is the *range* of $\sigma$. The set $\mathcal{V}(\mathcal{R}(\sigma))$ represents the set of all variables occurring in

---

[1] It is often written as $\{x_1/t_1, \ldots, x_n/t_n\}$ [3,10,13].

$\mathcal{R}(\sigma)$. The identity mapping $\varepsilon$ over $Var$ is the *empty substitution*. A bijection $\rho$ from $Var$ to $Var$ is a *renaming* of variables. The set of all renamings is denoted by $Ren$ (where $Ren \subset Sub$).

**Definition 2 ($E\sigma$).** Let $\sigma \in Sub$ and $E \in Exp$. Then $E\sigma$ is defined as follows:

$$E\sigma = \begin{cases} \sigma(x) & \text{if } E = x \text{ for } x \in Var, \\ a & \text{if } E = a \text{ for a constant } a, \\ f(t_1\sigma, ..., t_m\sigma) & \text{if } E = f(t_1, ..., t_m) \in Term, \\ P(t_1\sigma, ..., t_n\sigma) & \text{if } E = P(t_1, ..., t_n) \in Atom. \end{cases}$$

**Definition 3 (composition).** For $\sigma, \lambda \in Sub$, the *composition* of $\sigma$ and $\lambda$ (denoted by $\sigma\lambda$) is a function from $Var$ to $Term$ such that

$$\sigma\lambda(x) = (x\sigma)\lambda \quad \text{for any } x \in Var.$$

For any $e \in Exp$, it holds that $e(\sigma\lambda) = (e\sigma)\lambda$. The composition operation has the properties: $(\sigma\lambda)\mu = \sigma(\lambda\mu)$ and $\sigma\varepsilon = \varepsilon\sigma = \sigma$ for any $\sigma, \lambda, \mu \in Sub$. Note that $\sigma\lambda \neq \lambda\sigma$ in general.

**Definition 4 (idempotent).** A substitution $\sigma$ is *idempotent* if $\sigma\sigma = \sigma$. The set of all idempotent substitutions is denoted by $ISub$.

**Proposition 1 ([4,9]).** *A substitution $\sigma$ is idempotent iff $D(\sigma) \cap \mathcal{V}(\mathcal{R}(\sigma)) = \emptyset$.*

**Definition 5 (order on $Atom$).** Let $A, B \in Atom$. A preorder relation $\leq$ over $Atom$ is defined as follows:

- $A \leq \top$,
- $\bot \leq A$,
- $A \leq B$ if $A = B\theta$ for some $\theta \in Sub$.

We write $A \sim B$ if $A \leq B$ and $B \leq A$.

When $A \leq B$, we say that $A$ is an *instance* of $B$ (or $B$ is a *generalization* of $A$). It holds that $A \sim B$ iff $A = B\rho$ for some $\rho \in Ren$. Let $\mathcal{Q}$ be the quotient set $Atom/\sim$. Then the ordered set $(\mathcal{Q}, \leq)$ constitutes a complete lattice [16].

**Definition 6 (gci, lcg).** Let $\Sigma \subseteq Atom$. An atom $A \in Atom$ is a *common instance* of $\Sigma$ if $A \leq B$ for any $B \in \Sigma$. In particular, $A$ is a *greatest common instance* (gci) of $\Sigma$ if $A$ is a common instance of $\Sigma$ and $A' \leq A$ for any common instance $A'$ of $\Sigma$.

An atom $A \in Atom$ is a *common generalization* of $\Sigma$ if $B \leq A$ for any $B \in \Sigma$. In particular, $A$ is a *least common generalization* (lcg) of $\Sigma$ if $A$ is a common generalization of $\Sigma$ and $A \leq A'$ for any common generalization $A'$ of $\Sigma$.

Least common generalization is simply called *least generalization* hereafter.

**Definition 7 (order on *Sub*).** Let $\sigma, \theta \in Sub$. A preorder relation $\leq$ over *Sub* is defined as:[2]

$$\sigma \leq \theta \text{ if } \sigma = \theta\lambda \text{ for some } \lambda \in Sub.$$

We write $\sigma \sim \theta$ if $\sigma \leq \theta$ and $\theta \leq \sigma$.

By definition, $\sigma \leq \rho$ for any $\sigma \in Sub$ and $\rho \in Ren$. It holds that $\sigma \sim \theta$ iff $\sigma = \theta\rho$ for some $\rho \in Ren$.

**Definition 8 (unifier, mgu, mgsu).** Let $\Sigma = \{A_1, \ldots, A_n\}$ be a set of atoms. A substitution $\sigma \in Sub$ is a *unifier* for $\Sigma$ if $A_1\sigma = \cdots = A_n\sigma$ holds. A unifier $\sigma$ for a set $\Sigma$ is a *most general unifier* (mgu) (written $\sigma = mgu(\Sigma)$) if $\theta \leq \sigma$ for any unifier $\theta$ for the set $\Sigma$. For a finite set $\mathcal{S}$ of finite sets of atoms, $\sigma \in Sub$ is a *most general simultaneous unifier* (mgsu) of $\mathcal{S}$ (written $mgsu(\mathcal{S})$) if $\sigma = mgu(\Sigma)$ for any $\Sigma \in \mathcal{S}$.

**Proposition 2** ([4, Prop.4.5]). *For any finite set $\Sigma \subseteq Atom$, $\sigma = mgu(\Sigma)$ for some $\sigma \in Sub$ iff there is $\lambda \in ISub$ such that $\lambda = mgu(\Sigma)$ and $\lambda \sim \sigma$.*

By Proposition 2 mgus are assumed to be idempotent in this paper without loss of generality. Let $\mathcal{IS}$ be the quotient set $ISub/\sim$, completed with the bottom element $\perp$. Denote the relation $\leq/\sim$ simply by $\leq$. Then the ordered set $(\mathcal{IS}, \leq)$ constitutes a complete lattice [4].

**Definition 9 (combination).** For $\Theta \subseteq \mathcal{IS}$, the glb of $(\Theta, \leq)$ is called a *combination*. When $\Theta = \{\theta_1, \ldots, \theta_n\}$, it is written as $\theta_1 + \cdots + \theta_n$.

For any $\sigma, \lambda, \mu \in ISub$, it holds that (i) $(\sigma + \sigma) \sim \sigma$, (ii) $(\sigma + \lambda) \sim (\lambda + \sigma)$, (iii) $((\sigma + \lambda) + \mu) \sim (\sigma + (\lambda + \mu))$, and (iv) $(\sigma + \varepsilon) \sim \sigma$.

Chang and Lee [1] provide another definition of combination. Given $\theta_1, \ldots, \theta_n \in ISub$ where $\theta_i = \{t_1^i/x_1^i, \ldots, t_{k_i}^i/x_{k_i}^i\}$ $(1 \leq i \leq n)$, the combination $\theta_1 + \cdots + \theta_n$ is defined as the mgu of two atoms: $A_1 = P(x_1^1, \ldots, x_{k_1}^1, \ldots, x_1^n, \ldots, x_{k_n}^n)$ and $A_2 = P(t_1^1, \ldots, t_{k_1}^1, \ldots, t_1^n, \ldots, t_{k_n}^n)$. These two definitions are proved to be equivalent [17].[3]

*Example 1* ([1, p. 188]). Given $\theta_1 = \{f(g(x_1))/x_3, f(x_2)/x_4\}$ and $\theta_2 = \{x_4/x_3, g(x_1)/x_2\}$, define $A_1 = P(x_3, x_4, x_3, x_2)$ and $A_2 = P(f(g(x_1)), f(x_2), x_4, g(x_1))$. The mgu of $A_1$ and $A_2$ is $\{f(g(x_1))/x_3, f(g(x_1))/x_4, g(x_1)/x_2\}$, which is the combination of $\theta_1$ and $\theta_2$. Note that $\theta_1 + \theta_2 = \theta_1\theta_2$ but $\theta_1 + \theta_2 \neq \theta_2\theta_1 = \{f(x_2)/x_3, g(x_1)/x_2, f(x_2)/x_4\}$.

The next proposition immediately holds by definition.

**Proposition 3.** *For $\sigma, \lambda \in ISub$, $\sigma + \lambda = \sigma \cup \lambda$ if $\mathcal{D}(\sigma) \cap \mathcal{D}(\lambda) = \emptyset$.*

**Proposition 4** ([4,17]). *Let $\mathcal{E} = \{\Sigma_1, \ldots, \Sigma_n\}$ be a set of finite sets of atoms.*

---

[2] We use the same symbol $\leq$ over *Atom*, but the meaning is clear from the context. Note that the relation is often used reversely in the literature, e.g. $\sigma \geq \theta$ if $\sigma = \theta\lambda$ [4].

[3] Combination is called *parallel composition* in [13].

**(i)** $mgsu(\mathcal{E}) \sim \sigma_1 \cdots \sigma_n$ where $\sigma_1 = mgu(\Sigma_1)$ and $\sigma_i = mgu(\Sigma_i \sigma_1 \cdots \sigma_{i-1})$ $(2 \leq i \leq n)$.

**(ii)** $mgsu(\mathcal{E}) \sim mgu(\Sigma_1) + \cdots + mgu(\Sigma_n)$.

Proposition 4 presents two different ways of computing $mgsu(\mathcal{E})$. The one (i) presents that computing $\sigma_1, \ldots, \sigma_n$ in a sequential manner and composing them to get $mgsu(\mathcal{E})$. This method is usually employed in binary resolution. The other one (ii) presents that computing $mgu(\Sigma_i)$ for each $\Sigma_i$ and combining them to get $mgsu(\mathcal{E})$. Comparing two methods, computation of $\sigma_i$ uses the results of $\sigma_1, \ldots, \sigma_{i-1}$ in (i). By contrast, in (ii) each $mgu(\Sigma_i)$ is computed independently, so that combination has potential for computing gci in parallel.

*Example 2* Consider the set of atoms $\Sigma = \{P(x, f(y)),\ P(z, f(b)),\ P(c, w)\}$. Let $\Sigma_1 = \{P(x, f(y)),\ P(z, f(b))\}$ and $\Sigma_2 = \{P(z, f(b)),\ f(c, w)\}$. Then $\sigma_1 = mgu(\Sigma_1) = \{b/y, x/z\}$ and $\sigma_2 = mgu(\Sigma_2 \sigma_1) = \{c/x, f(b)/w\}$. The mgsu of $\{\Sigma_1, \Sigma_2\}$ is then obtained by the composition $\sigma_1 \sigma_2 = \{c/x, b/y, c/z, f(b)/w\}$, and the gci of $\Sigma_1 \cup \Sigma_2$ is $P(c, f(b))$ (Fig. 1(a)). Similar computation is done by first computing $\lambda_1 = mgu(\Sigma_2) = \{c/z, f(b)/w\}$ and then computing $\lambda_2 = mgu(\Sigma_1 \lambda_1) = \{c/x, b/y\}$, which produces the same mgsu and the gci (Fig. 1(b)). On the other hand, the mgsu is computed by the combination $\sigma_1 + \lambda_1 = \{c/x, b/y, c/z, f(b)/w\}$ which produces the gci (Fig. 1(c)).

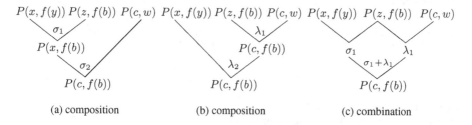

(a) composition          (b) composition          (c) combination

**Fig. 1.** Composition and combination

## 3   Computing Least Generalization by Anti-combination

### 3.1   Anti-unification Algorithm

For a set $\Sigma \subseteq Atom$, its *least (common) generalization* (written $lg(\Sigma)$) is defined as the least upper bound of the set $(\Sigma, \leq)$ (Definition 6). $lg(\Sigma)$ is obtained from $\Sigma$ by anti-unification, that is a dual of unification.

**Definition 10 (anti-unifier, msau) ([11]).** Let $\Sigma = \{A_1, \ldots, A_k\}$ be a set of atoms. Then, a tuple of substitutions $\tau = (\sigma_1, \ldots, \sigma_k)$ where $\sigma_i \in Sub$ $(1 \leq i \leq k)$ is an *anti-unifier* of $\Sigma$ if $A_i = lg(\Sigma)\sigma_i$ for $i = 1, \ldots, k$. An anti-unifier $\tau$ of $\Sigma$ is a *most specific anti-unifier* (msau) if for each anti-unifier $(\theta_1, \ldots, \theta_k)$ there is a substitution $\lambda_i \in Sub$ such that $\sigma_i = \lambda_i \theta_i$ $(1 \leq i \leq k)$. We define $\mathcal{D}(\tau) = \mathcal{D}(\sigma_1) \cup \cdots \cup \mathcal{D}(\sigma_k)$.

An anti-unifier always exists, but is not necessarily unique. There is a unique most specific anti-unifier that produces the least generalization, which is unique up to renaming of variables [11]. Like an mgu, an msau is also assumed to be idempotent.

**Proposition 5.** *Let $\Sigma$ be a set of atoms. Then $(\sigma_1, \ldots, \sigma_k)$ such that $\sigma_i \in Sub$ $(1 \leq i \leq k)$ is an msau of $\Sigma$ iff there is an msau $(\lambda_1, \ldots, \lambda_k)$ such that $\lambda_i \in ISub$ and $\lambda_i \sim \sigma_i$ for $i = 1, \ldots, k$.*

*Proof.* When $\mathcal{D}(\sigma_i) \cap \mathcal{V}(\mathcal{R}(\sigma_i)) \neq \emptyset$, let $\lambda_i = \sigma_i \rho_i$ where $\rho_i \in Ren$ and $\mathcal{D}(\lambda_i) \cap \mathcal{V}(\mathcal{R}(\lambda_i)) = \emptyset$. In this case, $A_i = lg(\Sigma)\sigma_i$ implies $A_i \sim lg(\Sigma)\lambda_i$, and vice-versa. □

Now we recall the *anti-unification algorithm* [3, Algorithm 13.1] for computing a least generalization of two atoms which is originally introduced in [14, 16]. Given an atom $A = P(t_1, \ldots, t_n)$, a term $t_i$ $(1 \leq i \leq n)$ has *position* $\langle i \rangle$ in $A$. If a term $f(s_1, \ldots, s_m)$ has position $\langle p_1, \ldots, p_k \rangle$ in $A$, then $s_j$ within this term has position $\langle p_1, \ldots, p_k, j \rangle$ in $A$. The algorithm is described in Fig. 2.

Since the lub of $(\Sigma, \leq)$ is associative, the anti-unification algorithm is iteratively applied for computing a least generalization of a set $\Sigma$ of atoms. In this case, an anti-unifier is computed by a composition of substitutions.

*Example 3.* Let $\Sigma = \{A_1, A_2, A_3\}$, $G_1 = lg(\{A_1, A_2\})$ and $G_2 = lg(\{A_1, A_2, A_3\}) = lg(\{G_1, A_3\})$. Then $A_1 = G_1\theta_1$, $A_2 = G_1\theta_2$, $G_1 = G_2\sigma_1$, and $A_3 = G_2\sigma_2$ for some $\theta_1, \theta_2, \sigma_1, \sigma_2 \in Sub$. Then $A_1 = G_2\sigma_1\theta_1$, $A_2 = G_2\sigma_1\theta_2$, and $A_3 = G_2\sigma_2$. So $(\sigma_1\theta_1, \sigma_1\theta_2, \sigma_2)$ is an anti-unifier of $(A_1, A_2, A_3)$.

---

**Input** : Two compatible atoms $A_1$ and $A_2$
**Output** : $G = lg(\{A_1, A_2\})$ and an msau $\tau = (\theta_1, \theta_2)$

1. Set $A'_1 = A_1$ and $A'_2 = A_2$, $\theta_1 = \theta_2 = \varepsilon$, and $i = 0$.
   Let $z_1, z_2, \ldots$ be a sequence of variables not appearing in $A_1$ or $A_2$.
2. If $A'_1 = A'_2$, then output $G := A'_1$, $\tau := (\theta_1, \theta_2)$ and stop.
3. Let $p$ be the leftmost symbol position where $A'_1$ and $A'_2$ differ. Let $s$ and $t$ be the terms occurring at this position in $A'_1$ and $A'_2$, respectively.
4. If, for some $j$ with $1 \leq j \leq i$, $z_j\theta_1 = s$ and $z_j\theta_2 = t$, then replace $s$ at the position $p$ in $A'_1$ by $z_j$, replace $t$ at the position $p$ in $A'_2$ by $z_j$, and go to 2.
5. Otherwise set $i$ to $i + 1$, replace $s$ at the position $p$ in $A'_1$ by $z_i$, and replace $t$ at the position $p$ in $A'_2$ by $z_i$. Set $\theta_1$ to $\theta_1 \cup \{s/z_i\}$, $\theta_2$ to $\theta_2 \cup \{t/z_i\}$, and go to 2.

---

**Fig. 2.** Anti-unification algorithm [3]

The above algorithm computes a substitution $\theta_i$ such that $A_i = G\theta_i$ $(i = 1, 2)$ for $G = lg(\{A_1, A_2\})$. Then an lg $G$ is also computed by $G = A_i\theta_i^{-1}$ where $\theta_i^{-1}$ is an *inverse substitution* of $\theta_i$. An inverse substitution $\theta^{-1}$ is well-defined if $\theta$ is injective.

**Definition 11 (inverse substitution)** ([12]). Let $\theta \in Sub$ be injective and $t \in Term$. If $\mathcal{D}(\theta) \cap \mathcal{V}(t) = \emptyset$, then an *inverse substitution* $\theta^{-1} : Term \rightarrow Var$ is defined as follows.

$$t\theta^{-1} = x \qquad \text{if } (t/x) \in \theta,$$
$$f(t_1, \ldots, t_n)\theta^{-1} = f(t_1\theta^{-1}, \ldots, t_n\theta^{-1}) \text{ if } (f(t_1, \ldots, t_n)/x) \notin \theta \text{ for any } x \in Var,$$
$$y\theta^{-1} = y \qquad \text{if } (y/x) \notin \theta \text{ for any } x \in Var.$$

If $\mathcal{D}(\theta) \cap \mathcal{V}(t) \neq \emptyset$, a renaming substitution $\rho \in Ren$ is applied to $t$ in such a way that $\mathcal{D}(\theta) \cap \mathcal{V}(t\rho) = \emptyset$. Then we can apply $\theta^{-1}$ to $t\rho$ if $\theta$ is injective. If a substitution $\theta$ is not injective, we use the technique of [3] to constitute $\theta^{-1}$. For instance, when $t = f(x, y)$ and $\theta = \{a/x, a/y\}$, it becomes $t\theta = f(a, a)$. The inverse substitution $\theta^{-1} = \{x/a, y/a\}$ is ill-defined, then it is modified as $\theta^{-1} = \{(x/a, \langle 1 \rangle), (y/a, \langle 2 \rangle)\}$ meaning that $a$ at position $\langle 1 \rangle$ is mapped to $x$ and $a$ at position $\langle 2 \rangle$ is mapped to $y$. With this mechanism, $f(a, a)\theta^{-1} = f(x, y)$. For any non-injective $\theta \in Sub$, we constitute $\theta^{-1}$ in this way.

**Definition 12 (anti-combination).** Let $\sigma = \theta_1 + \cdots + \theta_n$ be a combination of $\theta_i \in ISub$ $(1 \leq i \leq n)$. Then the inverse substitution $\sigma^{-1}$ is called an *anti-combination* of $\theta_1, \ldots, \theta_n$.

Combining injective substitutions may produce a non-injective substitution. For instance, $\theta_1 = \{a/x\}$ and $\theta_2 = \{a/y\}$ produce $\theta_1 + \theta_2 = \{a/x, a/y\}$. To compute its inverse substitution, we incorporate information of substitutions from which each binding comes from: $(\theta_1 + \theta_2)^{-1} = \{(x/a, \langle \theta_1 \rangle), (y/a, \langle \theta_2 \rangle)\}$ which means that $a$ from $\theta_1$ is mapped to $x$ and $a$ from $\theta_2$ is mapped to $y$. With this technique, anti-combination is well-defined for non-injective combination.

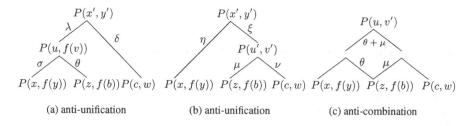

**Fig. 3.** Anti-unification and anti-combination

**Lemma 1.** *Let $\Sigma = \{A_1, A_2, A_3\}$ be a set of atoms, $\tau_{12} = (\sigma_{12}, \lambda_{12})$ an msau of $\{A_1, A_2\}$, and $\tau_{13} = (\sigma_{13}, \lambda_{13})$ an msau of $\{A_1, A_3\}$ such that $\mathcal{D}(\tau_{12}) \cap \mathcal{D}(\tau_{13}) = \emptyset$. Then $lg(\Sigma) = A_1\theta^{-1}$ where $\theta \sim (\sigma_{12} + \sigma_{13})$.*

*Proof.* Let $G_1 = lg(\{A_1, A_2\})$ and $G_2 = lg(\{A_1, A_3\})$. Then $lg(\Sigma) = lg(\{G_1, G_2\})$, and $G_1\sigma_{12} = A_1$ and $G_2\sigma_{13} = A_1$. By $\mathcal{D}(\sigma_{12}) \cap \mathcal{D}(\sigma_{13}) = \emptyset$, $G_1\sigma_{12} = G_1(\sigma_{12} + \sigma_{13}) = A_1$ and $G_2\sigma_{13} = G_2(\sigma_{12} + \sigma_{13}) = A_1$. Then $lg(\Sigma) = lg(\{G_1, G_2\}) = lg(\{A_1(\sigma_{12} + \sigma_{13})^{-1}, A_1(\sigma_{12} + \sigma_{13})^{-1}\}) = A_1(\sigma_{12} + \sigma_{13})^{-1}$.  □

Since combination is associative, the result of Lemma 1 is extended to a set containing $n$ atoms $(n \geq 3)$.

**Theorem 1.** *Let* $\Sigma = \{A_1, \ldots, A_n\}$ $(n \geq 3)$ *be a set of atoms,* $\tau_{1k} = (\sigma_{1k}, \lambda_{1k})$ $(2 \leq k \leq n)$ *an msau of* $\{A_1, A_k\}$ *such that* $\mathcal{D}(\tau_{1i}) \cap \mathcal{D}(\tau_{1j}) = \emptyset$ $(1 \leq i, j \leq n; i \neq j)$. *Then,* $lg(\Sigma) = A_1\theta^{-1}$ *where* $\theta \sim (\sigma_{12} + \cdots + \sigma_{1n})$.

Theorem 1 shows that a least generalization of atoms is computed by anti-combination of substitutions.

*Example 4.* Consider the set $\Sigma = \{ P(x, f(y)), \ P(z, f(b)), \ P(c, w) \}$ of atoms. Then $lg(\{ P(x, f(y)), \ P(z, f(b)) \}) = P(u, f(v))$ with the msau $(\sigma, \theta)$ where $\sigma = \{x/u, y/v\}$ and $\theta = \{z/u, b/v\}$. In this case, $P(u, f(v))\sigma = P(x, f(y))$ and $P(u, f(v))\theta = P(z, f(b))$.

Next, $lg(\{P(u, f(v)), P(c, w)\}) = P(x', y')$ with the msau $(\lambda, \delta)$ where $\lambda = \{u/x', f(v)/y'\}$ and $\delta = \{c/x', w/y'\}$. In this case, $P(x', y')\lambda = P(u, f(v))$ and $P(x', y')\delta = P(c, w)$. Then, $lg(\Sigma) = P(x', y')$ where $P(x', y')\lambda\sigma = P(x, f(y))$ with $\lambda\sigma = \{x/x', f(y)/y'\}$ and $P(x', y')\lambda\theta = P(z, f(b))$ with $\lambda\theta = \{z/x', f(b)/y'\}$ (Fig. 3(a)). Similar computation is done by first computing $lg(\{ P(z, f(b)), P(c, w)\})$ with $(\mu, \nu) = (\{z/u', f(b)/v'\}, \{c/u', w/v'\})$, and then computing $lg(\{ P(x, f(y)), lg(\{ P(z, f(b)), P(c, w)\}) \})$ with $(\eta, \xi) = (\{x/x', f(y)/y'\}, \{u'/x', v'/y'\})$ (Fig. 3(b)).

By contrast, $\theta + \mu = \{z/u, b/v, z/u', f(b)/v'\}$. Then

$$(\theta + \mu)^{-1} = \{ (u/z, \langle \theta \rangle), (v/b, \langle \theta \rangle), (u'/z, \langle \mu \rangle), (v'/f(b), \langle \mu \rangle) \}.$$

Applying it to $P(z, f(b))$, $lg(\Sigma) = P(u, v')$ $(\sim P(x', y'))$ is obtained (Fig. 3(c)). Note that by the second condition of Definition 11, $(v/b, \langle \theta \rangle)$ is not applied to $b$ in $P(z, f(b))$.

## 3.2   Algorithms for Computing Least Generalization of a Set of Atoms

The algorithm for computing anti-unification (Fig. 2) is extended to computing a least generalization of a set of atoms. Given a set $\Sigma$, $\Sigma[i]$ means the $i$-th element of $\Sigma$.

---

**Algorithm 1: AntiUnif**

**Input** : A set $\Sigma = \{A_1, \ldots, A_n\}$ ($n \geq 2$) of compatible atoms
**Output** : a least generalization of $\Sigma$

1. Put $G := \Sigma[1]$.
2. Put $i := 2$; while $i \leq n$ do:
   Compute $G := lg(\{G, \Sigma[i]\})$ by the anti-unification algorithm (Fig. 2).
   Put $i := i + 1$.
3. Return $G$.

---

The algorithm for computing a least generalization of a set of atoms by anti-combination is described as follows.

---

**Algorithm 2: AntiComb**

**Input** : A set $\Sigma = \{A_1, \ldots, A_n\}$ ($n \geq 2$) of compatible atoms
**Output** : a least generalization of $\Sigma$

1. Put $\theta := \varepsilon$ (empty substitution).
2. Put $i := 2$; while $i \leq n$ do:
   Compute $G_i = lg(\{A_1, A_i\})$ by the anti-unification algorithm.
   Get a substitution $\theta_i$ such that $A_1 = G_i\theta_i$, $\mathcal{D}(\theta_i) \cap \mathcal{D}(\theta) = \emptyset$ and
   $\mathcal{D}(\theta_i) \cap \mathcal{V}(\mathcal{R}(\theta_i)) = \emptyset$.
   Put $\theta := \theta + \theta_i$ and $i := i + 1$.
3. Compute the inverse substitution $\theta^{-1}$.
4. Compute $G = A_1\theta^{-1}$ and return $G$.

---

In $\theta_i$ we store information about the substitution and the position of each element as $[t_i/z_i, \langle p, q \rangle, \theta_i]$, meaning that $t_i/z_i$ in $\theta_i$ happens at the $q$-th position of the $p$-th arity.

When $k$ ($2 \leq k < n$) processors are available, the step 2 of Algorithm 2 is split into $k$ procedures. First, $\Sigma$ is partitioned into $k$ subsets $\Sigma_1 \cup \cdots \cup \Sigma_k$ such that $\Sigma_1 = \{A_1, \ldots, A_{m_1}\}$, $\Sigma_2 = \{A_{m_1}, A_{m_1+1}, \ldots, A_{m_2}\}$, $\ldots$, $\Sigma_k = \{A_{m_{k-1}}, A_{m_{k-1}+1}, \ldots, A_{m_k}\}$ where each $\Sigma_i$ and $\Sigma_{i+1}$ share an element $A_{m_i}$ in common. After computing a combination $\theta^i$ for each $\Sigma_i$ ($1 \leq i \leq k$) in parallel, they are combined into one substitution $\theta = \theta^1 + \cdots + \theta^k$. Then, its inverse substitution is computed at the step 3. Formally, such a spliting is done by

$$\Sigma_j = \{\Sigma[(j-1) \times \lfloor \frac{n}{k} \rfloor + 1], \ldots, \Sigma[j \times \lfloor \frac{n}{k} \rfloor + 1]\} \ (1 \leq j \leq k - 1),$$

$$\Sigma_k = \{\Sigma[(k-1) \times \lfloor \frac{n}{k} \rfloor + 1], \ldots, \Sigma[n]\}$$

where $\lfloor \ \rfloor$ is the floor function.

According to [7] the complexity of the anti-unification algorithm of Fig. 2 is computed in $O(N \log N)$ where $N$ is the size of the lub of $\theta_1$ and $\theta_2$. Using the result, the complexity of **AntiUnif** is $O(n \times N \log N)$ where $n$ is the number of atoms in $\Sigma$. Step 2 of **AntiComb** is also done in $O(n \times N \log N)$, since combination of substitution is computed by merging $\theta \cup \theta_i$ (Proposition 3). If $k$-processors $(k \geq 2)$ are available for computing Step 2 in parallel, the lower bound of computation is given as $O(\frac{n \times N \log N}{k})$.

*Example 5.* Suppose the set $\Sigma$ of atoms such that $|\Sigma| = 5$ and each atom has a ternary predicate $P$.[4]

$E := \{$

$A_1 = P(\underline{f_9(x_2, x_2, x_1)}, \; \underline{f_{10}(x_2, f_7(f_5(f_{10}(x_1, x_1)), f_7(f_2(x_2, x_2, x_1), f_3(x_1)))), \; \underline{x_1}),$

$A_2 = P(\underline{f_9(x_2, x_2, x_1)}, \; \underline{f_{10}(f_3(f_4(f_8(x_2, x_1)), x_2, f_7(x_2, x_1))), f_1(x_1, x_1, x_1)), \; \underline{f_3(x_2)}),$

$A_3 = P(\underline{f_9(x_2, x_2, x_1)}, \; \underline{f_{10}(f_5(x_1), f_5(f_5(f_6(x_2, x_1)))), \; \underline{f_3(f_{10}(x_2, x_1)))},$

$A_4 = P(\underline{f_9(f_1(x_1, x_2, x_2), x_1, f_2(x_1, x_1, x_1))}, \; \underline{f_{10}(f_7(f_9(f_6(x_1, x_1), f_6(x_1, x_2), x_1), x_1), x_1), \; \underline{x_1}),$

$A_5 = P(\underline{f_9(f_4(x_2, x_2, x_1), f_4(x_2, x_1, x_2), f_{10}(x_1, x_1))},$

$\qquad\qquad\qquad \underline{f_{10}(x_2, f_4(f_5(f_9(x_1, x_2, x_1)), x_2, f_5(f_5(x_1)))), \; \underline{x_2})$

$\}.$

## Using **AntiUnif:**

$G_1 := lg(A_1, A_2) = P(f_9(x_2, x_2, x_1), f_{10}(z_1, z_2), z_3)$  % **Compute** $lg(A_1, A_2)$

$G_2 := lg(G_1, A_3) = P(f_9(x_2, x_2, x_1), f_{10}(z_4, z_5), z_6)$  % **Compute** $lg(G_1, A_3)$

$G_3 := lg(G_2, A_4) = P(f_9(z_7, z_8, z_9), f_{10}(z_{10}, z_{11}), z_{12})$  % **Compute** $lg(G_2, A_4)$

$G_4 := lg(G_3, A_5) = P(f_9(z_{13}, z_{14}, z_{15}), f_{10}(z_{16}, z_{17}), z_{18})$  % **Compute** $lg(G_3, A_5)$

## Using **AntiComb:**

$G_1 := lg(A_1, A_2) = P(f_9(x_2, x_2, x_1), f_{10}(z_1, z_2), z_3)$  % **Compute** $lg(A_1, A_2)$

$\theta_1 := \{[x_2/z_1, \langle 2, 1 \rangle, \theta_1], [f_7(f_5(f_{10}(x_1, x_1)), f_7(f_2(x_2, x_2, x_1), f_3(x_1)))/z_2, \langle 2, 2 \rangle, \theta_1],$
$\qquad [x_1/z_3, \langle 3 \rangle, \theta_1] \};$

$G_2 := lg(A_1, A_3) = P(f_9(x_2, x_2, x_1), f_{10}(z_4, z_5), z_6)$  % **Compute** $lg(A_1, A_3)$

$\theta_2 := \{[x_2/z_4, \langle 2, 1 \rangle, \theta_2], [f_7(f_5(f_{10}(x_1, x_1)), f_7(f_2(x_2, x_2, x_1), f_3(x_1)))/z_5, \langle 2, 2 \rangle, \theta_2],$
$\qquad [x_1/z_6, \langle 3 \rangle, \theta_2] \};$

$G_3 := lg(A_1, A_4) = P(f_9(z_7, z_8, z_9), f_{10}(z_{10}, z_{11}), x_1)$  % **Compute** $lg(A_1, A_4)$

$\theta_3 := \{[x_2/z_7, \langle 1, 1 \rangle, \theta_3], [x_2/z_8, \langle 1, 2 \rangle, \theta_3], [x_1/z_9, \langle 1, 3 \rangle, \theta_3], [x_2/z_{10}, \langle 2, 1 \rangle, \theta_3],$
$\qquad [f_7(f_5(f_{10}(x_1, x_1)), f_7(f_2(x_2, x_2, x_1), f_3(x_1)))/z_{11}, \langle 2, 2 \rangle, \theta_3] \};$

$G_4 := lg(A_1, A_5) = P(f_9(z_{12}, z_{13}, z_{14}), f_{10}(x_2, z_{15}), z_{16})$  % **Compute** $lg(A_1, A_5)$

$\theta_4 := \{[x_2/z_{12}, \langle 1, 1 \rangle, \theta_4], [x_2/z_{13}, \langle 1, 2 \rangle, \theta_4], [x_1/z_{14}, \langle 1, 3 \rangle, \theta_4],$
$\qquad [f_7(f_5(f_{10}(x_1, x_1)), f_7(f_2(x_2, x_2, x_1), f_3(x_1)))/z_{15}, \langle 2, 2 \rangle, \theta_4], [x_1/z_{16}, \langle 3 \rangle, \theta_4] \};$

---

[4] Here we draw underlines to help distinguishing 3 terms in $P$.

$\theta := \theta_1 + \theta_2 + \theta_3 + \theta_4$ % **Compute combination**

$= \{[x_2/z_1, \langle 2,1 \rangle, \theta_1], [f_7(f_5(f_{10}(x_1, x_1)), f_7(f_2(x_2, x_2, x_1), f_3(x_1)))/z_2, \langle 2,2 \rangle, \theta_1],$
$[x_1/z_3, \langle 3 \rangle, \theta_1], [x_2/z_4, \langle 2,1 \rangle, \theta_2], [f_7(f_5(f_{10}(x_1, x_1)), f_7(f_2(x_2, x_2, x_1), f_3(x_1)))/z_5, \langle 2,2 \rangle, \theta_2],$
$[x_1/z_6, \langle 3 \rangle, \theta_2], [x_2/z_7, \langle 1,1 \rangle, \theta_3], [x_2/z_8, \langle 1,2 \rangle, \theta_3], [x_1/z_9, \langle 1,3 \rangle, \theta_3],$
$[x_2/z_{10}, \langle 2,1 \rangle, \theta_3], [f_7(f_5(f_{10}(x_1, x_1)), f_7(f_2(x_2, x_2, x_1), f_3(x_1)))/z_{11}, \langle 2,2 \rangle, \theta_3],$
$[x_2/z_{12}, \langle 1,1 \rangle, \theta_4], [x_2/z_{13}, \langle 1,2 \rangle, \theta_4], [x_1/z_{14}, \langle 1,3 \rangle, \theta_4],$
$[f_7(f_5(f_{10}(x_1, x_1)), f_7(f_2(x_2, x_2, x_1), f_3(x_1)))/z_{15}, \langle 2,2 \rangle, \theta_4], [x_1/z_{16}, \langle 3 \rangle, \theta_4] \};$

$\theta^{-1} :=$ % **Compute anti-combination**

$\{[z_1/x_2, \langle 2,1 \rangle, \theta_1], [z_2/f_7(f_5(f_{10}(x_1, x_1)), f_7(f_2(x_2, x_2, x_1), f_3(x_1))), \langle 2,2 \rangle, \theta_1],$
$[z_3/x_1, \langle 3 \rangle, \theta_1], [z_4/x_2, \langle 2,1 \rangle, \theta_2], [z_5/f_7(f_5(f_{10}(x_1, x_1)), f_7(f_2(x_2, x_2, x_1), f_3(x_1))), \langle 2,2 \rangle, \theta_2],$
$[z_6/x_1, \langle 3 \rangle, \theta_2], [z_7/x_2, \langle 1,1 \rangle, \theta_3], [z_8/x_2, \langle 1,2 \rangle, \theta_3], [z_9/x_1, \langle 1,3 \rangle, \theta_3],$
$[z_{10}/x_2, \langle 2,1 \rangle, \theta_3], [z_{11}/f_7(f_5(f_{10}(x_1, x_1)), f_7(f_2(x_2, x_2, x_1), f_3(x_1))), \langle 2,2 \rangle, \theta_3],$
$[z_{12}/x_2, \langle 1,1 \rangle, \theta_4], [z_{13}/x_2, \langle 1,2 \rangle, \theta_4], [z_{14}/x_1, \langle 1,3 \rangle, \theta_4],$
$[z_{15}/f_7(f_5(f_{10}(x_1, x_1)), f_7(f_2(x_2, x_2, x_1), f_3(x_1))), \langle 2,2 \rangle, \theta_4], [z_{16}/x_1, \langle 3 \rangle, \theta_4] \};$

$A_1\theta^{-1} := P(f_9(z_{12}, z_{13}, z_{14}), f_{10}(z_{10}, z_{15}), z_{16})$. % **Compute least generalization**

When there are different replacements $z_i/t_i$ from different $\theta_j$'s at the same position $\langle m, n \rangle$ in $\theta^{-1}$, for instance, $[z_7/x_2, \langle 1,1 \rangle, \theta_3]$ and $[z_{12}/x_2, \langle 1,1 \rangle, \theta_4]$, they are equivalent modulo variable renaming and one of them is selected.

## 4 Experimental Evaluation

In this section, we compare runtime for computing least generalizations by two algorithms **AntiUnif** and **AntiComb**.

### 4.1 Generating Test Data

We use randomly created data sets $Prog$ satisfying the following conditions.

1. Each element in $Prog$ is an atom of the form: $P(t_1, t_2, t_3)$ where $P$ is a ternary predicate and $t_1, t_2, t_3$ are terms. Every atom in $Prog$ has the same predicate.
2. $Prog$ has two parameters: $n$ is the number of elements in $Prog$, and $m$ is the number of function symbols appearing in $Prog$. The number of different variables appearing in $Prog$ is set to $\frac{n}{2}$, while there is no constant in $Prog$.
3. For an atom $A = P(t_1, t_2, t_3)$, the $depth$ of $A$ is defined as $d(A) = 1 + max\{d(t_1), d(t_2), d(t_3)\}$ where $d(t_i)$ $(1 \leq i \leq 3)$ is the number of function symbols appearing in $t_i$. For instance, the depth of $P(x, y, z)$ is 1, the depth of $P(f(x), y, g(h(z)))$ is 3, and so on. We set the depth of each atom $A$ in $Prog$ as $d(A) \leq 5$.
4. For any atom $P(t_1, t_2, t_3)$ in $Prog$, if a function $f$ appears in the outermost of the term $t_i$ $(1 \leq i \leq 3)$, then the outermost function appearing in the corresponding term $s_i$ of another atom $P(s_1, s_2, s_3)$ in $Prog$ is set to the same function $f$.

An explanation is in order for the above 4th condition on $Prog$. For instance, two atoms: $P(f(g(x)), y, g(z))$ and $P(f(h(x)), g(y), g(h(z)))$ have the same outermost function $f$ in terms appearing in the 1st arity of $P$ and the same outermost function $g$ in the 3rd arity. This is because we randomly generate a set $Prog$ then it is very unlikely that the same function appears in the corresponding positions of more than two elements. Without this assumption, computation of anti-unification will be simple and the results are likely to contain no function. For instance, the result of anti-unification of $P(f_1(g_1(x)), y, g_2(z))$ and $P(f_2(h_1(x)), g_3(y), g_4(h_2(z)))$ becomes $P(x, y, z)$. Note that it may happen that no function appears in the $i$-th arity $(1 \leq i \leq 3)$ of $P$ as in the 2nd element of $P(f(g(x)), y, g(z))$.

## 4.2    Experimental results

We compare runtime for computing a least generalization of $Prog$ using **AntiUnif** and **AntiComb**. We implement two algorithms by Maple 2018, 64 bit. The testing is done on a computer with the following configuration: Intel(R) Core$^{TM}$ i7-4750HQ CPU@ 2.0 GHz, RAM 8.00 GB, Operating system: Windows 10, 64-bit.

In the experiments, we set the parameters $n$ and $m$ as follows:

- The number of atoms in $Prog$ is set to: $n = 500, 1000, 3000, 5000, 10000$.
- The number of functions appearing in $Prog$ is set to: $m = n/2$; $m = n$; $m = 2n$.

Based on $(n, m)$, generate the set of atoms $Prog$ randomly. In **AntiComb**, the number of processors $k$ is set to $k = 10; 30; 50$. For each $(n, m, k)$ we measure runtime at least four times and pick average values.

In experiments, we do not have many computers for parallel computing. So we compute the time for $k$-parallel processing by $max\{t_1, \ldots, t_k\}$ where $t_i$ $(1 \leq i \leq k)$ is the time for computing a combination $\theta^i$ for $\Sigma_i$. After computing each $\theta^i$, they are combined into $\theta = \theta^1 + \cdots + \theta^k$. This process is denoted by Stage 1. After Stage 1, produce the inverse $\theta^{-1}$ and compute $A_1\theta^{-1}$ that is the least generalization $lg(\Sigma)$ of the input set $\Sigma$. This process is denoted by Stage 2.

Table 1 shows the experimental results that are displayed in Figs. 4 and 5.

By the results of testing, it is observed that **AntiComb** is faster than **AntiUnif** in general. This is because **AntiComb** can compute least generalization in parallel. The time of computing a least generalization by **AntiComb** decreases by increasing the number of processors for parallel computing. Note that runtime $T_{AC}$ for **AntiComb** is greater than the value $T_{AU}/k$ where $T_{AU}$ is runtime for **AntiUnif**. This is because the relation $T_{AU}/k < T_{AC} < T_{AU}/k + T_\infty$ holds by *Brent's law* [6], where $T_\infty$ is runtime using an idealized machine with an infinite number of processors. It is known that parallel computing is effective when the number of processors is small, or when the problem is perfectly parallel (*Amdahl's law*) [5]. In **AntiComb**, Stage 1 is (partly) computed in parallel while Stage 2 is serial. Hence, the *speedup* of the algorithm $S = T_{AU}/T_{AC}$ is limited by the time needed for the serial fraction of the problem. The *efficiency* of parallel computing $E = S/k$ also decreases by increasing $k$. Moreover, we compute runtime for parallel processing by $max\{t_1, \ldots, t_k\}$. These factors make the speedup of **AntiComb** seemingly smaller than the number of processors used.

**Table 1.** Experimental results

| n | m | AntiUnif (sec) | k | AntiComb (sec) Stage 1 | Stage 2 | Total |
|---|---|---|---|---|---|---|
| 500 | 250 | 0.203 | 10 | 0.047 | 0.031 | 0.078 |
| | | | 30 | 0.032 | 0.031 | 0.063 |
| | | | 50 | 0.016 | 0.031 | 0.047 |
| 500 | 500 | 0.218 | 10 | 0.032 | 0.015 | 0.047 |
| | | | 30 | 0.016 | 0.031 | 0.047 |
| | | | 50 | 0.016 | 0.016 | 0.032 |
| 500 | 1000 | 0.406 | 10 | 0.141 | 0.031 | 0.172 |
| | | | 30 | 0.031 | 0.047 | 0.078 |
| | | | 50 | 0.016 | 0.047 | 0.063 |

| n | m | AntiUnif (sec) | k | AntiComb (sec) Stage 1 | Stage 2 | Total |
|---|---|---|---|---|---|---|
| 1000 | 500 | 0.406 | 10 | 0.063 | 0.25 | 0.313 |
| | | | 30 | 0.032 | 0.062 | 0.094 |
| | | | 50 | 0.032 | 0.047 | 0.079 |
| 1000 | 1000 | 0.422 | 10 | 0.266 | 0.078 | 0.344 |
| | | | 30 | 0.016 | 0.078 | 0.094 |
| | | | 50 | 0.016 | 0.062 | 0.078 |
| 1000 | 2000 | 0.61 | 10 | 0.063 | 0.063 | 0.126 |
| | | | 30 | 0.032 | 0.062 | 0.094 |
| | | | 50 | 0.016 | 0.047 | 0.063 |

| n | m | AntiUnif (sec) | k | AntiComb (sec) Stage 1 | Stage 2 | Total |
|---|---|---|---|---|---|---|
| 3000 | 1500 | 0.719 | 10 | 0.281 | 0.093 | 0.374 |
| | | | 30 | 0.219 | 0.078 | 0.297 |
| | | | 50 | 0.125 | 0.078 | 0.203 |
| 3000 | 3000 | 0.922 | 10 | 0.359 | 0.093 | 0.452 |
| | | | 30 | 0.047 | 0.109 | 0.156 |
| | | | 50 | 0.016 | 0.094 | 0.11 |
| 3000 | 6000 | 0.953 | 10 | 0.437 | 0.109 | 0.546 |
| | | | 30 | 0.219 | 0.11 | 0.329 |
| | | | 50 | 0.172 | 0.094 | 0.266 |

| n | m | AntiUnif (sec) | k | AntiComb (sec) Stage 1 | Stage 2 | Total |
|---|---|---|---|---|---|---|
| 5000 | 2500 | 1.218 | 10 | 0.547 | 0.125 | 0.672 |
| | | | 30 | 0.297 | 0.141 | 0.438 |
| | | | 50 | 0.276 | 0.125 | 0.401 |
| 5000 | 5000 | 2.125 | 10 | 0.829 | 0.204 | 1.033 |
| | | | 30 | 0.5 | 0.234 | 0.734 |
| | | | 50 | 0.328 | 0.219 | 0.547 |
| 5000 | 10000 | 2.891 | 10 | 1.109 | 0.234 | 1.343 |
| | | | 30 | 0.641 | 0.25 | 0.891 |
| | | | 50 | 0.453 | 0.234 | 0.687 |

| n | m | AntiUnif (sec) | k | AntiComb (sec) Stage 1 | Stage 2 | Total | Speedup [†] | Efficiency [‡] |
|---|---|---|---|---|---|---|---|---|
| 10000 | 5000 | 1.641 | 10 | 1.313 | 0.141 | 1.454 | 1.13 | 0.11 |
| | | | 30 | 0.515 | 0.125 | 0.64 | 2.56 | 0.09 |
| | | | 50 | 0.359 | 0.125 | 0.484 | 3.39 | 0.07 |
| 10000 | 10000 | 2.359 | 10 | 1.047 | 0.187 | 1.234 | 1.91 | 0.19 |
| | | | 30 | 0.547 | 0.188 | 0.735 | 3.21 | 0.11 |
| | | | 50 | 0.485 | 0.203 | 0.688 | 3.43 | 0.07 |
| 10000 | 20000 | 2.953 | 10 | 1.406 | 0.266 | 1.672 | 1.77 | 0.18 |
| | | | 30 | 0.579 | 0.297 | 0.876 | 3.37 | 0.11 |
| | | | 50 | 0.422 | 0.282 | 0.704 | 4.19 | 0.08 |

[†] Speedup:= AntiUnif / AntiComb(Total)
[‡] Efficiency:=Speedup / k

## 5    Discussion

Palamidessi [13] uses the least upper bound (that is called the glb in the context of [13]) of substitutions for *parallel factorization* that corresponds to least generalization. Given two substitutions $\theta$ and $\sigma$ with different bindings for the same variable, say $t/x \in \theta$ and $u/x \in \sigma$, she eliminates the difference by replacing $t$ and $u$ by $x$ in $\theta$ and $\sigma$ respectively. For instance, given two substitutions $\theta = \{a/x, f(a)/y\}$ and $\sigma = \{b/x, f(b)/y\}$, $\lambda = \{f(x)/y\}$ is computed as the least upper bound of $\theta$ and $\sigma$ by replacing $a$ and $b$ by $x$. This corresponds to computing a least generalization of two atoms $A_1 = P(a, f(a))$ and $A_2 = P(b, f(b))$

using the anti-unification algorithm, which outputs $lg(\{A_1, A_2\}) = P(x, f(x))$ and the msau $(\{a/x\}, \{b/x\})$. In the anti-combination algorithm **AntiComb**, on the other hand, given the set of $n$ atoms $\{A_1, \ldots, A_n\}$ such that $A_1 = P(a, f(a))$ and $A_2 = P(b, f(b))$, $lg(\{A_1, A_2\}) = P(x, f(x))$ and the substitution $\theta_2 = \{a/x\}$ is computed. $\theta_2$ is then combined with other substitution $\theta_i$ such that $A_1 = G_i\theta_i$ and $G_i = lg(\{A_1, A_i\})$ for $3 \leq i \leq n$. As such, anti-combination is different from parallel factorization. In fact, the parallel factorization algorithm introduced in [13] outputs the lub of two substitutions, in other words, it computes anti-unification of two terms by manipulating substitutions.

Several algorithms for anti-unification are proposed in the literature. Kuper *et al.* [8] show that anti-unification of two terms represented in the form of trees of size $n$ is carried out in time $O(\log^2 n)$ using $n$ processors (or $n/\log^2 n$ processors

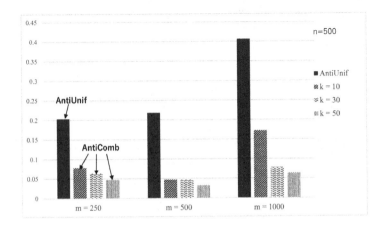

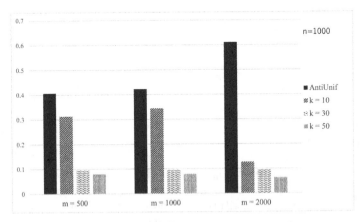

**Fig. 4.** Comparison of runtime by **AntiUnif** and **AntiComb** (1)

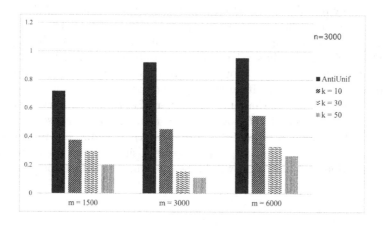

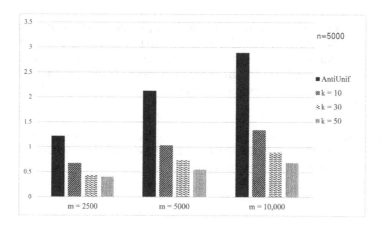

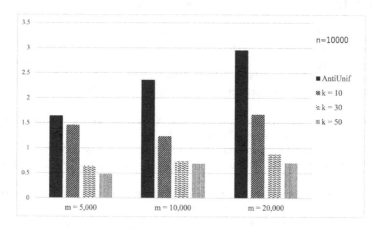

**Fig. 5.** Comparison of runtime by **AntiUnif** and **AntiComb** (2)

in [2]). Kostylev and Zakharov [7] represent two given terms by acyclic directed graphs, and compute their most specific term (or lg) in time $O(N \log N)$ where $N$ is the size of the most specific term it computes. In contrast to the algorithm proposed in this paper, those algorithms compute least generalization of two atoms (or terms). We use the Plotkin/Reynolds's algorithm in this paper, but **AntiComb** can use any algorithm of anti-unification of two atoms in the step 2. Kuper *et al.* [8] also analyze that anti-unification of $m$ terms, each having at most $O(n)$ symbols, is computed in $O(\log mn + \log^2 n)$ using $mn$ processors. If we use their anti-unification algorithm of two atoms in **AntiComb**, anti-unification of $m$ atoms takes $O(m \times \log^2 n)$ using $n$ processors. Using $mn$ processors, it is done in $O(\log^2 n)$. Hence, **AntiComb** will be faster than anti-unification of $m$ terms in [8].

## 6   Conclusion

This paper introduced a new algorithm for computing a least generalization of a set of atoms based on anti-combination. Experimental results show that the proposed algorithm has potential to compute induction from big data in the form of relational facts in parallel. Future study includes extending the framework to generalization of clauses and exploiting other opportunities for parallelisation in practical ILP applications.

**Acknowledgment.** This research is funded by Vietnam National University – Ho Chi Minh city (VNU-HCM) under grant number C2019-26-01. We thank Mikio Yoshida for useful discussion on the subject of this paper.

## References

1. Chang, C.L., Lee, R.T.C.: Symbolic Logic and Mechanical Theorem Proving. Academic Press, New York (1973)
2. Delcher, A.L., Kasif, S.: Efficient parallel term matching and anti-unification. J. Autom. Reason. **9**, 391–406 (1992)
3. Nienhuys-Cheng, S.-H., De Wolf, R.: Foundations of Inductive Logic Programming. LNAI, vol. 1228. Springer, Berlin, Heidelberg (1997)
4. Eder, E.: Properties of substitutions and unifications. J. Symb. Comput. **1**, 31–46 (1985)
5. Grama, A., Karypis, G., Kumar, V., Gupta, A.: Introduction to Parallel Computing, 2nd edn. Addison Wesley, Boston (2003)
6. Gustafson, J.L.: Brent's theorem. In: Padua, V. (ed.) Encyclopedia of Parallel Computing, pp. 182–185. Springer, Boston (2011). https://doi.org/10.1007/978-0-387-09766-4_80
7. Kostylev, E.V., Zakharov, V.A.: On the complexity of the anti-unification problem. Discrete Math. Appl. **18**(1), 85–98 (2008)
8. Kuper, G.M., McAloon, K.W., Palem, K.V., Perry, K.J.: A note on the parallel complexity of anti-unification. J. Autom. Reason. **9**, 381–389 (1992). https://doi.org/10.1007/BF00245297

9. Lassez, J.-L., Maher, M.J., Marriott, K.: Unification revisited. In: Mikner, J. (ed.) Foundations of Deductive Databases and Logic Programming, pp. 587–625. Morgan Kaufmann, Burlington (1988)
10. Lloyd, J.W.: Foundations of Logic Programming, 2nd edn. Springer, Berlin (1987)
11. Oancea, C., So, C., Watt, S.M.: Generalization in maple. In: Maple Conference, pp. 377–382 (2005)
12. Østvold, B.M.: A functional reconstruction of anti-unification. Technical report DART/04/04, Norwegian Computing (2004)
13. Palamidessi, C.: Algebraic properties of idempotent substitutions. In: Paterson, M.S. (ed.) ICALP 1990. LNCS, vol. 443, pp. 386–399. Springer, Heidelberg (1990). https://doi.org/10.1007/BFb0032046
14. Plotkin, G. D.: A note on inductive generalization. In: Machine Intelligence, vol. 5, pp. 153–163. Edinburgh University Press (1970)
15. Prawitz, D.: Advances and problems in mechanical proof procedures. In: Machine Intelligence, vol. 4, pp. 59–71. Edinburgh University Press (1969)
16. Reynolds, J.C.: Transformational systems and the algebraic structure of atomic formulas. In: Machine Intelligence, vol. 5, pp. 135–151. Edinburgh University Press (1970)
17. Yamasaki, S., Yoshida, M., Doshita, S.: A fixpoint semantics of Horn sentences based on substitution sets. Theor. Comput. Sci. **51**, 309–324 (1986)
18. Yoshida, M., Sakama, C.: Computing least generalization by anti-combination (short paper). Presented at ILP-14 (formally unpublished) (2014)

# LazyBum: Decision Tree Learning Using Lazy Propositionalization

Jonas Schouterden[(✉)][iD], Jesse Davis[iD], and Hendrik Blockeel[iD]

Department of Computer Science, KU Leuven, Celestijnenlaan 200A,
Box 2402, 3001 Leuven, Belgium
{jonas.schouterden,jesse.davis,hendrik.blockeel}@cs.kuleuven.be

**Abstract.** Propositionalization is the process of summarizing relational data into a tabular (attribute-value) format. The resulting table can next be used by any propositional learner. This approach makes it possible to apply a wide variety of learning methods to relational data. However, the transformation from relational to propositional format is generally not lossless: different relational structures may be mapped onto the same feature vector. At the same time, features may be introduced that are not needed for the learning task at hand. In general, it is hard to define a feature space that contains all and only those features that are needed for the learning task. This paper presents LazyBum, a system that can be considered a lazy version of the recently proposed OneBM method for propositionalization. LazyBum interleaves OneBM's feature construction method with a decision tree learner. This learner both uses and guides the propositionalization process. It indicates when and where to look for new features. This approach is similar to what has elsewhere been called dynamic propositionalization. In an experimental comparison with the original OneBM and with two other recently proposed propositionalization methods (nFOIL and MODL, which respectively perform dynamic and static propositionalization), LazyBum achieves a comparable accuracy with a lower execution time on most of the datasets.

**Keywords:** LazyBum · Inductive logic programming · Propositionalization

## 1 Introduction

There is a renewed interest in analyzing data stored in relational databases. In 2017, Tan et al. proposed the "One Button Machine" (OneBM) [15], which automatically constructs features from a relational database. In ILP terms, one would say that OneBM performs propositionalization [14]. It summarizes a relational database into a single table by defining features that are derived from the database by joining multiple tables. It handles one-to-many and many-to-many relationships by using specific aggregation functions that aggregate the information in a set of multiple related tuples into a single tuple.

© Springer Nature Switzerland AG 2020
D. Kazakov and C. Erten (Eds.): ILP 2019, LNAI 11770, pp. 98–113, 2020.
https://doi.org/10.1007/978-3-030-49210-6_9

An obvious disadvantage of propositionalization is that there is usually a loss of information: the resulting table provides a summary of the original database, from which that database cannot uniquely be reconstructed. Defining more features means that less information is lost.

Viewed from an ILP perspective, propositionalization is equivalent to defining a (usually relatively small) set of clauses, and associating with each clause one particular feature. A typical ILP system searches a space that is much larger than the number of features typically constructed by propositionalization approaches.

In this paper, we propose a variant of OneBM that performs dynamic, or "lazy", propositionalization. It considers the same types of features as OneBM, but constructs these features in a lazy manner that is guided by the learner. We begin by only considering that are based on the target table. But when another table's relevance to the learner becomes more evident, it expands its feature space to consider features based on information contained in that table.

The gradual expansion of the feature table is somewhat similar to how ILP systems gradually construct longer clauses by first constructing shorter ones and considering only the promising ones for extension. An important difference, however, is that ILP systems, when evaluating a clause, typically re-evaluate the whole clause, which includes re-discovering answer substitutions for the subclause that has already been evaluated earlier. The lazy propositionalization methods proposed in this paper caches these instantiations.

The hypothesis underlying this paper is that a method like OneBM can be made more efficient in both memory and time by implementing a lazy version of its feature construction, without a loss of accuracy. At the same time, one might hope that it is faster than ILP systems that use the same implicit search space.

The remainder of this paper is structured as follows. Section 2 briefly presents OneBM. Section 3 introduces our new algorithm, including two available strategies for defining new features, and discusses related work. Section 4 experimentally compares this algorithm to other propositionalization approaches, in terms of predictive and run-time performance, and Sect. 5 presents conclusions.

## 2 OneBM

The "One Button Machine" or OneBM [15] is a relational learning system that works on data stored in a relational database. It takes as input a set of tables, connected with each other through foreign keys. A single attribute is selected to serve as the target attribute, and the table containing this attribute is called the target table. OneBM produces as output a modified target table that contains newly constructed features which summarize the other tables. Figure 1 shows an example of what the input may look like.

The OneBM paper defines a "joining path" as a sequence of tables $T_0 \xrightarrow{c_1} T_1 \xrightarrow{c_2} T_2 \xrightarrow{c_3} \cdots T_k \mapsto A$ where $T_0$ is the target table, $c_i$ is the condition on which $T_{i-1}$ and $T_i$ are (equi-)joined, and $A$ is an attribute of the last table in the sequence. Note that this definition considers the projection onto one single attribute at the end as part of the "joining path." In this paper, we will use the

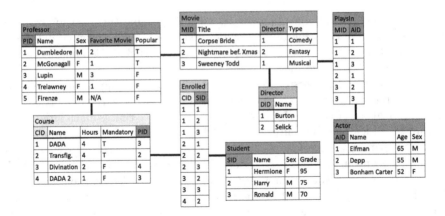

**Fig. 1.** An example database representing teachers and students in a fictional school. *Professor* is the target table and the target attribute is *popular*.

term "join path", or J-path, for the joining path without the final projection, and "join-project path", or JP-path, for the joining path as originally defined. Given a $T_0$-tuple $t$, we will write $t.P$ for the set of $T_k$-tuples associated with it through the join path $P$, and $t.P.A$ for the multiset of $A$-values in $t.P$.

Figure 2 shows, for the database shown in Fig. 1 and the JP-path *Professor* $\xrightarrow{PID}$ *Course* $\xrightarrow{CID}$ *Enrolled* $\xrightarrow{SID}$ *Student* $\mapsto$ *Grade*, the multiset of grades associated with Prof. Lupin (we use *PID* as shorthand notation for *Professor.PID* = *Course.PID* here, and similar for *CID* and *SID*).

If all the joins in $P$ are one-to-one or many-to-one, then $t.P.A$ is guaranteed to be a singleton; otherwise, it is not. In the first case, we call $P$ determinate, and in the second case we call it non-determinate.

OneBM derives features from JP-paths as follows. A determinate path defines one feature, whose value (for a given tuple $t$) is the single element of $t.P.A$. A non-determinate path defines a fixed-sized feature vector whose components are defined by predefined aggregation functions applied to $t.P.A$. Which aggregation functions are used depends on the type of $A$. If $A$ is numerical, the feature vector contains the mean, variance, min, max, sum and count of the numbers in the multiset. If $A$ is categorical, the feature vector contains the cardinality of the multiset and the corresponding set (in SQL terms, the count and count distinct functions). OneBM defines other aggregation functions for values that are texts, timestamps, etc.

The features defined by a JP-path can be collected using a single SQL query. For example, the multiset from Fig. 2 and its corresponding features can be computed using the following SQL query:

```
SELECT count(grade), sum(grade), average(grade),
       variance(grade), min(grade), max(grade)
FROM Professor
     JOIN Course ON Professor.PID = Course.PID
```

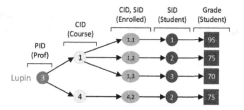

**Fig. 2.** The multiset of grades for students taking one of professor Lupin's courses. OneBM transforms this multiset to multiple features for Lupin. Example transformations include the average and standard deviation.

```
    JOIN Enrolled ON Course.CID = Enrolled.CID
    JOIN Student ON Student.SID = Enrolled.SID
GROUP BY Professor.PID
```

OneBM defines the depth of a table $T_i$, $d(T_i)$, as the length of the shortest join path between $T_0$ and $T_i$. It has two options for generating join paths: in "forward-only" mode, consecutive tables must be increasingly farther from the target table (that is, $i < j \Rightarrow d(T_i) < d(T_j)$), whereas in "full" mode this restriction is dropped, allowing for what the authors of OneBM call "backward traversal".

Given a database, OneBM constructs a table that contains for each join path all the defined features. As the number of join paths can grow exponentially with their length, OneBM has a MaxDepth parameter that limits this length.

OneBM uses a relatively restrictive bias. For instance, it does not mix selections into the join path, as, e.g., Van Assche et al. do [25]. Doing so would result in an exponential blowup of the already large feature table.

The lazy version of OneBM that we propose does not attempt to lift this restriction or address any other limitations; it constructs features lazily, but in all other respects is meant to behave as much as possible like OneBM. It is currently limited to numerical and categorical values, and only implements the forward-only approach.

## 3  LazyBum

Our lazy version of OneBM is called Lazy Button Machine, or LazyBum. The main motivation for developing LazyBum is that, by constructing all features in advance, OneBM may invest much work into computing features that afterwards will not be used by the learner. LazyBum takes a more cautious approach: it first computes features based on short join paths, and only extends join paths when (1) the simpler features turn out to be insufficient, and (2) there is reason to believe the extension will help. In principle, LazyBum can construct every feature that OneBM can construct, as it explores the same feature space. In practice, it avoids constructing the large majority of them.

As the lazy feature construction somehow needs to be informed about which tables are useful additions to the current path, it is natural to integrate a learning system into the feature construction process. LazyBum is based on relational decision tree learning (such as Tilde [1] or Relational Probability Trees [20]).

### 3.1   The LazyBum Algorithm

LazyBum learns a decision tree in a top-down fashion. When deciding on the test to include in a node, it evaluates possible tests using a "local data table" (LDT), which just like in traditional tree learning contains all instances sorted into this node, with one row per instance. Unlike traditional tree learning, the LDT does not have a fixed schema (set of attributes) as the learner may extend the schema with new features as needed. Each LDT is associated with a decision tree node and contains all the features constructed along the path from the root to that node. We now explain the learning process in detail.

At the root node of the tree, the LDT is the target table extended with all features derived from join paths of length 1 (i.e., the tables directly connected to the target table). LazyBum uses information gain to select the most informative feature in the LDT to split on. If a good enough split is found, it splits the LDT into two subsets of rows based on this: one for each child. If no good split can be found, LazyBum tries to extend the LDT by introducing new features. These new features are defined by extending some of the join paths used to build the current LDT. Information from the current decision tree branch can guide the selection of which join paths to extend, which is discussed in Subsect. 3.2. LazyBum finds the best split based on the new features, and splits the extended LDT into two subsets. If none of the new features is good enough, the node is turned into a leaf. This procedure is recursively repeated for all subsets created. Algorithm 1 summarizes the entire procedure.

The way LDTs are extended is somewhat similar to the way in which the relational decision tree learner Tilde extends its clausal queries. In Tilde, a query $Q$ is associated with the current node ($Q$ contains all the tests from the root to this node), and this query is extended with one or more literals, chosen among many candidates. After the most informative extension $e$ is found, the set of instances satisfying $Q$ (i.e., all instances at this node) is partitioned into a subset of instances that satisfy $Q \wedge e$, and a subset of instances that do not. Important differences between Tilde and LazyBum are:

- In Tilde, for each candidate extension $e$, the query $Q \wedge e$ is evaluated. This means the sub-query $Q$ is computed many times. The "query pack" implementation of Tilde [2] avoids this to some extent: within a single node, the search for all answer substitutions for query $Q$ is done only once, not once for each extension.

  While query packs avoid rerunning $Q$ multiple times inside one node, $Q$ must still be rerun in that node's children. LazyBum differs in this respect. Lazy-Bum caches the join paths corresponding to a node's LDT. A join path is cached using the primary keys identifiers of the tables on its path, for the

---

**Algorithm 1.** Main LazyBum algorithm.

---

**Require:**

    *MaxDepth*, max tree depth,

    *MinInst*, minimum nb of instances in a leaf

    *MinIG*, minimum information gain threshold

1:  **procedure** GROW_TREE(node $N$, table $LDT$)
2:    **if** depth($N$) = $MaxDepth$ **or** #rows($LDT$) < $MinInst$ **then**
3:       Make $N$ a leaf node
4:    **else**
5:       Find the test $\tau$ with highest information gain to split $LDT$ on
6:       **if** IG($\tau$) > $MinIG$ **then**
7:          Split $LDT$ into tables $LDT_L$, $LDT_R$
8:          Turn $N$ into an inner node with children $N_L, N_R$
9:          Call grow_tree($N_L, LDT_L$) and grow_tree($N_R, LDT_R$)
10:      **else**
11:        **if** table $LDT$ can be extended **then**
12:           $LDT^{ext}$ ← extend_data_table($LDT, N$)
13:           Find the test $\tau$ with highest information gain to split $LDT^{ext}$ on
14:           **if** IG($\tau$) > $MinIG$ **then**
15:             Split $LDT^{ext}$ in tables $LDT_L^{ext}$, $LDT_R^{ext}$
16:             Make $N$ an inner node with children $N_L, N_R$
17:             Call grow_tree($N_L, LDT_L^{ext}$) and grow_tree($N_R, LDT_R^{ext}$)
18:           **else**
19:             Make $N$ a leaf node
20:        **else**                      ▷ $LDT$ cannot be extended
21:          Make $N$ a leaf node

---

instances in the LDT. When extending a node's LDT, it reuses the join paths of its ancestor nodes to avoid recomputing these joins. Only the joins with the extension tables need to be calculated. This is similar to caching all answer substitutions of $Q \land e$ for all possible extensions $e$, and reusing the cached results in all child nodes.

In addition, when extending a LDT, LazyBum derives all features for each join path extension and adds them to the LDT. Therefore, if a feature is relevant but not chosen immediately because a better feature exists, this feature will appear in the LDT for all descendant nodes and hence can be used as split criteria in one of these nodes (without having to be recomputed). In comparison, Tilde with query packs does not cache the 'features' it does not split on for use in child nodes.

– Tilde uses a more flexible language bias, largely specified by the user, whereas LazyBum uses a predefined and more restrictive bias. LazyBum's bias is intended to be restrictive enough to make the storage of the LDT feasible.

## 3.2 LDT Extension Strategies

We call two tables **neighbors** if they are connected by a foreign key relationship.

LazyBum defines two different strategies for extending an LDT. Let $P = T_0 \rightarrow T_1 \rightarrow \cdots \rightarrow T_k$ be a J-path used to construct the LDT. A table is called a candidate for extension of $P$ if (a) it does not occur in $P$ and (b) it neighbors on $T_k$. In the **unrestricted** strategy, every path used to construct the current LDT gets extended with each candidate for extension. In the **restricted** strategy, only those paths get extended from which at least one feature actually occurs in an ancestor node of the decision tree node currently being considered. Hence, the decision tree guides the selections of which join paths should be extended. The difference between the two strategies is that for the unrestricted strategy, it suffices that the features defined by the join path have been introduced in the LDT, while for the restricted strategy they must also have been used at least once. The motivation for the latter condition is that LazyBum should preferentially introduce relevant features, and the underlying assumption is that tables are more likely to be relevant if their neighbors are.

The LDT is then extended by considering for each extended J-path all JP-paths (that is, considering each attribute of the newly added tables), computing the features defined by these JP-paths, and adding these features to the LDT. Table 1 lists the aggregation functions that are currently used by LazyBum. Most of them speak for themselves. The "contains" aggregation function introduces for each possible value of a categorical domain a Boolean feature that is true if and only if the value occurs in the multiset. To avoid problems with "categorical" variables that have a very large domain (e.g., because they are in fact strings), these features are only introduced for variables whose domain size is below both an absolute threshold $DomSize_{abs}$ and a relative threshold $DomSize_{rel}$ (relative to the number of rows in the table).

Figure 3 illustrates how the schemas of LDTs are extended in the restricted strategy, guided by their corresponding decision tree branches.

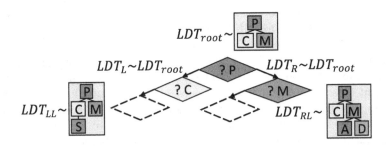

**Fig. 3.** Example of a LDT schema extension in the restricted strategy based on the splits chosen in the decision tree nodes, using the example database from Fig. 1. The partial decision tree shows the root node, its left child and its right child splitting on features from *Professor*, *Professor* $\xrightarrow{PID}$ *Course* and *Professor* $\xrightarrow{MID}$ *Movie*, respectively. The schemas of the LDTs of the root and its two children are the same. For both left children of the roots two children, no good split is found and their LDTs are extended.

**Table 1.** The functions supported by LazyBum to aggregate multisets.

| Join result | Data type | Aggregation function |
|---|---|---|
| Single value | Numerical | Identity function |
| | Categorical | |
| Multi-set | Numerical | Avg, standard deviation, variance, max, min, sum, count |
| | Categorical | Count, distinct count, contains |

### 3.3 Special Cases

*Associative Tables.* LazyBum normally extends join paths with a single table, but there is one exception to this rule. Many-to-many relationships are usually implemented with an intermediate associative table that does nothing else than connect two other tables in an m-to-n manner (for an example, see the table Enrolled in Fig. 1). The intermediate table has no attributes of its own, and is more of an implementation artifact than a conceptual table. For this reason, when an intermediate table is selected, the tables it connects to is immediately added as well. This is somewhat similar to lookahead in ILP.

*Empty Multisets.* For some tuples $t$ and join paths $P$, $t.P.A$ may be empty. Not all aggregation functions are defined on the empty set. To deal with this, LazyBum uses the following strategy when evaluating features to split on. For any test, the instance set is split into three subsets Pass, Fail, and Undefined, which respectively contain the instances that pass the test, fail the test, or are untestable because the feature is undefined. This ternary partition is transformed into a binary partition by merging Undefined with either Pass or Fail, depending on which of these two yields the highest scoring test. If that test is eventually chosen, the node stores which option was chosen, so that it can correctly handle instances with undefined values at prediction time. Apart from this, LazyBum also introduces a Boolean feature that indicate whether a multiset is empty or not, as this by itself may be relevant information.

*Missing Values.* Missing values may occur in the input data. Missing values are quite different from undefined values, and must be treated differently. When the original database has missing values, these are included as separate elements in $t.P.A$. Except for count and count distinct, all aggregation functions are computed on the sub-multiset of the multiset that excludes missing values. When that sub-multiset is empty, while the multiset itself is not, a default value is included as the feature's value.

### 3.4 Comparison with Related Work

Many propositionalization approaches have been proposed in the past and successfully applied to various domains, such as information extraction and word sense disambiguation [4, 10, 14, 23, 24]. To better position LazyBum with respect to the state of the art, we categorize these approaches along four dimensions.

*ILP vs Databases.* A first dimension is the perspective that they take. Some approaches take an ILP-based first-order logic perspective, other approaches take a relational database perspective [11]. Although the logical and database representations are strongly related, logic and database query engines are typically optimized for different types of queries (essentially, determining the existence of at least one answer substitution, versus computing the set of all answer substitutions). LazyBum is set in the database setting. The motivation for this is that the features it computes are indeed based on entire sets of answer substitutions.

*Types of Features.* We distinguish among three types of features. The first type is existential features, which simply check the existence of an answer substitution of a particular type. These features are typically constructed by propositionalization approaches that are closely related to ILP learners. Examples of such systems are LINUS [18], DINUS [17], SINUS [11], RSD [28], RelF [13] and nFOIL [16]. They often focus on categorical attributes, with numerical attributes getting discretized.

The second type of features is based on simple aggregation functions, which summarize information in neighboring tables [21]. Most initial relational-database oriented propositionalization approaches focus on this type of feature. Examples of such systems are POLKA [9], RELAGGS [12], Deep Feature Synthesis [8] and OneBM [15].

The third type of features consists of complex aggregates [25, 26]. A complex aggregate combines an aggregation function with a selection condition. The ILP learners Tilde and FORF included in the ACE system [25] allow for complex aggregates to be used. A recent propositionalization approach that considers complex aggregates is MODL [3, 4], which is included in the Khiops data mining tool. MODL was designed to deal with a possibly infinite feature space. The approach it takes is two-fold. First, it postulates a hierarchical prior distribution over all possible constructed features. This prior distribution penalizes complex features. It takes into account the recursive use of feature construction rules[1], being uniform at each recursion level. Second, it samples this distribution to construct features.

LazyBum does not construct complex aggregates, but focuses on simple aggregates as used in OneBM. However, LazyBum does build some features using the existential quantifier.

*Indirectly Linked Complementary Tables.* This dimension is specific to database-oriented propositionalization approaches and concerns how they handle complementary tables that are not directly connected to the target table. Like OneBM, LazyBum joins tables over a path through the database, aggregating information for each instance using a single aggregation function. In contrast, POLKA

---

[1] A constructed feature can be used as an argument for another construction rule.

and Deep Feature Synthesis use aggregation functions recursively, aggregating in between joins. RELAGGS uses a form of identifier propagation similar to CrossMine [27] to directly relate all complementary tables to the target table.

*Static vs. Dynamic Propositionalization.* Static propositionalization approaches perform the following two-step process: (1) convert the relational database to a data table, and (2) apply any propositional learner to the data table. In contrast, dynamic approaches [5,7,16] interleave feature construction and model learning. LazyBum is a dynamic version of OneBM, constructing a data table gradually, as needed. LazyBum differs from existing dynamic propositionalization systems like SAYU [5–7] and nFOIL [16] in three important ways. First, LazyBum takes a database perspective, whereas SAYU and nFOIL come from an ILP-perspective. Second, LazyBum considers a much wider array of aggregations whereas prior approaches focus on existence [5,16] or possible simple counts [7]. Finally, Lazy-Bum guides the propositionalization by learning a decision tree, while nFOIL and SAYU use Bayesian network classifiers.

# 4    Evaluation

The goal of the empirical evaluation is to compare LazyBum's predictive and run-time performance to that of other propositionalization approaches.

## 4.1    Methodology

**Table 2.** The datasets used in the experiments.

|  | Hepatitis | UW-CSE | University | IMDb |
|---|---|---|---|---|
| # examples | 500 | 278 | 38 | 12000 |
| # classes | 2 | 4 | 3 | 3 |
| # rows (in total) | 12927 | 712 | 145 | 442698 |
| # tables | 7 | 5 | 5 | 8 |
| Target table | Dispat | Person | Student | Movies |
| Target variable | Type | Inphase | Intelligence | Rating |

The following datasets were used in the evaluation, which were collected from the CTU Prague Relational Dataset Repository [19]:

- The Hepatitis dataset describes patients with hepatitis B and C. The goal is to predict the type of hepatitis.
- The UW-CSE dataset contains information about the University of Washington's computer science department. The goal is to predict the phase a person is in.

- The University dataset is a small dataset containing information about students. The classification task is to predict the intelligence of a student.
- The IMDb (Internet Movie Database) dataset contains information relating movies, directors and actors. A possible regression task is to predict the rating of a movie, which is a real number between 0 and 10. We turned this into a classification problem by divided the examples into 3 groups: those with a rating lower than 3.3 (bad movies), those with a rating between 3.3 and 6.6 (average movies) and those with a rating higher than 6.6. The original dataset contained 67245 instances, with 5219 bad, 39599 average and 22427 good movies. From this dataset, we sampled 12000 examples, with 4000 examples of each class.

The datasets vary in size and number of instances (Table 2). For each dataset, we removed the feature columns from the main table, leaving only the primary key and the target attribute (and foreign keys). This ensures that the systems must use information from the secondary tables to result in a model that performs better than a majority class predictor.

We compare two versions of LazyBum (using respectively the restricted and unrestricted strategy) to the following alternative approaches:

- OneBM is the static propositionalization system on which LazyBum is based. As the original OneBM could not be made available to us, we implemented our own version, which shares the same code base as LazyBum. As a result, our OneBM and LazyBum versions are able to generate the same features.
- MODL [3,4] is a recent static propositionalization approach included in the Khiops data mining tool.
- nFOIL [16]. Like LazyBum, nFOIL performs dynamic propositionalization. However, nFOIL uses a naive Bayes learner instead of a decision tree to guide its search for features. nFOIL uses conjunctive clauses to represent features, while LazyBum uses simple aggregation functions.
- Wordification [22] is another recent static propositionalization method. Each instance in a dataset is viewed as a text document, with as words the constructed features. Wordification converts each instance in a feature vector using a bag-of-words representation for its corresponding document.
- Tilde [1] is a relational decision learner; it produces a model but no propositionalization of the data. Since LazyBum is inspired by Tilde and uses a decision tree learner to guide its feature construction, we compare with Tilde as a baseline.

For each of the systems, we performed 10-fold cross-validation. The same 10 folds were used for all systems except for nFOIL and Tilde. For nFOIL and Tilde, we used their builtin 10-fold cross-validation, which choose their own 10 folds. On each dataset, we measure both predictive accuracy and run-time performance. However, OneBM, MODL and Wordification are static propositionalization approaches. They only flatten the database into a table without building a predictive model, while LazyBum also learns a decision tree. To compare predictive accuracy for these methods with LazyBum, we learn a single decision tree on their output tables. For OneBM and MODL, we used WEKA's C4.5 decision tree implementation. For Wordification, we used a default scikit-learn tree.

To compare run-time performance, we measure the model induction time, averaged over the different folds. For OneBM, MODL and Wordification, this includes both the propositionalization time and the time to learn a decision tree.

LazyBum and OneBM were run with their default parameter settings. For LazyBum, this corresponds $MinIG = 0.001$, $MaxDepth = \infty$ an $MinInst = 3$ (see Algorithm 1). LazyBum and OneBM share their feature generation code, which uses default thresholds $DomSize_{abs} = 40$ and $DomSize_{rel} = 0.2$ for the "contains" aggregation function.

For MODL, the number of constructed features was set to 1000. Its default feature construction rules were used, without recoding the categorical or numerical features, while keeping the initial target table attributes as features.

For Wordification, we based our experiments on the included sample scripts, using the default weighting method.

Both nFOIL and Tilde were used with their default options. As input, nFOIL expects a list of ground facts, together with a language bias of types and refinement mode definitions. The datasets were converted by using each table row as a predicate instance. In the rmode definitions used, primary and foreign key attributes were marked as possible input variables (on which unification can be performed), the other attributes were marked as output variables. If a regular column has at most five different values, it was added as a possible selection condition to the rmodes. For Tilde, we used the same language bias as for nFOIL.

## 4.2   Results

We had to modify the nFOIL setup for two datasets. For Hepatitis, nFOIL ran for four days without finishing when using a language bias containing constants. Hence, nFOIL's reported results for Hepatitis use a language bias without constants. For IMDb, the largest of the datasets, nFOIL always crashed, and Wordification did not succeed in propositionalising the first fold in eight hours, after which it was canceled. At that point, it was using 15.5 gigabytes of memory.

*Predictive Accuracy.* When comparing propositionalization methods, both Lazy-Bum versions have the highest accuracy on the UW-CSE and IMDb datasets (Fig. 4a). On Hepatitis, both LazyBum versions are almost as accurate as nFOIL, and they outperform the static approaches. On University, the smallest of our datasets, nFOIL and Tilde noticeably outperform all other approaches. Inspecting their models for University shows that a large part of their generated feature clauses or node queries contain multiple instances of some predicate. That is, features contain self-joins of tables. In comparison, our LazyBum and OneBM implementations only allow each table to occur once in a join path; they cannot generate these features. This may be why nFOIL performs better on University.

It is noteworthy that LazyBum outperforms OneBM+C4.5 on all datasets. Given that LazyBum introduces a subset of the features that OneBM uses, the

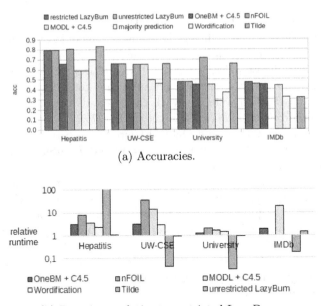

(a) Accuracies.

(b) Run times relative to restricted LazyBum.

**Fig. 4.** Accuracy and run-time measurements for each of the datasets. For OneBM, MODL and Wordification, this includes both propositionalization and learning a tree using C4.5 (averaged over the 10 folds).

only plausible explanation for this is that OneBM generates so many features that it harms the performance of C4.5.

*Run-Time Performance.* Tilde is faster than all other approaches on three out of four datasets (Fig. 4b). Tilde was 665 times slower than restricted LazyBum on Hepatitis. This is likely due to the high number of refinements for each clause, as nFOIL did not even finish without modifying the language bias. Possibly contributing to Tilde's relative speed is that it does not propositionalize.

When comparing between the propositionalization methods, the restricted LazyBum is between 1.2 and 35.8 times faster than its competitors. The smallest speedups are for the University dataset, which is substantially smaller than the other datasets. Remarkably, the restricted LazyBum is only noticeably faster than the unrestricted version on the IMDb dataset. As IMDb is the largest dataset, there is the most to gain from using fewer joins. For the smaller University and UW-CSE datasets, the restricted version is slightly slower due to having a more complex extension strategy.

*General Discussion.* In summary, LazyBum always results in significant run time improvements compared to the other propositionalization methods, while still achieving equivalent predictive performance on three of the four datasets. While Tilde often outperforms the propositionalizers in terms of both accuracy and speed, it only produces a model, whereas the propositionalizers produce a table that enables the generation of many different models. For the OneBM, MODL and Wordification settings, most of the time is spent building the data table, with the decision tree induction time being almost negligible in comparison. LazyBum has the advantage of possibly not having to propositionalize the whole table.

## 5 Conclusion

We have implemented LazyBum, a lazy version of OneBM, a recently proposed system for propositionalizing relational databases, and evaluated its performance relative to OneBM and to several other propositionalization methods. Our experimental results suggest that LazyBum outperforms all other systems in terms of speed, sometimes by an order of magnitude, and this usually without significant loss of accuracy. Moreover, LazyBum systematically outperforms OneBM in terms of accuracy, which can only be explained by the fact that OneBM's eager generation of (many irrelevant) features is harmful to the subsequent learning process. These results suggest that lazy propositionalization by interleaving a decision tree learner with the feature generation process is an effective approach to mining relational data.

**Acknowledgments.** Work supported by the KU Leuven Research Fund (C14/17/070, "SIRV"), Research Foundation – Flanders (project G079416N, MERCS), and the Flanders AI Impulse Program. The authors thank Marc Boullé for his responsiveness and help with the Khiops system.

## References

1. Blockeel, H., De Raedt, L.: Top-down induction of first-order logical decision trees. Artif. Intell. **101**(1–2), 285–297 (1998)
2. Blockeel, H., Dehaspe, L., Demoen, B., Janssens, G., Ramon, J., Vandecasteele, H.: Improving the efficiency of inductive logic programming through the use of query packs. J. Artif. Intell. Res. **16**, 135–166 (2002)
3. Boullé, M.: Towards Automatic Feature Construction for Supervised Classification. In: Calders, T., Esposito, F., Hüllermeier, E., Meo, R. (eds.) ECML PKDD 2014. LNCS (LNAI), vol. 8724, pp. 181–196. Springer, Heidelberg (2014). https://doi.org/10.1007/978-3-662-44848-9_12
4. Boullé, M., Charnay, C., Lachiche, N.: A scalable robust and automatic propositionalization approach for Bayesian classification of large mixed numerical and categorical data. Mach. Learn. **108**(2), 229–266 (2018). https://doi.org/10.1007/s10994-018-5746-9
5. Davis, J., Burnside, E., de Castro Dutra, I., Page, D., Costa, V.S.: An Integrated Approach to Learning Bayesian Networks of Rules. In: Gama, J., Camacho, R., Brazdil, P.B., Jorge, A.M., Torgo, L. (eds.) ECML 2005. LNCS (LNAI), vol. 3720, pp. 84–95. Springer, Heidelberg (2005). https://doi.org/10.1007/11564096_13
6. Davis, J., Costa, V.S., Ray, S., Page, D.: An integrated approached to feature invention and model construction for drug activity prediction. In: 24th International Conference on Machine Learning, pp. 217–224 (2007)

7. Davis, J., Ong, I., Struyf, J., Burnside, E., Page, D., Costa, V.S.: Change of representation for statistical relational learning. In: 20th International Joint Conference on Artificial Intelligence, pp. 2719–2726 (2007)
8. Kanter, J.M., Veeramachaneni, K.: Deep feature synthesis: towards automating data science endeavors. In: 2015 IEEE International Conference on Data Science and Advanced Analytics, pp. 1–10 (2015)
9. Knobbe, A.J., de Haas, M., Siebes, A.: Propositionalisation and aggregates. In: De Raedt, L., Siebes, A. (eds.) PKDD 2001. LNCS (LNAI), vol. 2168, pp. 277–288. Springer, Heidelberg (2001). https://doi.org/10.1007/3-540-44794-6_23
10. Krogel, M.A.: On propositionalization for knowledge discovery in relational databases. Ph.D. thesis, Otto-von-Guericke University Magdeburg, Germany (2005)
11. Krogel, M.A., Rawles, S., Železný, F., Flach, P.A., Lavrač, N., Wrobel, S.: Comparative evaluation of approaches to propositionalization. In: 13th International Conference on Inductive Logic Programming, vol. 2835, pp. 194–217 (2003)
12. Krogel, M.-A., Wrobel, S.: Transformation-based learning using multirelational aggregation. In: Rouveirol, C., Sebag, M. (eds.) ILP 2001. LNCS (LNAI), vol. 2157, pp. 142–155. Springer, Heidelberg (2001). https://doi.org/10.1007/3-540-44797-0_12
13. Kuželka, O., Železný, F.: Block-wise construction of tree-like relational features with monotone reducibility and redundancy. Mach. Learn. 83(2), 163–192 (2011)
14. Lachiche, N.: Propositionalization. In: Sammut, C., Webb, G.I. (eds.) Encyclopedia of Machine Learning and Data Mining, pp. 1025–1031. Springer, Boston (2017). https://doi.org/10.1007/978-0-387-30164-8
15. Lam, H.T., Thiebaut, J.M., Sinn, M., Chen, B., Mai, T., Alkan, O.: One button machine for automating feature engineering in relational databases. CoRR abs/1706.0 (2017)
16. Landwehr, N., Kersting, K., Raedt, L.D.: nFOIL: integrating Naïve Bayes and FOIL. AAAI, pp. 795–800 (2005)
17. Lavrač, N., Džeroski, S.: Inductive Logic Programming: Techniques and Applications. Ellis Horwood series in artificial intelligence, Ellis Horwood (1994)
18. Lavrač, N., Džeroski, S., Grobelnik, M.: Learning nonrecursive definitions of relations with linus. In: Kodratoff, Y. (ed.) EWSL 1991. LNCS, vol. 482, pp. 265–281. Springer, Heidelberg (1991). https://doi.org/10.1007/BFb0017020
19. Motl, J., Schulte, O.: The CTU Prague relational learning repository. CoRR abs/1511.0, 1–7 (2015)
20. Neville, J., Jensen, D.D., Friedland, L., Hay, M.: Learning relational probability trees. In: 9th International Conference on Knowledge Discovery and Data Mining, pp. 625–630. ACM (2003)
21. Perlich, C., Provost, F.: Aggregation-based feature invention and relational concept classes. In: 9th International Conference on Knowledge Discovery and Data Mining, pp. 167–176. ACM (2003)
22. Perovšek, M., Vavpetič, A., Kranjc, J., Cestnik, B., Lavrač, N.: Wordification: propositionalization by unfolding relational data into bags of words. Expert Syst. Appl. 42(17), 6442–6456 (2015)
23. Ramakrishnan, G., Joshi, S., Balakrishnan, S., Srinivasan, A.: Using ILP to construct features for information extraction from semi-structured text. In: Blockeel, H., Ramon, J., Shavlik, J., Tadepalli, P. (eds.) ILP 2007. LNCS (LNAI), vol. 4894, pp. 211–224. Springer, Heidelberg (2008). https://doi.org/10.1007/978-3-540-78469-2_22

24. Specia, L., Srinivasan, A., Ramakrishnan, G., Volpe Nunes, M.G.: Word sense disambiguation using inductive logic programming. In: Muggleton, S., Otero, R., Tamaddoni-Nezhad, A. (eds.) ILP 2006. LNCS (LNAI), vol. 4455, pp. 409–423. Springer, Heidelberg (2007). https://doi.org/10.1007/978-3-540-73847-3_37
25. Van Assche, A., Vens, C., Blockeel, H., Džeroski, S.: First order random forests: learning relational classifiers with complex aggregates. Mach. Learn. **64**(1–3), 149–182 (2006)
26. Vens, C.: Complex aggregates in relational learning. AI Commun. **21**(2–3), 219–220 (2008)
27. Yin, X., Han, J., Yang, J., Yu, P.S.: CrossMine: efficient classification across multiple database relations. In: 20th International Conference on Data Engineering, pp. 399–410. IEEE (2004)
28. Železný, F., Lavrač, N.: Propositionalization-based relational subgroup discovery with RSD. Mach. Learn. **62**(1), 33–63 (2006)

# Weight Your Words: The Effect of Different Weighting Schemes on Wordification Performance

Tatiana Sciammarella$^{(\boxtimes)}$ and Gerson Zaverucha$^{(\boxtimes)}$

COPPE-PESC/Federal University of Rio de Janeiro,
Rio de Janeiro, RJ 21941-972, Brazil
{scit,gerson}@cos.ufrj.br
https://www.cos.ufrj.br

**Abstract.** Relational data models are usually used by researchers and companies when a single-table model is not enough to describe their system. Then, when it comes to classification, there are mainly two options: apply the corresponding relational version of classification algorithms or use a propositionalization technique to transform the relational database into a single-table representation before classification. In this work, we evaluate a fast and simple propositionalization algorithm called Wordification. This technique uses the table name, attribute name and value to create a feature. Each feature is treated as a word and the instances of the database are represented by a Bag-Of-Words (BOW) model. Then, a weighting scheme is used to weight the features for each instance. The original implementation of Wordification only explored the TF-IDF, the term-frequency and the binary weighting schemes. However, works in the text classification and data mining fields show that the proper choice of weighting schemes can boost classification. Therefore, we empirically experimented different term weighting approaches with Wordification. Our results show that the right combination of weighting scheme and classification algorithm can significantly improve classification performance.

**Keywords:** Propositionalization · Relational data mining · Term weighting · Wordification · Classification

## 1 Introduction

A relational data model is used when we desire to not only store attributes of our entities, but also their relationships. In this case, we can apply two strategies to learn from the stored data: apply multi-relational learners or use a propositionalization technique to transform the relational dataset into a single-table representation, and then apply standard propositional learners. In this work, we focus on the latter approach and evaluate a propositionalization method called Wordification [25]. Because Wordification creates much simpler features than other propositionalization techniques, it can achieve greater scalability [25].

© Springer Nature Switzerland AG 2020
D. Kazakov and C. Erten (Eds.): ILP 2019, LNAI 11770, pp. 114–128, 2020.
https://doi.org/10.1007/978-3-030-49210-6_10

Besides, statistical tests showed that the classification performance of Wordification is equivalent to more complex propositionalization techniques, albeit the algorithm being much faster [25].

Wordification uses a weighting scheme to assign numerical values to features according to their relevance [25]. Then the resulting vector can be used as input to propositional learners. In the original Wordification paper [25] only the TF-IDF [31], and two other simpler weighting schemes, the term-frequency (TF) and binary scheme, were used. The term-frequency performs a simple count of each term and the binary (0/1) scheme just indicates the absence or presence of a term in a document. This paper aims to evaluate the Wordification performance using other weighting schemes, which performed better than TF-IDF in information retrieval [23, 27] and text classification scenarios [8, 14, 17].

The rest of this paper is organized as follows. Section 2 describes the background and the related work. Section 3 explains the necessary tools for implementation. Then Sect. 4 presents the experimental results. Lastly, Sect. 5 presents our conclusions.

## 2    Background and Related Work

The study of the impact of different term weighting schemes to a propositionalization approach is not commonly done. Usually, weighting schemes are a subject of information retrieval [30] and text classification [29] fields, while propositionalization is an established approach of Relational Data Mining (RDM) and Inductive Logic Programming (ILP) [10]. Due to the particular behavior of Wordification algorithm, however, we have the opportunity to join these very distinct themes in this work. We provide below an overview of Wordification methodology and the term weighting schemes studied in this paper.

### 2.1    Propositionalization

Propositionalization techniques can transform a relational database into a propositional single-table format. Therefore, the process of learning with a propositionalization technique can be divided into the two following steps: first, the relational data have to be transformed into a single-table dataset; secondly, we apply a propositional learner on the resulting dataset [25].

**Wordification.** Generally, propositionalization algorithms construct complex first-order features [11, 13, 16, 35], which act as binary attributes of the new propositional dataset. Compared to other propositionalization techniques, Wordification generates much simpler features with the aim of achieving greater scalability. It takes as input a relational database and outputs a set of feature vectors, where each vector represents a document in the Bag-of-Words (BOW) [7] vector format.

A relational database can be described as a set of relations $\{R_1, ..., R_n\}$ and a set of foreign-key connections between the relations denoted by $R_i \rightarrow R_j$ [25]. In Fig. 1's diagram, the relations are represented as tables and the arrows are the foreign-keys linking them. Table 1 shows part of the tables of the *Trains* database [19]. The link between these tables is established by the *train* attribute in the *CAR* table, which is referred by *trainID* in the *TRAIN* table.

As a first step of the Wordification, the user has to choose the target table from the database. This table must contain the column with the class labels that will be used later in the classification step. Each row of the target table originates a text document, which is described by a set of words (or features). The features are formed by the combination of the table name, attribute name and its discretized value as shown below:

$$[table\ name]\_[attribute\ name]\_[value]$$

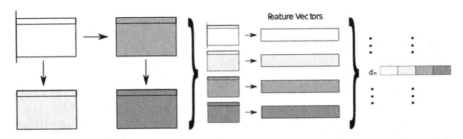

**Fig. 1.** The Wordification process of creating a document $d_n$. The upper-left table is the target table, which is related to the other tables. For each individual entry of the target table one Bag-Of-Words (BOW) vector $d_n$ of weights of "words" is constructed. The "words" correspond to the generated features of the target table and the related tables. Modified from [25].

The features of each document are first generated for the target table and then for each entry from the related tables. Finally, the generated features are joined together according to the relational schema of the database, as illustrated in Fig. 1. Figure 2 shows the generated features for two instances of the *Trains* database. For example, the feature *Cars_Position_1* is created from the join of attribute *Position* with value equal to *1* of table *CAR*.

After generating the documents for every entry of the target table, we assign numerical values to the features of each document using a weighting scheme. The original Wordification paper [25] included the results for three weighting methods: TF-IDF, term-frequency and binary weighting scheme. However, as these different weighting schemes did not perform significantly differently on the classification task, the paper focused on the TF-IDF scheme since this method is prevalent in text mining applications. In order to investigate further the influence of the weighting schemes to the final classification performance, we selected some term

**Table 1.** Example of two related tables before Wordification.

| trainID | direction |
|---------|-----------|
| 1       | east      |
| ...     | ...       |
| 15      | west      |
| ...     | ...       |

(a) Trains table

| carID | train | position | shape | len | sides | roof | wheels | load_shape | load_num |
|-------|-------|----------|-------|-----|-------|------|--------|------------|----------|
| 1 | 1 | 1 | rectangle | short | not_double | none | 2 | circle | 1 |
| 2 | 1 | 2 | rectangle | long | not_double | none | 3 | hexagon | 1 |
| 3 | 1 | 3 | rectangle | short | not_double | peaked | 2 | triangle | 1 |
| 4 | 1 | 4 | rectangle | long | not_double | none | 2 | rectangle | 3 |
| ... | ... | ... | ... | ... | ... | ... | ... | ... | ... |
| 48 | 15 | 1 | rectangle | long | not_double | none | 2 | rectangle | 2 |
| 49 | 15 | 2 | u_shaped | short | not_double | none | 2 | rectangle | 1 |
| ... | ... | ... | ... | ... | ... | ... | ... | ... | ... |

(b) Cars table

!1 Cars_Position_1, Cars_Shape_Rectangle, Cars_Len_Short, Cars_Sides_NotDouble,
Cars_Roof_None Cars_Wheels_2, Cars_LoadShape_Circle, Cars_LoadNum_1,
Cars_Position_2, Cars_Shape_Rectangle, Cars_Len_Long, Cars_Sides_NotDouble,
Cars_Roof_None, Cars_Wheels_3, Cars_LoadShape_Hexagon, Cars_LoadNum_1,
Cars_Position_3, Cars_Shape_Rectangle, Cars_Len_Short, Cars_Sides_NotDouble,
Cars_Roof_Peaked, Cars_Wheels_2, Cars_LoadShape_Triangle, Cars_LoadNum_1,
Cars_Position_4, Cars_Shape_Rectangle, Cars_Len_Long, Cars_Sides_NotDouble,
Cars_Roof_None, Cars_Wheels_2, Cars_LoadShape_Rectangle, Cars_LoadNum_3

!0 Cars_Position_1, Cars_Shape_Rectangle, Cars_Len_Long, Cars_Sides_NotDouble,
Cars_Roof_None, Cars_Wheels_2, Cars_LoadShape_Rectangle, Cars_LoadNum_2,
Cars_Position_2, Cars_Shape_UShaped, Cars_Len_Short, Cars_Sides_NotDouble,
Cars_Roof_None, Cars_Wheels_2, Cars_LoadShape_Rectangle, Cars_LoadNum_1

**Fig. 2.** Example of generated features per instance using *Trains* as the target table. The !1 and !0 at the beginning of the text represents the class positive (east) or negative (west) of the instance.

weighting methods that statistically outperformed TF-IDF [8,14,17,23] and compared the classification performance. The following section presents a detailed description of each weighting scheme used in our experiments, including the TF-IDF.

## 2.2    Term Weighting Schemes

Weighting schemes can be divided into two groups: unsupervised and supervised [9]. In the group of unsupervised weighting schemes, we have the TF-IDF and BM25 algorithms, which come from the information retrieval field. First, they are used to weight the terms and then, a ranking function is computed by summing the assigned weights for each query [26]. On the other hand, the supervised weighting schemes DELTA TF-IDF, TF-RF and CRED-TF-IDF were specially designed to be applied in the text classification field [8,14,17]. They use the available class information of each document in their formula to improve the classification performance [15].

**TF-IDF.** This scheme is often used as a weighting function in information retrieval searches [31]. It is intended to reflect how important a word is to a document in a collection or *corpus*. The TF part is the *term frequency* and is simply a count of how many times a word $w$ appears in a document $d$. If a word appears many times in a document, then that word may be relevant to that document. The IDF, a short for *inverse document frequency*, measures the weight of a term on corpus level. It diminishes the weight of terms that occur very frequently in the corpus $D$ and increases the weight of terms that occur rarely. The TF-IDF measure is defined as follows:

$$tfidf(w,d) = tf(w,d) * log\frac{|D|}{|d \in D : w \in d|} \tag{1}$$

where $|D|$ is the total number of documents in the corpus and $|d \in D : w \in d|$ is the number of documents where the word $w$ appears.

**BM25.** Also known as Okapi BM25 [27], the BM25 is a state-of-the-art term weighting for information retrieval [18]. Its structure is very similar to TF-IDF, however, its term-frequency component is nonlinear. This characteristic is desirable due to the statistical dependence of term occurrences: the information gained on observing a term the first time is greater than the information gained on subsequently seeing the same term. As a result, the term weight saturates after a few occurrences. The IDF calculation is also slightly different as shown below:

$$bm25(w,d) = tf'(w,d) * idf'(w) \tag{2}$$

$$tf'(w,d) = \frac{tf(w,d) * (k_1 + 1)}{tf(w,d) + k_1 * (1 - b + b * \frac{dl}{avgdl})} \tag{3}$$

$$idf'(w) = \frac{|D| - n(w) + 0.5}{n(w) + 0.5} \tag{4}$$

where $dl$ is the length of the document $d$ in words, $avgdl$ is the average document length in the collection, and $n(w)$ is the number of documents containing $w$. The values of the free parameters $k_1$ and $b$ are usually chosen as $k_1 \in [1.2, 2.0]$ and $b \in [0.5, 0.8]$ [26].

**DELTA TF-IDF.** This weighting scheme takes into account the class of each document. It assigns feature values for a document by calculating the difference of the TF-IDF scores of that word in the positive and negative training corpus [17] as shown below:

$$delta.tfidf(w, d) = tf(w, d) * log_2 \frac{|P|}{(P_w + 1)} - tf(w, d) * log_2 \frac{|N|}{(N_w + 1)} \quad (5)$$

where $|P|$ is the number of documents in the positively labeled training set and $P_w$ is the number of documents in the positively labeled training set with word $w$. In the same way, $|N|$ in the number of documents in the negatively labeled training set, and $N_w$ is the number of documents in the negatively labeled training set with word $w$.

**TF-RF.** The TF-RF proposes a substitute to the IDF part in order to improve the term's discriminating power for the text classification field [14]. The TF factor is the same, but the new factor $rf$, the *relevance frequency*, is defined as follow:

$$rf = log_2(2 + \frac{P_w}{N_w + 1}) \quad (6)$$

**CRED-TF-IDF.** The CRED-TF-IDF uses a different *term frequency* factor, which assigns a credibility adjusted score to each word [8]. Let $C_{i,k}$ be the count of word $i$ in class $k$, with $k \in \{-1, 1\}$, and $C_i$ to be the count of words $i$ over both classes. Then, we assign a score to word $i$ as follows:

$$\hat{s}_i = \frac{1}{C_i} \sum_{n=1}^{C_i} \frac{C_{i,k}}{C_i} \quad (7)$$

This $\hat{s}_i$ score is the average likelihood of making the correct classification for a given word $i$ in a document if $i$ was the only word in the document. As we are treating binary classification cases, this reduces to:

$$\hat{s}_i = \frac{C_{i,1}^2 + C_{i,-1}^2}{C_i^2} \quad (8)$$

Now, consider a case where we have two different words $i$ and $j$, for which $\hat{s}_i = \hat{s}_j = 0.75$ and $C_i = 5$ and $C_j = 100$. Intuitively, $\hat{s}_j$ seems a more credible score than $\hat{s}_i$ and $\hat{s}_i$ should be shrunk towards the population mean. Then, the weighted population means $\hat{s}$ is defined as:

$$\hat{s} = \sum_i \frac{C_i * \hat{s}_i}{C} \quad (9)$$

where C in the total count of words in the corpus. Now, based on the Bühlmann credibility adjustment [1] from the actuarial literature, the resulting *credibility adjusted score* for word $i$ is:

$$\overline{s}_i = \frac{C_{i,1}^2 + C_{i,-1}^2 + \hat{s} * \lambda}{C_i^2 + \lambda} \tag{10}$$

where $\lambda$ is an additive smoothing parameter. When $C_{i,1}$ and $C_{i,-1}$ are small, $\overline{s}_i \approx \hat{s}$ (otherwise, $\overline{s}_i \approx \hat{s}_i$) [8]. Finally, the modified *credibility adjusted term frequency* is defined as given by:

$$\overline{tf}_{i,d} = (0.5 + \overline{s}_i) * tf_{i,d} \tag{11}$$

## 3    Implementation

In this section, we present the datasets, platforms, weighting schemes, classifiers and additional configurations used to perform our experiments.

### 3.1    Datasets

We perform the experiments using 13 relational datasets. The datasets *Trains, IMDB, Mutagenesis 188, Mutagenesis 42, Carcinogenesis* and *Financial* were used in the original Wordification paper[1]. We also added to our experiments the *Bupa, Hepatitis, Musk Large, Mask Small, NBA, Pima* and *Facebook* databases[2] [20]. Each instance of these datasets are labelled as positive or negative. Table 2 shows the distribution of instances according to their classes.

### 3.2    Clowdflow

In order to test the weighting schemes, we first need to transform the relational database into a single-table dataset applying the Wordification algorithm. In this step, we used the Clowdflow platform [12], which is an open-source, web-based data mining platform. The Clowdflow offers many widgets to build data mining workflows, including a widget with the Wordification implementation.

Figure 3 shows our workflow. First, we use the *Database Connect* to access a database on a MySQL [22] database server. Then we use the *Database Context* to select the target table and the tables that we will be used in the following steps. The *Dataset Discretization* widget convert continuous attributes of the selected database to categorical, by discretizing the continuous attributes. It supports three discretization methods: equal-width interval, equal-frequency intervals, and class-aware discretization [3]. We use the equi-width discretization, the same used in Wordification paper [25]. Then, the Wordification widget takes as input the target table, the list of additional tables and the database context with information about the relation between tables to generate the features. We save the list of features generated per instance, as shown in Fig. 2, to a text file.

---

[1] Datasets available at http://kt.ijs.si/janez_kranjc/ilp_datasets/.

[2] Datasets available at https://relational.fit.cvut.cz/.

**Table 2.** Class Distributions.

| Database | Positive | Negative |
|----------|----------|----------|
| IMDB | 122 | 44 |
| Trains | 10 | 10 |
| Mutagenesis 188 | 125 | 63 |
| Mutagenesis 42 | 13 | 29 |
| Carcinogenesis | 182 | 147 |
| Financial | 606 | 76 |
| Bupa | 145 | 200 |
| Hepatitis | 294 | 206 |
| Musk Large | 39 | 63 |
| Musk Small | 47 | 45 |
| NBA | 15 | 15 |
| Pima | 268 | 500 |
| Facebook | 206 | 341 |

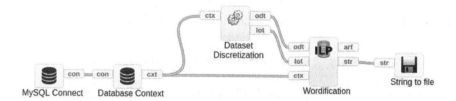

**Fig. 3.** Wordification workflow on Clowdflow.

## 3.3   Term Weighting and Classifiers

In possession of the text file, we use a weighting scheme to weight the features of each instance. Then, we can create the propositional table, where each column is a generated feature of the Wordification algorithm, and each row is a vector of weights that represents an instance of a database. Finally, the resulting table can be used as input to our classifiers, for which we apply the 10-fold cross-validation to estimate the area under the receiver operating characteristic curve (AUC ROC ) [6]. We chose this performance metric because most of our databases are imbalanced, as shown in Table 2. We repeat this process for each combination of dataset, weighting scheme, and classifier.

The BM25 free parameters are set to $k_1 = 1.2$ and $b = 0.75$. For the CRED-TF-IDF, we use the default value of $\lambda = 1$ [8]. Besides, we use Python 3.6 [28] to manipulate the text files and implement the weighting schemes functions. The classifiers are set to the default configurations of SVM with linear kernel, KNN, Random Forest and Decision Tree classifiers from the library scikit-learn [24]. KNN and SVM are justified by its frequent use, in works related to text classification [14,15,34]. The Random Forest and SVM are known to have the best performance among the classifiers [4,36]. Besides, Decision Tree and SVM were the two learners used in the Wordification paper [25].

## 3.4  Statistical Testing

We statistically compare the classification AUC of the Wordification output using different weighting schemes on multiple datasets, separately for each classifier, applying the Friedman test [5] with significance level $\alpha = 0.05$. The Friedman test ranks the algorithms for each dataset and then compares the average rank of the algorithms. If the null hypothesis, which states that all algorithms are equivalent, is rejected, we can proceed with the Nemenyi *post-hoc* test [21] to compare the multiple algorithms to each other. The Nemenyi test performs a pair-wise test of performance. In this case, if the average ranks of the algorithms differ by at least the critical distance (CD), as defined by Demsar [2], we say that the performance of the algorithms is significantly different.

## 4  Experimental Results

The results from the 10-fold cross-validation are shown in Tables 3, 4, 5 and 6.

**Table 3.** Average AUC ROC Scores for Decision Tree.

| Database | TF-IDF | BM25 | DELTA-TF-IDF | TF-RF | CRED-TF-IDF |
|---|---|---|---|---|---|
| IMDB | **0.61** | 0.60 | 0.50 | 0.50 | 0.50 |
| Trains | **0.95** | **0.95** | **0.95** | 0.85 | 0.90 |
| Mutagenesis 188 | **0.93** | 0.92 | 0.92 | **0.93** | 0.92 |
| Mutagenesis 42 | **0.95** | 0.93 | **0.95** | **0.95** | **0.95** |
| Carcinogenesis | 0.50 | 0.52 | **0.57** | 0.53 | 0.52 |
| Financial | **0.61** | **0.61** | **0.61** | **0.61** | **0.61** |
| Bupa | 0.64 | 0.64 | **0.65** | 0.64 | **0.67** |
| Hepatitis | **0.66** | **0.66** | **0.66** | **0.66** | **0.66** |
| Musk Large | 0.57 | **0.63** | 0.55 | 0.59 | 0.55 |
| Musk Small | 0.59 | 0.59 | 0.59 | **0.63** | 0.62 |
| NBA | **0.60** | 0.58 | 0.43 | 0.40 | **0.60** |
| Pima | 0.52 | 0.52 | **0.53** | **0.53** | **0.53** |
| Facebook | 0.94 | 0.94 | 0.94 | 0.94 | **0.95** |

**Table 4.** Average AUC ROC Scores for Random Forest.

| Database | TF-IDF | BM25 | DELTA-TF-IDF | TF-RF | CRED-TF-IDF |
|---|---|---|---|---|---|
| IMDB | **0.58** | **0.58** | 0.46 | 0.54 | 0.57 |
| Trains | 0.75 | **0.90** | 0.80 | **0.90** | 0.80 |
| Mutagenesis 188 | 0.97 | **0.98** | 0.96 | 0.97 | 0.97 |
| Mutagenesis 42 | 0.87 | **1.00** | 0.95 | 0.92 | **1.00** |
| Carcinogenesis | 0.53 | 0.59 | 0.59 | **0.61** | 0.56 |
| Financial | 0.60 | **0.62** | 0.60 | 0.61 | 0.61 |
| Bupa | **0.68** | 0.66 | 0.67 | 0.63 | 0.65 |
| Hepatitis | **0.66** | 0.65 | **0.66** | **0.66** | **0.66** |
| Musk Large | 0.68 | 0.68 | **0.75** | 0.71 | 0.67 |
| Musk Small | 0.63 | 0.69 | 0.61 | **0.71** | 0.67 |
| NBA | 0.61 | 0.56 | **0.63** | 0.39 | 0.56 |
| Pima | 0.64 | 0.62 | 0.65 | **0.67** | 0.64 |
| Facebook | **0.97** | **0.97** | **0.97** | **0.97** | 0.96 |

**Table 5.** Average AUC ROC Scores for SVM.

| Database | TF-IDF | BM25 | DELTA-TF-IDF | TF-RF | CRED-TF-IDF |
|---|---|---|---|---|---|
| IMDB | **0.65** | **0.65** | **0.65** | **0.65** | **0.65** |
| Trains | 0.40 | 0.80 | **0.90** | 0.80 | 0.40 |
| Mutagenesis 188 | 0.93 | 0.95 | 0.96 | **0.97** | 0.93 |
| Mutagenesis 42 | 0.95 | 0.95 | **1.00** | 0.93 | 0.95 |
| Carcinogenesis | 0.60 | 0.61 | **0.62** | 0.61 | 0.60 |
| Financial | **0.61** | 0.45 | 0.54 | 0.44 | 0.55 |
| Bupa | 0.68 | 0.67 | **0.83** | 0.68 | 0.69 |
| Hepatitis | 0.61 | 0.56 | 0.61 | 0.56 | **0.65** |
| Musk Large | 0.76 | 0.81 | **0.92** | 0.76 | 0.84 |
| Musk Small | 0.78 | 0.81 | **1.00** | 0.79 | 0.88 |
| NBA | 0.43 | 0.53 | **0.75** | 0.48 | 0.48 |
| Pima | 0.67 | 0.67 | **0.79** | 0.68 | 0.73 |
| Facebook | 0.95 | 0.92 | 0.96 | **0.97** | 0.95 |

Each row of these tables shows the average AUC ROC score for a given database. Based on these results, we apply the statistical tests to compare the performance of different combinations of weighting schemes and classifiers. Moreover Table 7 summarizes the occurrences of best scores for each combination of classifier and weighting scheme. From this table, we can see that for the Decision Tree, the TF-IDF and CRED-TF-IDF achieved the highest scores in 7 of the 13 databases, while the BM25 and TF-RF scored better in 6 cases for the Random Forest. On the other hand, the DELTA-TF-IDF performed better in 9 and 8 databases, for the SVM and KNN respectively.

**Table 6.** Average AUC ROC Scores for KNN.

| Database | TF-IDF | BM25 | DELTA-TF-IDF | TF-RF | CRED-TF-IDF |
|---|---|---|---|---|---|
| IMDB | 0.57 | 0.58 | 0.50 | 0.50 | **0.61** |
| Trains | 0.50 | 0.90 | 0.85 | **0.95** | 0.45 |
| Mutagenesis 188 | 0.81 | 0.80 | 0.92 | **0.93** | 0.83 |
| Mutagenesis 42 | 0.68 | 0.54 | **0.85** | 0.80 | 0.54 |
| Carcinogenesis | **0.62** | 0.61 | 0.61 | 0.53 | **0.62** |
| Financial | **0.56** | **0.56** | **0.56** | 0.55 | **0.56** |
| Bupa | 0.63 | 0.64 | **0.74** | 0.73 | 0.68 |
| Hepatitis | 0.59 | 0.58 | **0.63** | 0.58 | 0.58 |
| Musk Large | 0.57 | 0.57 | **0.79** | 0.60 | 0.64 |
| Musk Small | 0.60 | 0.64 | **0.83** | 0.64 | 0.63 |
| NBA | 0.54 | 0.50 | 0.66 | 0.33 | **0.69** |
| Pima | 0.63 | 0.64 | **0.69** | 0.67 | 0.68 |
| Facebook | 0.91 | 0.88 | **0.97** | **0.97** | 0.93 |

**Table 7.** Summary of best scores for each combination of classifier and weighting scheme.

| Database | TF-IDF | BM25 | DELTA-TF-IDF | TF-RF | CRED-TF-IDF |
|---|---|---|---|---|---|
| Decision Tree | **7/13** | 4/13 | 6/13 | 6/13 | **7/13** |
| Random Forest | 4/13 | **6/13** | 4/13 | **6/13** | 2/13 |
| SVM | 2/13 | 1/13 | **9/13** | 3/13 | 2/13 |
| KNN | 2/13 | 1/13 | **8/13** | 3/13 | 4/13 |

## 4.1   Decision Tree and Random Forest

For Decision Tree and Random Forest classifiers, the null hypothesis could not be rejected (p-value > 0.05; Decision Tree: 0.255; Random Forest: 0.62). Therefore, the final results are statistically equivalent even if the weighting scheme is changed. This result shows that these classifiers are robust against the choice of weighting schemes.

**Table 8.** Mean rank of Friedman test for Decision Tree and Random Forest classifiers.

| Weighting scheme | Mean rank |
|---|---|
| TF-IDF | 2.92 |
| BM25 | 3.58 |
| DELTA-TF-IDF | 3.35 |
| TF-RF | 2.69 |
| CRED-TF-IDF | **2.46** |

(a) Decision Tree

| Weighting scheme | Mean rank |
|---|---|
| TF-IDF | 3.31 |
| BM25 | **2.58** |
| DELTA-TF-IDF | 3.19 |
| TF-RF | 2.65 |
| CRED-TF-IDF | 3.27 |

(b) Random Forest

Table 8 shows the mean rank for each weighting scheme for the decision tree and random forest classifiers. Although there is not a significant difference in performance, the decision tree classifier achieved a better average rank using the CRED-TF-IDF weighting scheme, while the random forest performed better using the BM25.

## 4.2 SVM and KNN

For both SVM and KNN classifiers, the null hypothesis was successfully rejected (p-value $< 0.05$; SVM $= 0.003$; KNN $= 0.007$). It means that the performance of these classifiers significantly differs according to the choice of weighting scheme. The Table 9 shows that both performed better using the DELTA-TF-IDF weighting scheme.

**Table 9.** Mean rank of Friedman test for SVM and KNN classifiers.

| Weighting scheme | Mean rank |
|---|---|
| TF-IDF | 3.77 |
| BM25 | 3.35 |
| DELTA-TF-IDF | **1.62** |
| TF-RF | 3.35 |
| CRED-TF-IDF | 2.92 |

(a) SVM

| Weighting scheme | Mean rank |
|---|---|
| TF-IDF | 3.65 |
| BM25 | 3.73 |
| DELTA-TF-IDF | **1.73** |
| TF-RF | 3.12 |
| CRED-TF-IDF | 2.77 |

(b) KNN

The results of the Nemenyi test can be visualized compactly with the critical distance diagram. The diagram interconnects the algorithms which performance are statistically equivalent. For the SVM classifier, the diagram in Fig. 4a shows that the performance using DELTA-TF-IDF was significantly better than the performance using the traditional TF-IDF weighting scheme. The Fig. 4b shows that the performance of KNN was significantly better using DELTA-TF-IDF compared to TF-IDF and BM25.

### 4.3   SVM with DELTA-TF-IDF vs Decision Tree with TF-IDF

In the original Wordification paper, the best-reported results were achieved using the weights from TF-IDF as an input of a Decision Tree classifier [25]. On the other hand, our best average results occurred when we used the weights from the DELTA-TF-IDF weighting scheme as an input of an SVM classifier. In order to compare these two configurations, we applied the Wilcoxon signed ranked test [33] using the AUC as the performance metric. This test shows that the results of SVM with DELTA-TF-IDF are significantly better than the Decision Tree with TF-IDF (p-value = 0.0478; $\alpha = 0.05$).

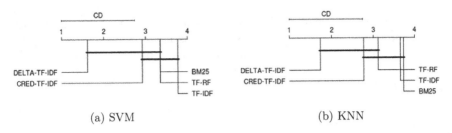

**Fig. 4.** Critical distance diagram for the reported (a) SVM and (b) KNN's classification AUC.

## 5   Conclusions

This paper intended to analyze the impact of changing the weighting schemes of Wordification in the performance of the classification. Our experiments showed that some classifiers, such as Decision Tree and Random Forest, are very robust and are not impacted by the choice of weighting scheme. However, the performance of other classifiers, such as SVM and KNN, can greatly differ according to this choice. SVM and KNN performed significantly better using DELTA-TF-IDF rather than the traditional TF-IDF. We also showed that the use of SVM with the DELTA-TF-IDF weighting scheme can result in better results than the choice of the original proposal of Wordification, where the weights of the features were given by the TF-IDF and were used as input to a Decision Tree classifier. In other words, we can say that the right combination of weighting schemes and the classifier can lead to a significantly different outcome.

**Acknowledgment.** We would like to thank the financial support of the Brazilian Research Agencies CAPES and CNPq, Janez Kranjc for some clarifications regarding Clowdflow, and to all the authors of Wordification for making it available.

# References

1. Bühlmann, H., Gisler, A.: A Course in Credibility Theory and its Applications. Springer, Heidelberg (2006). https://doi.org/10.1007/3-540-29273-X
2. Demšar, J.: Statistical comparisons of classifiers over multiple data sets. J. Mach. Learn. Res. JMLR **7**, 1–30 (2006). http://www.jmlr.org/papers/volume7/demsar06a/demsar06a.pdf
3. Fayyad, U.M., Irani, K.B.: Multi-Interval discretization of Continuous-Valued attributes for classification learning. In: Proceedings of the Conference of International Joint Conferences on Artificial Intelligence (1993). https://www.semanticscholar.org/paper/1dc53b91327cab503acc0ca5afb9155882b717a5
4. Fernández-Delgado, M., Cernadas, E., Barro, S., Amorim, D.: Do we need hundreds of classifiers to solve real world classification problems? J. Mach. Learn. Res. (2014). http://www.jmlr.org/papers/volume15/delgado14a/delgado14a.pdf
5. Friedman, M.: The use of ranks to avoid the assumption of normality implicit in the analysis of variance. J. Am. Stat. Assoc. **32**(200), 675–701 (1937). https://www.tandfonline.com/doi/abs/10.1080/01621459.1937.10503522
6. Hanley, J.A., McNeil, B.J.: The meaning and use of the area under a receiver operating characteristic (ROC) curve. Radiology **143**(1), 29–36 (1982). http://dx.doi.org/10.1148/radiology.143.1.7063747
7. Joulin, A., Grave, E., Bojanowski, P., Mikolov, T.: Bag of tricks for efficient text classification, July 2016. http://arxiv.org/abs/1607.01759
8. Kim, Y., Zhang, O.: Credibility adjusted term frequency: a supervised term weighting scheme for sentiment analysis and text classification. In: Proceedings of the 5th Workshop on Computational Approaches to Subjectivity, Sentiment and Social Media Analysis, May 2014
9. Kołcz, A., Teo, C.H.: Feature weighting for improved classifier robustness. In: CEAS 2009: Sixth Conference on Email and Anti-spam (2009)
10. Kramer, S., Lavrač, N., Flach, P.: Propositionalization approaches to relational data mining. In: Džeroski, S., Lavrač, N. (eds.) Relational Data Mining, pp. 262–291. Springer, Heidelberg (2001), https://doi.org/10.1007/978-3-662-04599-2_11
11. Kramer, S., Pfahringer, B., Helma, C.: Stochastic propositionalization of non-determinate background knowledge. In: Page, D. (ed.) ILP 1998. LNCS, vol. 1446, pp. 80–94. Springer, Heidelberg (1998). https://doi.org/10.1007/BFb0027312
12. Kranjc, J., Podpečan, V., Lavrač, N.: ClowdFlows: A Cloud Based Scientific Workflow Platform. In: Flach, P.A., De Bie, T., Cristianini, N. (eds.) ECML PKDD 2012. LNCS (LNAI), vol. 7524, pp. 816–819. Springer, Heidelberg (2012). https://doi.org/10.1007/978-3-642-33486-3_54
13. Kuželka, O., Železný, F.: Block-wise construction of tree-like relational features with monotone reducibility and redundancy. Mach. Learn. **83**(2), 163–192 (2011). https://doi.org/10.1007/s10994-010-5208-5
14. Lan, M., Tan, C.L., Low, H.B.: Proposing a new term weighting scheme for text categorization. In: AAAI, vol. 6, pp. 763–768 (2006). https://www.aaai.org/Papers/AAAI/2006/AAAI06-121.pdf
15. Lan, M., Tan, C.L., Su, J., Lu, Y.: Supervised and traditional term weighting methods for automatic text categorization. IEEE Trans. Pattern Anal. Mach. Intell. **31**(4), 721–735 (2009). https://doi.org/10.1109/TPAMI.2008.110
16. Lavrač, N., Džeroski, S., Grobelnik, M.: Learning nonrecursive definitions of relations with linus. In: Kodratoff, Y. (ed.) EWSL 1991. LNCS, vol. 482, pp. 265–281. Springer, Heidelberg (1991). https://doi.org/10.1007/BFb0017020

17. Martineau, J.C., Finin, T.: Delta TFIDF: an improved feature space for sentiment analysis. In: Third International AAAI Conference on Weblogs and Social Media (2009). https://www.aaai.org/ocs/index.php/ICWSM/09/paper/viewPaper/187
18. Mirończuk, M.M., Protasiewicz, J.: A recent overview of the state-of-the-art elements of text classification. Expert Systems Appl. **106**, 36–54 (2018). https://doi.org/10.1016/j.eswa.2018.03.058
19. Michie, D., Muggleton, S., Page, D., Srinivasan, A.: To the international computing community: A new East-West challenge. Technical report, Oxford University Computing laboratory, Oxford, UK (1994)
20. Motl, J., Schulte, O.: The ctu prague relational learning repository. arXiv preprint arXiv:1511.03086 (2015)
21. Nemenyi, P.: Distribution-free multiple comparisons. Biometrics **18**, 263 (1962)
22. Oracle Corporation: MySQL (2019). https://www.mysql.com/
23. Paik, J.H.: A novel TF-IDF weighting scheme for effective ranking. In: Proceedings of the 36th International ACM SIGIR Conference on Research and Development in Information Retrieval, pp. 343–352. SIGIR 2013, ACM, New York, NY, USA (2013). http://doi.acm.org/10.1145/2484028.2484070
24. Pedregosa, F., et al.: Scikit-learn: machine learning in Python. J. Mach. Learn. Res. JMLR **12**, 2825–2830 (2011). http://www.jmlr.org/papers/volume12/pedregosa11a/pedregosa11a.pdf
25. Perovšek, M., Vavpetič, A., Kranjc, J., Cestnik, B., Lavrač, N.: Wordification: propositionalization by unfolding relational data into bags of words. Expert Syst. Appl. **42**(17), 6442–6456 (2015). https://doi.org/10.1016/j.eswa.2015.04.017
26. Robertson, S., Zaragoza, H.: The probabilistic relevance framework: BM25 and beyond. Foundations and Trends® in Information Retrieval 3(4), 333–389 (2009). http://dx.doi.org/10.1561/1500000019
27. Robertson, S.E., Walker, S., Jones, S., Hancock-Beaulieu, M.M., Gatford, M.: Others: Okapi at TREC-3. NIST Special Publication **109**, 109 (1995)
28. Sanner, M.F.: Python: a programming language for software integration and development. J. Molecular Graph. Modell. **17**(1), 57–61 (1999). https://www.ncbi.nlm.nih.gov/pubmed/10660911
29. Sebastiani, F.: Machine learning in automated text categorization. ACM Comput. Surv. **34**(1), 1–47 (2002). https://doi.org/10.1145/505282.505283
30. Singhal, A., et al.: Modern information retrieval: a brief overview. IEEE Data Eng. Bull. **24**(4), 35–43 (2001). http://sifaka.cs.uiuc.edu/course/410s12/mir.pdf
31. Sparck Jones, K.: A statistical interpretation of term specificity and its application in retrieval. Journal of Documentation (1972). https://www.emeraldinsight.com/doi/abs/10.1108/eb026526
32. Trotman, A.: Learning to rank. Inf. Retrieval **8**(3), 359–381 (2005). https://doi.org/10.1007/s10791-005-6991-7
33. Wilcoxon, F.: Individual comparisons by ranking methods (1945). http://dx.doi.org/10.2307/3001968
34. Yang, Y., Liu, X., et al.: A re-examination of text categorization methods. In: Sigir. vol. 99, p. 99 (1999). http://people.csail.mit.edu/jim/temp/yang.pdf
35. Železný, F., Lavrač, N.: Propositionalization-based relational subgroup discovery with RSD. Mach. Learn. **62**(1), 33–63 (2006). https://doi.org/10.1007/s10994-006-5834-0
36. Zhang, C., Liu, C., Zhang, X., Almpanidis, G.: An up-to-date comparison of state-of-the-art classification algorithms. Expert Syst. Appl. **82**, 128–150 (2017). https://doi.org/10.1016/j.eswa.2017.04.003

# Learning Probabilistic Logic Programs over Continuous Data

Stefanie Speichert[1]([⊠]) and Vaishak Belle[1,2]

[1] University of Edinburgh, Edinburgh, UK
s.speichert@ed.ac.uk
[2] Alan Turing Institute, London, UK

**Abstract.** The field of statistical relational learning aims at unifying logic and probability to reason and learn from data. Perhaps the most successful paradigm in the field is probabilistic logic programming (PLP): the enabling of stochastic primitives in logic programming. While many systems offer inference capabilities, the more significant challenge is that of learning meaningful and interpretable symbolic representations from data. In that regard, inductive logic programming and related techniques have paved much of the way for the last few decades, but a major limitation of this exciting landscape is that only discrete features and distributions are handled. Many disciplines express phenomena in terms of continuous models.

In this paper, we propose a new computational framework for inducing probabilistic logic programs over continuous and mixed discrete-continuous data. Most significantly, we show how to learn these programs while making no assumption about the true underlying density. Our experiments show the promise of the proposed framework.

## 1 Introduction

The field of statistical relational learning (SRL) aims at unifying logic and probability to reason and learn from relational data. Perhaps the most successful paradigm here is probabilistic (logic) programming (PLP): the enabling of stochastic primitives in (logic) programming, which is now increasingly seen to provide a declarative basis to complex machine learning applications [14, 20].

While many PLP systems offer inference capabilities [4, 14, 31], the more difficult task is that of learning meaningful and interpretable symbolic representations from data. *Parameter learning* attempts to obtain the probabilities of atoms from observational traces (e.g., number of heads observed in a sequence of coin tosses). *Structure learning* goes a step further and attempts to learn deterministic or probabilistic rules (that is, logic programs) from data. In that regard, *inductive logic programming (ILP)* and first-order logic (FOL) rule learning have paved much of the way for the last few decades [13, 32, 38], with important applications for Web and biomedical data [12, 44], among others.

This work is partly supported by the EPSRC grant *Towards Explainable and Robust Statistical AI: A Symbolic Approach.*

© Springer Nature Switzerland AG 2020
D. Kazakov and C. Erten (Eds.): ILP 2019, LNAI 11770, pp. 129–144, 2020.
https://doi.org/10.1007/978-3-030-49210-6_11

A major limitation of this exciting landscape is that only discrete features and distributions are handled. This is somewhat surprising, as many disciplines express phenomena in terms of continuous models. The heart of the matter is that *inference is already very challenging*. Indeed, inference schemes often assume parametric families (e.g., Gaussians) [22, 28], or are approximate offering asymptotic guarantees that only ensure correctness in the limit [33]. The learning of models is analogously restricted, as learning uses inference as a sub-routine [25]. Consequently, there is very little treatment on continuous distributions, both on the inference and learning fronts. (We discuss some notable exceptions in the penultimate section.)

*In this work, we study the problem of parameter and structure learning for PLPs over continuous and mixed discrete-continuous data.* Critically, we will not assume that these distributions are taken from known parametric families. To the best of our knowledge, this is the first such attempt and we hope it will make probabilistic knowledge representation systems more widely applicable for uncertain hybrid data. In particular, we propose a computational framework for inducing probabilistic logic programs over continuous and mixed discrete-continuous data. Rather than needing to define a new learning paradigm, we show that it is possible to leverage existing structure learners by appealing to the formulation of *weighted model integration* (WMI). WMI has been proposed recently as a computational abstraction for inference in discrete-continuous domains [6]. It generalizes *weighted model counting* [9], which is used for inference in ProbLog [18], for example. The resulting system is then a new dialect of the popular PLP language ProbLog [18], which we call *WMIProbLog*. On the one hand, WMIProbLog supports learning with hybrid distributions, and on the other, it enables *efficient exact inference*. We remark that our framework is very general, and could easily be adapted to other PLP languages.

## 2   Framework

Our framework consists of a generic weight and structure learner for hybrid data (i.e., data containing continuous and discrete attributes), to yield weighted hybrid atoms and thus, hybrid programs. As mentioned above, our approach piggybacks on existing structure learners, including techniques for density estimation that impose no restrictions on the true density that generated the data.

Overall, our algorithmic pipeline is as follows:

1. Intervals that best represent the data are constructed and polynomial weights for these intervals are learned, based on algorithms for *basis splines*. Basically, the attributes are split into mutually exclusive intervals. Then, a piecewise polynomial (PP) approximation of the density is learned by the algorithm with the understanding that each piece represents the probability density function (PDF) for that interval. The constructed intervals lead to "invented" predicates.
2. Relations between these atoms are constructed as clauses, subsequently yielding hybrid probabilistic programs. That is, rules to relate the newly invented

atoms are induced by adapting the inputs of two discrete probabilistic FOL rule learners.

3. Finally, the atoms, weights and rules are combined in a PLP language equipped with exact inference via WMI, which we call *WMIProbLog*. Exact inference is made possible by means of the PP representation, which admits efficient integration [3]. This is a major contribution in itself because most SRL languages with continuous distributions only support approximate inference over weak asymptotic guarantees [34].

The organization of the paper is as follows. We discuss the technical background for realizing the above steps, before turning to empirical evaluations, related work and conclusions.

## 2.1  Learning Weighted Atoms

We present a fully *unsupervised approach* to jointly learn intervals and their piecewise polynomial approximate densities from data. Our objective is defined as follows:

**Definition 1 (Weighted Atom Construction).** *Given:*

1. *a finite set of numeric data points $E = \{x_1, ..., x_n\}$ where $t(x_j)$ is a ground fact for the predicate $t$.[1]*
2. *A partition scheme $E_1, ..., E_l$ that partitions $E$ into $l$ parts where $\cup_i E_i = E$, $E_i \cap E_j = \emptyset$ and $E_i \subseteq E$.*
3. *An unknown distribution for each partition $i$, that is, $f_i : E_i \to \mathbb{R}_{\geq 0}$ such that $\sum_{i=1}^{l} \int_{E_i} f_i = 1$.*
4. *A hypothesis space $\mathbf{H}$ that consists of piecewise polynomials where $H \in \mathbf{H}$ is of the form $\langle h_1, ... h_l \rangle$, such that $\sum_{i=1}^{l} \int_{E_i} h_i = 1$.*
5. *A loss function measuring the loss/granularity tradeoff for a candidate density-estimator $h_i$: $loss(h_i, f_i)$ for each $i$.[2]*

**Find:** *A hypothesis $H$ such that $loss(f_i, h_i)$ is minimized for each $i$.*

The goal of this learner is to find an optimal piecewise polynomial density estimation that is as close to the unknown underlying distribution as possible. As a result, we obtain new weighted atoms of the form: $h_i :: t\_i(X) \leftarrow t(X), E_i(X)$ for each $i$. For example, we might learn the following for the `height(X)` predicate over the $[60, 91]$ region: $X^2/3 :: \text{height\_60\_91}(X) \leftarrow \text{height}(X), X \in [60, 91]$. This says that the atoms whose groundings lay between 60 and 91 such as `height_60_91(60.4)` have a probabilistic density given by the polynomial $X^2/3$. We provide an algorithm that induces such weighted predicates. It involves two steps: *partitioning* and *density estimation*.

---

[1] Imagine, for example, the predicate `height(X)` with examples such as `height(60.4)`, ..., `height(91.1)`, ..., `height(124.6)`.

[2] That is, we may want to penalise very granular representations that are defined over a large number of intervals and polynomials of a high degree. So, we would like to minimise the loss, but prefer simpler representations over granular ones.

**Step 1: Partitioning.** Partitioning refers to dividing the range of a continuous variable into $l$ mutually exclusive intervals according to selected criteria. Our motivation is to capture complex continuous data by offloading the continuity to the weight functions so as to yield meaningful hybrid atoms. Suppose $X$ is a real-valued variable – logically, think of the argument in $height(X)$ – and suppose $x_{min}, \ldots, x_{max}$ are the data points we observe. Partitioning yields $I = \{E_1, ..., E_l\}$ with $E_i = [c_{i-1}, c_i]$. The set of cutpoints $C = \{c_0, ..., c_l\}$ determine the interval such that $c_{i-1} < c_i$, $i \in \{1, ..., l\}$, $c_0 = x_{min}$ and $c_l = x_{max}$. The partiton step, therefore, defines intervals over the domain $\Omega = [x_{min}, x_{max}]$.

To restrict the interval search we chose to limit ourselves to two simple but effective schemes: *equal-width* and *equal-frequency* binning [16]. Both methods are regulated by the same parameter $l$ that determines the number of bins that is considered by the algorithm.

**Step 2: Density Estimation.** To enable exact inference over hybrid queries, we choose piecewise polynomial functions to approximate the density. The main advantage is that such PP densities can be learned from data without *any* prior information about the density while still capturing the true density very closely [46]. This section introduces the problem of approximating densities through PPs and shows how to learn the weighted atoms from data.

**Definition 2.** *A piecewise function over a real-valued variable $x$ is defined over $l$ pieces as:*

$$
\delta(X) = \begin{cases} 0 & x < c_0 \\ \delta_1(x) & c_0 \leq x \leq c_1 \\ \ldots \\ \delta_l(x) & c_{l-1} \leq x \leq c_l \\ 0 & x > c_l \end{cases}
$$

*where the intervals (expressed using cutpoints) are mutually exclusive, and each $\delta_i(x)$ is a polynomial with the same maximum polynomial order $k$ of the form: $\delta_i(x) = b_0^i + b_1^i * x + \ldots + b_k^i * x^k$. In order for $\delta(x)$ to form a valid density, the function must be non-negative and integrate to 1: $\sum_{i=1}^{l} \int_{c_{i-1}}^{c_i} \delta_i(x) dx = 1$.*

Our overall objective is to learn PP weights for each of the intervals. That is, suppose $f : \mathbb{R} \rightarrow \mathbb{R}_+$ is the density of an unknown distribution. We would like to find a candidate PP hypothesis $h$, defined over $l$ intervals such that the polynomial for each interval is of degree at most $d$. Let $P_{l,d}$ be the class of $l$-piecewise degree-$d$ polynomials. Then, we wish to find $m$ hypotheses $h_i^1, ..., h_i^m \in P_{l,d}$ for each interval $i$ and then select one that maximises the likelihood of the observed data. Since we also do not know the optimal degree to choose from, we let the same likelihood criterion also determine the best degree. For this, we leverage known techniques for learning polynomials [29] based on *basis splines* (B-Splines) [11]. B-Splines form a basis in the piecewise polynomial space. By considering linear combinations of splines, more complex polynomials can be obtained. The combination is adjusted by a set of mixing coefficients. By imposing constraints on these coefficients, polynomials can form a (valid) density: they are continuous, non-negative, differentiable and integrate to 1.

The parameters, the degree of the polynomial $d$ and the number of pieces $l$ are estimated by the Bayesian information criterion [29, 45]:

$$BIC(x, \delta(x)) = \mathcal{L}(x \mid \delta(x)) - \frac{log(|X|)}{2}$$

where $\mathcal{L}$ denotes the log-likelihood measure. The BIC score is known to be robust and avoids overfitting the model parameters. Moreover, in our empirical results, it was seen to favor smaller polynomial ranks which achieve the desired loss/granularity tradeoff discussed earlier.

Our algorithm is as follows:

1. **Input:** data points for real-valued variable $X$, and user-specified values for maximum number of intervals allowed ($maxSize = 40$), and maximum degree for polynomials allowed ($maxOrder = 9$).
2. Sort the points for $X$ in ascending order, initialize $B$ (the *best BIC score*) to $-\infty$, and $S$ (the *best polynomial structure*) to {}.
3. Loop the following steps for $2 \leq l \leq maxSize$ intervals.
4. Loop the following steps for partition choices $d \in \{equal\ width,\ equal\ frequency\}$.
5. Obtain cutpoint set $C$ from $(X, d)$.
6. Loop the following steps for polynomial degree $1 \leq k \leq maxOrder$.
7. Define temporary variables $s$ and $b$, the former containing a PP derived from $(C, k)$, and the latter the BIC score derived from $s$.
8. If $b$ exceeds $B$, then let $B = b$, and $S = s$.
9. Return to (6) with the next iteration of $k$ until completion, following which return to (4) with the next iteration of $d$ until completion, following which return to (3) with the next iteration of $l$ until completion.
10. **Output:** $(S, B)$.

**Theorem 1.** *The above algorithm realises Definition 1 with BIC measuring the loss and a PP hypothesis space defined over B-Splines.*

## 2.2   Learning Rules

We now move beyond simply learning weighted atoms to learning complex dependencies between subspaces in a mixed discrete-continuous setting, that is, probabilistic rules for the hybrid atoms. For this purpose, we leverage first-order relational rule learners. The basic idea is to augment the original dataset that uses continuous variables (such as `height(X)`) together with instances of the invented predicates (such as `height_low(X)`, standing for values in the lower range), as determined by the partitioning.

At this stage, there are multiple choices for rule learning. In the simplest setting, we ignore the learned densities and perform rule learning for one or many target predicate(s). In a more advanced setting, we integrate the rule learner directly into the pipeline, giving it not only the predicate but also the learned probabilities as input. Both schemes are considered in the literature. For example, [13] develop a case where parameters and the structure are optimized jointly. In contrast, [44] apply a deterministic rule-learner in a deterministic setting, and the weights are then obtained in a second step. In this section, we explore both settings as an illustration of our framework's generality.

**Definition 3 (Rule Learning with Hybrid Atoms).** *Given:*

1. *(a) a set of examples E, consisting of pairs $(x_i, p_i)$ where $x_i$ is a ground fact for the invented predicate t and $p_i$ is the integrated target probability; or*
   *(b) a set of examples E consisting of $\{x_1, ..., x_n\}$ where $x_i$ is a ground fact for the invented predicate t.*
2. *A background theory B containing information about the examples in the form of a ProbLog program;*
3. *A loss function loss(H, B, E), measuring the loss of a hypothesis (set of clauses) H w.r.t B and E;*
4. *A space of possible clauses $L_h$ specified using a declarative bias;*

***Find:*** *A hypothesis $H \subseteq L_H$ such that $H = arg\ min_H\ loss(H, B, E)$.*

In other words, (1) partitions an attribute into its pieces and adds each piece as an atom. The two cases decide whether the integrated probability is passed to the rule learner (e.g. 0.31 :: `height_low(X)`) or not (e.g. `height_low(X)`). Then, (2)–(4) realise standard first-order rule learning with the addition that rules (may) have a probability assigned to them. The loss function is, of course, determined by the rule learner itself. ProbFOIL+'s loss function, for example, is based on the error of predictions:

$$loss(H, B, E) = \sum_{x_i, p_i \in E} |P_s(H \cup B \models x_i) - p_i|$$

To compute probabilities for the first case we need to integrate the pieces over their respective polynomial. For each clause $c_i$ and each piecewise polynomial density $\delta_i(x)$ over cutpoints the integral is calculated as $[c_{i-1}, c_i]$, $i \in \{1, ..., l\}$: $p_i = \int_{c_{i-1}}^{c_i} \delta_i(x)dx$ where $p_i$ is a constant that denotes the probability over the interval $[c_{i-1}, c_i]$. The hybrid atom is now transformed into a discrete atom with a probability mass, that is, $p_i :: t\_i(X)$. This is then used instead of the polynomial, and analogously, such a transformation is applied to all invented predicates.

Once the weights are computed any discrete FOL rule learner can be used to induce the rules. We utilize ProbFOIL+ [13] and SLIPCOVER [8] for the case of probabilistic facts versus not. It should be clear that our architecture does not hinge on either learner and indeed, ProbFOIL+ also handles the case of non-probabilistic facts. Our choices are to be seen as illustrative of the generality of the framework. We immediately also get the following.

**Theorem 2.** *The algorithmic scheme described above realises both versions of Definition 3.*

*Proof.* It is immediate to see that by integrating the polynomials, we obtain standard probabilistic atoms of the form $p_i :: c_i$, where $p_i$ is a number and $c_i$ is an atom. It now follows that ProbFOIL+ (and SLIPCOVER respectively) performs rule induction over probabilistic examples (and non-probabilistic examples respectively) wrt to the appropriate loss function. ☐

As a final step, a WMIProbLog program (discussed in the following section) is obtained that combines the individual relations, their polynomial weights and the rules.

## 3 WMIProbLog

Learning rich representations is only appealing when it is also possible to efficiently query those representations. In particular, PLPs are particularly useful for computing conditional queries against structured models. Our learning regime culminates in the synthesis of WMIProbLog programs, a dialect of ProbLog and Hybrid ProbLog [21], the latter being a generalisation of ProbLog to continuous distributions in parametric forms. Hybrid ProbLog provides an inference scheme based on interval propagation and dynamic discretisation. WMIProbLog supports a generic (that is, applies to any density function approximated in PP form) and efficient exact inference methodology via WMI, and as will be discussed below, it does not involve any discretisation or rewriting of the program.

Syntactically, ProbLog vs Hybrid ProbLog vs WMIProbLog can be contrasted as follows. Consider a simple mixture model in ProbLog, where a biased coin toss yields either a 50% chance of success or a 25% chance of success:

```
0.7::heads. 0.5::a. 0.25::b.
tails :- \+heads.
mix :- heads, a.
mix :- tails, b.
```

To model the chance of success as continuous random variables in Hybrid ProbLog, we might change the corresponding clauses to:

```
(X,uniform(0,10))::a(X).
(X,uniform(0,20))::b(X).
mix(X) :- heads, a(X).
mix(X) :- tails, b(X).
```

In WMIProbLog, in line with our previous sections, those continuous variables over, say, polynomials of degree 0 (chosen for ease of presentation, although they can be of arbitrary degree in general) would be:

```
0.1::a(X) :- between(0,10,X).
0.05::b(X) :- between(0,20,X).
```

Querying for mix in the first, and for mix_chance:

```
mix_chance :- mix(X), between(0,5,X).
```

in the other programs yields .425, for example.

The semantics of Hybrid ProbLog and WMIProbLog is given by probability distributions over subsets of the facts and values for the numeric variables in the continuous facts, much like in ProbLog, except that these values may be drawn from an uncountable set. (See [21] for details.) But what is perhaps most interesting about WMIProbLog is that, on the one hand, it is simply a syntactic variant of the Hybrid ProbLog program in which continuous functions are not necessarily parametric, but on the other, by integrating probabilities as shown earlier, it is also a well-defined ProbLog program.

**Theorem 3.** *Given any WMIProbLog program $\Delta$ there is a syntactically well-defined ProbLog program $\Delta^-$ such that for all $q, e \in \Delta^-$, marginalization and probabilistic querying have the same values in $\Delta$ and $\Delta^-$.*

*Proof.* As in the previous theorem, we simply integrate the polynomials to obtain classic ProbLog probabilistic facts. Clearly, as the query and evidence atoms only refer to these *abstracted* facts, the values for marginalisation and conditional querying will be the same.                                        □

We write $q, e \in \Delta^-$ to mean that the query and evidence atoms only refer to the *abstract program* $\Delta^-$, where continuous atoms involving intervals and polynomials and replaced with integrated probabilities. This idea, of abstracting continuous features is at the very heart of WMI [6]. However, such a strategy would only allow the most trivial conditional probability computations in general (e.g., probability of mix given that heads), and would not be able to handle queries like mix_chance. Following Hybrid ProbLog, one approach would be to syntactically rewrite the program (or dynamically discretise at computation time), so as to involve every interval mentioned in a query in a well-defined manner; e.g., split the definition of $a(X)$ as:

```
.1::a(X) :- between(0,5,X).
.1::a(X) :- between(5,10,X).
```

Such a strategy is acceptable formally but can be seen to be a painful exercise. So, the next observation to make is that if the weights are dropped, we also immediately have a syntactically well-defined ProbLog (and Prolog) program: Given any WMIProbLog program $\Delta$ there is a syntactically well-defined ProbLog program $\Delta^*$ that is obtained by dropping all the (polynomial and numeric) weights.

What is the advantage of the reduction? To see this, consider that from a computational perspective, the ProbLog engine proceeds by grounding the input program and queries, breaking loops if necessary, to ultimately yield a propositional formula [18]. That formula is then compiled to a data structure such as a BDD or d-DNNF [10]. It is clearly useful to leverage that pipeline.

For example, contrast the BDD (below) obtained for the query `mix(X)`, with the one obtained for a query that uses intervals not explicitly mentioned in the original program (Fig. 1):

```
a_half :- a(X), between(0,5,X).
query(a_half).
```

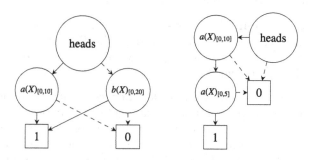

**Fig. 1.** Proofs of the query in BDD form.

So the only aspect that is needed to be resolved is the computation involving the densities and weights. This becomes possible because ProbLog's computational architecture is immediately generalisable to any commutative semiring [23].[3] (For example, polynomials with natural number coefficients form a commutative semiring.) So the densities can be thought of as abstract elements of a semiring, which can then be symbolically integrated. For example, `query(a_half)` would be computed: $\int_0^{10} .1 \cdot \mathbb{I}_{[0,5]}(x) dx = \int_0^5 .1 dx = .5$. Correspondingly, the probability for `mix_chance` can be computed as: $\int_0^{10} .1 \cdot \mathbb{I}_{[0,5]}(x) \cdot .6 dx + \int_0^{20} .05 \cdot \mathbb{I}_{[0,5]}(x) \cdot .4 = .425$.

## 4  Empirical Evaluations

We now evaluate our framework in this section. We reiterate that, *to the best of our knowledge, this is the first attempt to articulate a compositional PLP framework for arbitrarily complex distributions from continuous data.* Thus, our goal was to study the empirical behaviour of the implemented framework on various representational aspects to illustrate its capabilities.

### 4.1  Datasets

To carefully monitor the quality of the learned models, we mainly utilized the *University data set* [19,41]. Beyond this, we considered many more hybrid

---

[3] In an independent and recent effort, Martires et al. [30] have also considered the use of semirings to do WMI inference over propositional circuits.

datasets from the UCI repository [15]. The datasets capture domains ranging from health care to marketing, but not all of them are of the same quality. Some, especially *Anneal-U* and *CRX* contain many missing values. Some others contain duplicate entries.

### 4.2  Learning Representations

**On Piecewise Polynomials.** This section discusses our observations for the piecewise polynomial representation learning. The BIC score determined the model parameters such as the order of polynomials and bins. Table 1 lists statistics for the UCI datasets, which we contextualise further below.

**Q1: How does the polynomial learner compare to other density estimators?** We compared the polynomial learner to Gaussian mixture models (GMM), which is the current state-of-the-art for density estimation, by appealing to KL divergence in a controlled experiment. (Unimodal Gaussians are used by most PLPs, e.g, [35].) For the GMM learner, we use the one from Python *sklearn*, which also uses the BIC score as a model selection criterion. As polynomial densities are only defined in $\Omega = [cp_0, cp_l]$ the GMMs need to be normalised for a direct comparison. They are multiplied by a normalisation constant $1/\int_\Omega f(x)dx$.

As it is not feasible to calculate the KL divergence directly for GMMs we chose a sample size of $10^6$ for a sampling-based approximation. This is calculated as: $KL = \int_\Omega p(x) \log \frac{p(x)}{q(x)} dx \approx \frac{1}{N} \sum_{i=1}^{N} \log \frac{p(x_i)}{q(x_i)}$ where $x_1, ..., x_n \sim p(x)$. We compared different types of distributions and sample sizes. The distributions were generated randomly. Not surprisingly, the polynomial learner performs gradually better than the GMMs as the true distribution gets less similar to a mixture of Gaussians (see Table 2). What is perhaps more interesting is

**Table 1.** Statistics on UCI datsets and the polynomial learning component. It shows (in order) the number of training examples, the number of the continuous attributes (number of all attributes in brackets) the number of created bins separately learned for each attribute and then averaged over the number of features in the dataset (brackets show number when including missing values) and the maximum order learned.

| Dataset | Train | # C | # Bins | O |
|---|---|---|---|---|
| Anneal-U | 673 | 6 (39) | 10.7 (19) | 2 |
| Australian | 517 | 5 (15) | 7.5 (7.5) | 6 |
| Auto | 119 | 15 (26) | 6.7 (8.7) | 3 |
| Car | 294 | 6 (9) | 7 (9.2) | 4 |
| Crx | 488 | 6 (16) | 5.8 (11.7) | 4 |
| Diabetes | 576 | 7 (21) | 4.6 (9.1) | 4 |
| German | 750 | 3 (9) | 6.9 (6) | 7 |
| German-org | 750 | 3 (25) | 9.1 (6.3) | 7 |
| Iris | 112 | 4 (5) | 3.75 (3.75) | 3 |

**Table 2.** Approximation comparison of different distributions in terms of KL divergence. Here, $n$ denotes the sample size and $T$ the model type. Abbreviations: Gaussian Mixture Model estimation (G) and Piecewise Polynomial density estimation (P). We tested distributions following Exponential, Gaussian and Mixture of Gaussian with 2 (MoG-2) and 5 (MoG-5) components.

| n | T | Expon | Gauss | MoG-2 | MoG-5 |
|---|---|---|---|---|---|
| 100 | G | 0.10409 | 0.01028 | **0.00308** | 0.12795 |
|  | P | **0.01254** | **0.00300** | 0.05699 | **0.05701** |
| 1000 | G | 0.03633 | **0.00123** | **0.00335** | 0.01550 |
|  | P | **0.00860** | 0.00228 | 0.00830 | **0.01295** |
| 10000 | G | 0.02959 | **0.00001** | **0.00083** | 0.01142 |
|  | P | **0.00147** | 0.00045 | 0.00125 | **0.00419** |

how well the PP learner estimates Gaussians. For small sample sizes, the polynomial learner still outperforms GMMs when approximating a unimodal Gaussian. When estimating a more complex distribution such as a mixture of five Gaussian our learner fully outperforms the GMM learner even though the underlying distribution is a mixture of Gaussians. This is mainly because the BIC in combination with polynomial density can (a) handle small sample sizes, and (b) not be forced to determine the appropriate number of components for these samples. This shows that the learner generalises well even with small sample sizes thereby avoiding overfitting.

**Q2: Which trends in parameter learning can be observed for ...**
**Q2.1: ... the order?**

The order of the polynomials in the learned models stayed relatively low in a range from 2 to 5. In fact, only three attributes over all UCI datasets learned an order that was higher than 5 but never higher than 7 (see Table 1). The few outliers occurred when an attribute contained a high number of missing values. Naturally, low order polynomials are computationally simpler to integrate during inference.

**Q2.2: ... the number of intervals?**

The appropriate number of intervals to approximate a PDF increases with its non-uniformity, the unimodal Gaussian only needed 3 pieces, whereas the 5 Gaussian Mixture needed 6 or more (depending on the sample size). Furthermore, to achieve a close approximation, the cutpoints have to span the entire range of attribute values which is why our algorithm often preferred equal frequency over equal width partitions.

We also observed that the BIC is sensitive to the number of attribute instances. For under 100 data points, the smallest partition and order was often chosen (cf. Table 1). This observation helps to explain the behaviour when missing values are observed. If a dataset contained missing values, we filtered them out in a preprocessing step leading to less samples for the attribute so as to not skew the learner. However, our observations indicate that even though more values achieve a higher score, the smaller representation is still able to generalise well.

## 4.3   Rule Learning

Here, we report on how the invented predicates integrated with the discrete rule learners.

**Table 3.** Example rules learned by ProbFOIL+ (above horizontal line) and SLIP-COVER (below line) for the target `grade_high(A,B)`. Below these a sample predicate is shown, the polynomial is given as a weight before the rule head `iq_1(A,X)` and the body of the rule determines the interval start and end points where the polynomial density holds.

```
grade_high(A,B) :- sat_low(A,B), \+diff_hard(B), \+iq_1(A,X).
grade_high(A,B) :- takes(A,B), \+diff_hard(B).
grade_high(A,B) :- nrhours_4(B,Y), iq_1(A,X).
grade_high(A,B) :- nrhours_4(B,Y), course(B).
grade_high(A,B) :- sat_low(A,B)
```

```
0.056367 -0.001598* X + 1.25739e-05 * X ^ 2 ::
iq_1(A,X):-iq(A,X),between(52.6,103.4,X)
```

**Q3: How do the invented predicates interact with the rule learners?** The idea behind these invented predicates is to capture continuous data in terms of PP density approximations, which are ultimately adapted to the input format of the rule learners. Table 3 shows an example. The invented predicates are distinguished by the underscores followed by numbers. In the case of the `iq` predicate, higher number indicate higher values. The grade of a course being influenced by a student's intelligence is clearly intuitive: a student either gets a high grade if their intelligence is not low (rule 1) or if they have low intelligence and put in a lot of hours of study (rule 3), and so, the rules provide a logical way to make sense of dependencies between subspaces in a mixed discrete-continuous settings. We further see in Table 4 that the rule accuracy is not affected over larger domains, which is clearly desirable.

**Table 4.** Statistics for the predicates `grade_high`, `grade_mid`, `grade_low` for the two rule learners (L): SLIPCOVER (S) and ProbFOIL+ (P). Comparisons are drawn in terms of area under the precision/recall curve (AUCPR), area under the ROC curve (AUCROC), the number of rules in a theory (Th) and the average number of literals per rule for a theory (Pr).

| grade | L | AUCPR | AUCROC | Th | Pr |
|-------|---|-------|--------|----|----|
| high | S | 0.249906564 | 0.750555262 | 8 | 1.375 |
|      | P | **0.381490547** | **0.935926625** | 2 | 2.5 |
| mid | S | **0.404951538** | **0.940245155** | 7 | 1 |
|     | P | 0.3914379 | 0.936826911 | 2 | 2 |
| low | S | 0.152929751 | **0.813107006** | 10 | 1.4 |
|     | P | **0.166327753** | 0.654570657 | 1 | 3 |

**Q4: How do the rule learners compare?** As can be seen in Table 4, our setting is not necessarily indicative of any general trend for the two rule learners, but we did see, for example, that SLIPCOVER rules are shorter than ones learned via ProbFOIL+, on average. In terms of standard measures, we found both to be sufficient for inducing reasonable programs.

**Q5: How efficient is the query engine?** In order to test the efficiency of our inference engine over large programs, we generated 100 random continuous features and tested the query computation time. We fixed the number of bins to 2, 5, 10 and 15 in order to study the computation time. The query length, e.g. the number of terms in the query was set to 5, 10, 20, 50 and 100. The results are shown in Table 5. As can be seen, the system scales linearly with increasing sizes, which is desirable.

**Table 5.** Query execution time in seconds. P denotes the number of pieces of the underlying attributes, and t the amount of terms in the query.

| P | $t = 5$ | $t = 10$ | $t = 20$ | $t = 50$ | $t = 100$ |
|---|---------|----------|----------|----------|-----------|
| 2 | 0.9514 | 1.0506 | 1.2817 | 2.1540 | 4.0185 |
| 5 | 1.2804 | 1.4325 | 1.6293 | 2.5331 | 4.3767 |
| 10 | 1.4885 | 1.5773 | 1.8441 | 2.7239 | 4.6914 |
| 15 | 1.8313 | 1.9621 | 2.2031 | 3.1954 | 5.1372 |

## 5    Related Work

Inference and learning in probabilistic systems are the most fundamental problems in uncertainty reasoning within AI, to which our work here contributes. There is an important distinction to be made between graphical models (including relational counterparts such as Markov logic networks [42]) and the inductive logic programming machinery that we use here, the latter based on logical deduction and proof theory. A comprehensive discussion on the semantic subtleties would be out of scope, and orthogonal to the main thrust of the paper. We refer interested readers to the lineage discussion in [13,39], and the possible worlds perspective in [43]. Indeed, our fundamental contributions include the dynamic interval and the polynomial density construction, all of which can perhaps be easily applied to other formalisms. (Naturally, the choice of the underlying induction paradigm may affect the nature and interpretability of the rules learned.)

From an inference viewpoint, much of the literature is focused on discrete random variables for which approaches such as model counting and bucket elimination have strong runtime bounds [9,37]. In contrast, WMI serves as a computational abstraction for exact and approximate inference in hybrid domains [5,6] based on piecewise polynomial approximations. It is thus different in spirit to variational methods and analytic closed-form solutions for parametric families. We refer the reader to [6] for discussions.

On the learning front, several feature and structure induction techniques have been proposed primarily for discrete data (or discretised models of continuous data). Indeed, learning relational features from data is very popular in NLP and related areas [40,44]. Rule learning has been studied in many forms, e.g., [17,26].

We leverage ProbFOIL+ and SLIPCOVER in this paper. ProbFOIL+ is based on the mFOIL rule learner [17]. Later work, such as nFOIL [26] integrates FOIL with Bayesian learning, and kFOIL [27] admits the specification of kernel methods with FOIL. Early versions of Markov logic network structure learning algorithms, for example, combined ideas from ILP and stochastic greedy search from classical graphical modelling communities [24]. Approaches such as [2,36] have further applied rule learning to complex applications such as automated planning and affordances. SLIPCOVER, on the other hand, is based on SLIP-CASE [7]. In general, the structure is learned through an iterative search through the clause space.

Treating continuous and hybrid data in such contexts, however, is rare. Existing inference schemes for hybrid data are either approximate, e.g., [1,33], or make restrictive assumptions about the distribution family (e.g., Gaussian potentials [28]). Structure learning schemes, consequently, inherit these limitations, e.g., [35,41] where they learn rules by assuming Gaussian base atoms.

## 6    Conclusions

To the best of our knowledge, this is the first attempt to articulate a learning regime for inducing PLPs from continuous data. It contributes an algorithmic framework that learns piecewise polynomial representations which are then integrated with rule learning to obtain probabilistic logic programs, along with effective symbolic inference. In our view, this work takes a major step towards the difficult challenge of inducing representations from data, especially continuous and mixed discrete-continuous data. In the long term, we hope the declarative/interpretability aspect of our proposal will prove useful when reasoning and learning over uncertain hybrid data.

## References

1. Alberti, M., Bellodi, E., Cota, G., Riguzzi, F., Zese, R.: cplint on SWISH: probabilistic logical inference with a web browser. Intell. Arti. **11**(1), 47–64 (2017)
2. Antanas, L., Frasconi, P., Costa, F., Tuytelaars, T., De Raedt, L.: A relational kernel-based framework for hierarchical image understanding. In: Gimel'farb, G., et al. (eds.) SSPR /SPR 2012. LNCS, vol. 7626, pp. 171–180. Springer, Heidelberg (2012). https://doi.org/10.1007/978-3-642-34166-3_19
3. Baldoni, V., Berline, N., De Loera, J., Köppe, M., Vergne, M.: How to integrate a polynomial over a simplex. Math. Comput. **80**(273), 297–325 (2011)
4. Baral, C., Gelfond, M., Rushton, J.N.: Probabilistic reasoning with answer sets. TPLP **9**(1), 57–144 (2009)
5. Belle, V., Van den Broeck, G., Passerini, A.: Hashing-based approximate probabilistic inference in hybrid domains. In: UAI (2015)

6. Belle, V., Passerini, A., Van den Broeck, G.: Probabilistic inference in hybrid domains by weighted model integration. In: Proceedings of 24th International Joint Conference on Artificial Intelligence (IJCAI), pp. 2770–2776 (2015)

7. Bellodi, E., Riguzzi, F.: Learning the structure of probabilistic logic programs. In: Muggleton, S.H., Tamaddoni-Nezhad, A., Lisi, F.A. (eds.) ILP 2011. LNCS (LNAI), vol. 7207, pp. 61–75. Springer, Heidelberg (2012). https://doi.org/10.1007/978-3-642-31951-8_10

8. Bellodi, E., Riguzzi, F.: Structure learning of probabilistic logic programs by searching the clause space. Theory Pract. Logic Program. **15**(2), 169–212 (2015)

9. Chavira, M., Darwiche, A.: On probabilistic inference by weighted model counting. Artif. Intell. **172**(6–7), 772–799 (2008)

10. Darwiche, A., Marquis, P.: A knowledge compilation map. J. Artif. Intell. Res. **17**, 229–264 (2002)

11. De Boor, C., De Boor, C., Mathématicien, E.U., De Boor, C., De Boor, C.: A practical guide to splines, vol. 27. Springer, New York (1978)

12. De Maeyer, D., Renkens, J., Cloots, L., De Raedt, L., Marchal, K.: Phenetic: network-based interpretation of unstructured gene lists in E. coli. Mol. BioSyst. **9**(7), 1594–1603 (2013)

13. De Raedt, L., Dries, A., Thon, I., Van den Broeck, G., Verbeke, M.: Inducing probabilistic relational rules from probabilistic examples. In: Proceedings of 24th International Joint Conference on Artificial Intelligence (IJCAI), pp. 1835–1842 (2015)

14. De Raedt, L., Kimmig, A.: Probabilistic (logic) programming concepts. Mach. Learn. **100**(1), 5–47 (2015). https://doi.org/10.1007/s10994-015-5494-z

15. Dheeru, D., Karra Taniskidou, E.: UCI machine learning repository (2017). http://archive.ics.uci.edu/ml

16. Dougherty, J., Kohavi, R., Sahami, M., et al.: Supervised and unsupervised discretization of continuous features. In: Machine Learning: Proceedings of the Twelfth International Conference, vol. 12, pp. 194–202 (1995)

17. Džeroski, S., Cestnik, B., Petrovski, I.: Using the m-estimate in rule induction. J. Comput. Inf. Technol. **1**(1), 37–46 (1993)

18. Fierens, D., Van den Broeck, G., Thon, I., Gutmann, B., Raedt, L.D.: Inference in probabilistic logic programs using weighted CNF's. In: UAI, pp. 211–220 (2011)

19. Getoor, L., Friedman, N., Koller, D., Pfeffer, A.: Learning probabilistic relational models. In: Džeroski, S., Lavrač, N. (eds.) Relational data Mining, pp. 307–335. Springer, Heidelberg (2001). https://doi.org/10.1007/978-3-662-04599-2_13

20. Goodman, N.D., Mansinghka, V.K., Roy, D.M., Bonawitz, K., Tenenbaum, J.B.: Church: a language for generative models. In: Proceedings of UAI, pp. 220–229 (2008)

21. Gutmann, B., Jaeger, M., De Raedt, L.: Extending ProbLog with continuous distributions. In: Frasconi, P., Lisi, F.A. (eds.) ILP 2010. LNCS (LNAI), vol. 6489, pp. 76–91. Springer, Heidelberg (2011). https://doi.org/10.1007/978-3-642-21295-6_12

22. Islam, M.A., Ramakrishnan, C., Ramakrishnan, I.: Parameter learning in prism programs with continuous random variables. arXiv preprint arXiv:1203.4287 (2012)

23. Kimmig, A., Van den Broeck, G., De Raedt, L.: An algebraic prolog for reasoning about possible worlds. In: Proceedings of the AAAI (2011). http://www.aaai.org/ocs/index.php/AAAI/AAAI11/paper/view/3685

24. Kok, S., Domingos, P.: Learning the structure of Markov logic networks. In: Proceedings of the International Conference on Machine Learning, pp. 441–448 (2005)

25. Koller, D., Friedman, N.: Probabilistic Graphical Models: Principles and Techniques. MIT Press, Cambridge (2009)

26. Landwehr, N., Kersting, K., De Raedt, L.: nFOIL: integrating Naïve Bayes and FOIL. In: AAAI 2005, pp. 795–800 (2005)

27. Landwehr, N., Passerini, A., De Raedt, L., Frasconi, P., et al.: kFOIL: learning simple relational kernels. AAAI **6**, 389–394 (2006)

28. Lauritzen, S.L., Jensen, F.: Stable local computation with conditional gaussian distributions. Stat. Comput. **11**(2), 191–203 (2001)

29. López-Cruz, P.L., Bielza, C., Larrañaga, P.: Learning mixtures of polynomials of multidimensional probability densities from data using b-spline interpolation. Int. J. Approximate Reasoning **55**(4), 989–1010 (2014)

30. Martires, P.Z.D., Dries, A., Raedt, L.D.: Knowledge compilation with continuous random variables and its application in hybrid probabilistic logic programming (2018). http://arxiv.org/abs/1807.00614

31. Milch, B., Marthi, B., Russell, S.J., Sontag, D., Ong, D.L., Kolobov, A.: BLOG: probabilistic models with unknown objects. In: Proceedings of the IJCAI, pp. 1352–1359 (2005)

32. Muggleton, S.: Inverse entailment and progol. New Gener. Comput. **13**(3), 245–286 (1995)

33. Murphy, K.P.: A variational approximation for Bayesian networks with discrete and continuous latent variables. In: UAI, pp. 457–466 (1999)

34. Nitti, D., Laet, T.D., Raedt, L.D.: A particle filter for hybrid relational domains. In: IROS, pp. 2764–2771 (2013)

35. Nitti, D., Ravkic, I., Davis, J., De Raedt, L.: Learning the structure of dynamic hybrid relational models. In: ECAI 2016, vol. 285, pp. 1283–1290 (2016)

36. Pasula, H., Marthi, B., Milch, B., Russell, S.J., Shpitser, I.: Identity uncertainty and citation matching. In: NIPS, pp. 1401–1408 (2002). http://papers.nips.cc/paper/2149-identity-uncertainty-and-citation-matching

37. Poole, D., Bacchus, F., Kisyński, J.: Towards completely lifted search-based probabilistic inference. CoRR abs/1107.4035 (2011)

38. Quinlan, J.R.: Learning logical definitions from relations. Mach. Learn. **5**(3), 239–266 (1990)

39. Raedt, L.D., Kersting, K., Natarajan, S., Poole, D.: Statistical Relational Artificial Intelligence: Logic, Probability, and Computation. Synthesis Lectures on Artificial Intelligence and Machine Learning, vol. 10, no. 2, pp. 1–189 (2016)

40. Raghavan, S., Mooney, R.J., Ku, H.: Learning to read between the lines using Bayesian logic programs. In: Proceedings of the 50th Annual Meeting of the Association for Computational Linguistics: Long Papers-Volume 1, pp. 349–358. Association for Computational Linguistics (2012)

41. Ravkic, I., Ramon, J., Davis, J.: Learning relational dependency networks in hybrid domains. Mach. Learn. **100**(2–3), 217–254 (2015)

42. Richardson, M., Domingos, P.: Markov logic networks. Mach. Learn. **62**(1), 107–136 (2006)

43. Russell, S.: Unifying logic and probability. Commun. ACM **58**(7), 88–97 (2015)

44. Schoenmackers, S., Etzioni, O., Weld, D.S., Davis, J.: Learning first-order horn clauses from web text. In: Proceedings of the 2010 Conference on Empirical Methods in Natural Language Processing, pp. 1088–1098. Association for Computational Linguistics (2010)

45. Schwarz, G.: Estimating the dimension of a model. Ann. Stat. **6**(2), 461–464 (1978)

46. Zong, Z.: Information-Theoretic Methods for Estimating of Complicated Probability Distributions, vol. 207. Elsevier (2006)

# Author Index

Printed in the United States
By Bookmasters